Contents

Introduction

How this book will help you in your course

This book is designed to help students following AQA Specification A in Advanced English Literature through their course. Most students approaching this specification will already have studied AQA Specification A in AS English Literature, and so this book has been written with that in mind. It is important to recognise from the start, however, that A2 Level is different from AS Level, in that two of the Assessment Objectives change (see 'The key to success: the Assessment Objectives' on the next page). Remember too, that this book is not simply a guide to individual set texts – each of you will choose different texts to work on. Rather, it is a guide to what you have to do with your texts in order to succeed.

The rest of this introduction will deal with the Assessment Objectives for the specification. Don't overlook this introduction and go straight to the modules – the Assessment Objectives not only underpin all the work in the course, but an understanding of them is also the key to gaining good marks, as the marking is based entirely on them. The final module, Reading for Meaning, tests all the Objectives.

The main part of the book deals with each of the three assessment modules for the A2 course. For each module, the book will take you through its design and content, with practical advice and activities. The work you are asked to do will be tailored to the type of assessment involved in the module, which might be external assessment, either open or closed book, or coursework. There will also be examples of the sort of questions and tasks which will be used to test each module as part of the examination.

There is a Glossary on pages 216–219.

The key to success: the Assessment Objectives

Here are the Assessment Objectives for Advanced (A2) English Literature:

The examination will assess a candidate's ability to:
AO1 communicate clearly the knowledge, understanding and insight appropriate to literary study, using appropriate terminology and accurate and coherent written expression
AO2ii respond with knowledge and understanding to literary texts of different types and periods, exploring and commenting on relationships and comparisons between literary texts
AO3 show detailed understanding of the ways in which writers' choices of form, structure and language shape meanings
AO4 articulate independent opinions and judgements, informed by different interpretations of literary texts by other readers
AO5ii evaluate the significance of cultural, historical and other contextual influences on literary texts and study

What the new Assessment Objectives mean

The Assessment Objectives were dealt with in the book accompanying the AS specification, and you will have worked with them during your AS course. It is important to recognise, though, that at Advanced (A2) Level Assessment Objectives 2 and 5 change, and make new demands on students. At AS Level, Assessment Objective 2i asks candidates to **'respond with knowledge and understanding to literary texts of different types and periods'**. At A2 Level, **'exploring and commenting on relationships and comparisons between literary texts'** is added. As you can see, this is quite different, reintroducing the requirement to compare texts which you were probably used to in your GCSE English Literature course.

Assessment Objective 5i at AS Level asks candidates to **'show understanding of the contexts in which literary texts are written and understood'**. At A2 Level this becomes: **'evaluate the significance of cultural, historical and other contextual influences on literary texts and study'**. What you have to think about, therefore, is how various factors have shaped the writing of the texts you're studying – and how they affect your reading of them.

Here are some of the relevant types of context which you might look at:

• The context of a period or era, including significant social, historical, political and cultural processes, which might encompass period-specific styles. This might concern the period in which the work was written, or the period which is being written about. These may not be the same. A knowledge of the context of the Indian Mutiny of the 1850s, for instance, will certainly affect your reading of J. G. Farrell's *The Siege of Krishnapur*, even though it was written in 1973.

- The context of the work in terms of the writer's biography or **milieu**. This might include literary and generic factors – how a play could be seen as a revenge tragedy, for instance, though this is also partly a period-specific context.

- The language context, including relevant episodes in the development and use of literary language, or the question of colloquial and **dialect** styles.

- The different contexts for a work established by its reception over time – works may have different meanings and effects upon their audience in different periods.

Just recognising the contexts of a text is not enough, though, because you have to 'evaluate the significance' of them. You need to decide how much a knowledge of the contexts affects the ways in which you understand the texts. Is a particular context of marginal significance, or is it central to your reading of the text?

Breaking down the Assessment Objectives

As you can see, the Assessment Objectives define the literary skills which you have to show during the course. It is vital to understand that the Assessment Objectives have different numbers of marks in different modules, and even for different texts. For example, in Module 4, Texts in Time, the 30 marks available are divided like this:

AO1	6 marks
AO2ii	5 marks
AO3	6 marks
AO4	7 marks
AO5ii	6 marks

This looks as though the marks are equally divided for each question, but this isn't quite the case. In this module, you have to choose a pre-1770 drama text and a pre-1900 poetry text. You'll be assessed on Assessment Objectives 1, 2ii and 3 on both texts – but on the drama text, you will also be assessed on AO4, making it the dominant Assessment Objective. For the poetry, AO4 (interpretations) isn't tested, but AO5ii (contexts) is.

So, the marks depend on the Assessment Objectives, and the marks vary between modules, and sometimes between sections too. That's why there is a box at the beginning of each of the three modules to show you exactly which Assessment Objectives count in that module, and how many marks each one carries.

An exercise in the new Advanced Level Assessment Objectives

STOP ALL THE CLOCKS, CUT OFF THE TELEPHONE

Stop all the clocks, cut off the telephone,
Prevent the dog from barking with a juicy bone,
Silence the pianos and with muffled drum
Bring out the coffin, let the mourners come.

Let aeroplanes circle moaning overhead
Scribbling on the sky the message He Is Dead,
Put crêpe bows round the white necks of the public doves,
Let the traffic policemen wear black cotton gloves.

He was my North, my South, my East and West,
My working week and my Sunday rest,
My noon, my midnight, my talk, my song;
I thought that love would last for ever: I was wrong.

The stars are not wanted now: put out every one;
Pack up the moon and dismantle the sun;
Pour away the ocean and sweep up the wood.
For nothing now can ever come to any good.

W. H. Auden (1907–73)

VALENTINE

Not a red rose or a satin heart.

I give you an onion.
It is a moon wrapped in brown paper.
It promises light
like the careful undressing of love.

Here.
It will blind you with tears
like a lover.
It will make your reflection
a wobbling photo of grief.

I am trying to be truthful.

Not a cute card or a kissogram.

I give you an onion.
Its fierce kiss will stay on your lips,
possessive and faithful
as we are,
for as long as we are.

Take it.
Its platinum loops shrink to a wedding-ring,
if you like.
Lethal.
Its scent will cling to your fingers,
cling to your knife.

Carol Ann Duffy (*1955–*)

Sonnet 18

Shall I compare thee to a summer's day?
Thou art more lovely and more temperate.
Rough winds do shake the darling buds of May,
And summer's lease hath all too short a date:
Sometime too hot the eye of heaven shines,
And often is his gold complexion dimm'd;
And every fair from fair sometime declines,
By chance, or nature's changing course, un-trimm'd;
But thy eternal summer shall not fade
Nor lose possession of that fair thou ow'st;
Nor shall Death brag thou wand'rest in his shade,
When in eternal lines to time thou grow'st;
　So long as men can breathe, or eyes can see,
　So long lives this, and this gives life to thee.

William Shakespeare (*1564–1616*)

Although you might have come across these poems before, the aim here is to look at them in the context of the Advanced (A2) Level Assessment Objectives.

AO2ii	respond with knowledge and understanding to literary texts of different types and periods, exploring and commenting on relationships and comparisons between literary texts

The first step in comparing these poems is easy – all three are concerned with love and time. In addition, all three are personal, first-person poems: 'Stop All the Clocks' mourns the death of a loved one, and the other two make declarations of love, though not in a straightforward way. 'Valentine', particularly, concerns itself with the realities of love ('I am trying to be truthful'), meaning its difficulties and dangers.

To compare the poems in a detailed way, it's a good idea to use AO3 as a framework, comparing how the three poets use form, structure and language to shape their meanings. Work your way through the poems using the following suggestions.

Form

There are three different forms here – but remember, what you're interested in is comparing how form expresses meaning in each case.

1 The four separate verses of 'Stop All the Clocks' suggest each verse contains a separate aspect of the subject. Is this true here? How do punctuation and rhyme give a sense of finality?

2 'Sonnet 18' is unpunctuated by verse divisions. Is it one continuous argument? If it changes, is it marked by the form? How? Think about rhyme as well as the layout of the lines.

3 'Valentine' does not follow a set pattern of verse, or of rhyme, though there are repetitions and echoes. Can you find any of these? How does Carol Ann Duffy use the form to suggest unconnected but related thoughts about love, and about this relationship?

Now look back at your conclusions, and think about the relationships and comparisons between these texts.

Structure

Form is closely related to structure in all these poems.

4 You've already worked out the subjects of each of the verses in 'Stop All the Clocks'. Is there a logical structure here? How does the poem build to the last verse, and the last line in particular?

5 How does the first line of 'Sonnet 18' set the agenda for the whole poem? Where does the view of time alter, and which word at the beginning of a line marks the shift? The final change is to introduce the idea of the life of the poem, not just the person. Where does this begin, exactly?

6 'Valentine' looks different from the others on the page, not only because of the lack of verse pattern, but because of the varying line length. Look at the effects of some of the very short lines, and the three single lines. Why do you think the poem begins in the way it does, and ends in the way it does?

Now look back at your conclusions, and think about the relationships and comparisons between these texts.

Language

There's a lot to say about the ways in which language is used to express meaning in all of these poems. Here are a few questions to get you started.

7 Look at sentence forms in all three poems. Where can you find commands, or questions? Why have the poets used these forms?

8 Two of these poems make use of repetition, and one doesn't. What are the effects of the repetitions where they are used, and what does the lack of repetition tell you about the other one?

9 Each of the three poems has particular uses of language features. Look at the verbs in 'Stop All the Clocks', the unorthodox sentences in 'Valentine', and the word play in 'Sonnet 18'.

10 Imagery is a central feature of all three poems.

- Look at the imagery in the last two verses of 'Stop All the Clocks'. What is the effect of all of the images taken together? How does each one contribute to the whole? Notice particularly the line about the moon and the sun, bearing in mind the other two poems you're working on.

- The other two poems both take a single image and examine it. In 'Valentine', what gifts does the speaker reject? Why, do you think? Why does she find an onion appropriate, and what view of love does this reveal? Look at the further comparisons which stem from this central idea.

- 'Sonnet 18' also works on one image, introduced in the first line. As in 'Valentine', the conventional love comparison is rejected. Look at the ways in which Shakespeare uses the idea to praise the object of the poem, developing more imagery along the way.

Now look back at your conclusions, and think about the relationships and comparisons between these texts.

> AO5ii   evaluate the significance of cultural, historical and other contextual influences on literary texts and study

At Advanced (A2) Level it is not enough simply to recognise the contexts of each text studied. You also have to evaluate their significance for your reading of the text, particularly as you start to think about forming an interpretation. The ideas and questions which follow should help you to see what this might mean, and to see how the Assessment Objectives are interrelated.

'Stop All the Clocks' is an interesting poem to start with, when thinking about contexts. You might already have two contexts for your reading of the text: as part of GCSE English Literature study, in which case you probably studied it in the context of other poems, or its reading in the film *Four Weddings and a Funeral*. If you've seen and heard it in the film, the context may well be significant in your response to it. In the film, the reading at the funeral is an emotional moment, designed to affect the audience, who may well also associate it with homosexual love. However, these first two verses of the poem were originally published, in the prose/verse drama *The Ascent of F6*, by W. H. Auden and Christopher Isherwood. If you read the rest of the poem in this original version, you might arrive at a different interpretation of the verses.

ACTIVITY

1 Re-read the first two verses of 'Stop All the Clocks' on page vii, then read the following three verses, which completed the piece in *The Ascent of F6*.

> Hold up your umbrellas to keep off the rain
> From Doctor Williams while he opens a vein;
> Life, he pronounces, it is finally extinct.
> Sergeant, arrest that man who said he winked!
>
> Shawcross will say a few words sad and kind
> To the weeping crowds about the Master-Mind,
> While Lamp with a powerful microscope
> Searches their faces for a sign of hope.
>
> And Gunn, of course, will drive the motor-hearse:
> None could drive it better, most would drive it worse.
> He'll open up the throttle to its fullest power
> And drive him to the grave at ninety miles an hour.

2 The poem may well seem more like a satirical parody of love poetry now. How has the writer worked to create this tone? Think about:

- the effects of particular words
- the effects of particular rhymes
- the actions of the characters, and how they are described.

Clearly these two contexts give rise to interpretations which are quite opposed to each other. But this doesn't necessarily mean that the satirical reading of the poem is the 'right' one. If it did, it would mean that anybody's response to the poem based on the film alone would somehow be invalid. Assessment Objective 5i, the building block for this Objective, concerns 'the contexts in which literary texts are written and understood' – but these need not be the same. Here, the poem is written in one context, and understood in another by the film's audience. Two meanings – or interpretations – are generated, and both are valid. Nor does it make any difference that the writer did not intend, or indeed know about, the film context. Once a text is written, the writer is merely one interpreter of its meaning.

In the other two poems, gender provides an interesting context. Unlike 'Stop All the Clocks', neither poem identifies the gender of the person addressed. Some research could reveal significant contexts here. If you assume that the speaker in the poem – the persona – is the poet speaking (which might not be the case), what might the sexual preferences of the writers tell you? When you've looked at this, you might think about these issues:

1   Does this information make any difference to your reading of the poems? In other words, are the contexts significant?

2   If you respond to the poems differently when you know about these contexts, why do you respond differently? Is it to do with the poems, or with you?

3   What evidence are you using in reaching your conclusions about the poems? Context is a form of evidence in itself, as are the details of form, language and structure. The tone of 'Stop All the Clocks' can perhaps be read either way, depending on how you view the evidence. But what evidence of context can you find in the other two poems?

You could, of course, investigate other contexts, and if you were studying these texts as part of your Advanced (A2) Level course you would have to choose which to pursue – which contexts might prove to be significant in the writing and understanding of the texts. You could look at the features of each of the poems which place them in their historic and social contexts, for example. With the Shakespeare sonnet, you could look at the literary context of the sonnet form in Shakespeare's period, and how he uses it, or at how ambiguity appears in other Shakespeare sonnets. If you were tackling this as an Advanced (A2) Level task, you would also need to evaluate the significance of these contexts. Which are most central to your understanding of the texts, and why?

You will have noticed that as you investigated and thought about contexts, more relationships and comparisons between the three texts occurred to you, taking you back to AO2ii. The Advanced (A2) Level course, like the AS course, divides the subject into Assessment Objectives to test your knowledge of the ways that English Literature works, but these areas are very closely interrelated and sometimes overlap. In the final module in the course, Reading for Meaning, all the Assessment Objectives are tested, to show what you've learned about the study of English Literature during the whole Advanced Level course. In working through these three poems in this Introduction, you've done exactly that – you've read texts for meaning, using each of the Assessment Objectives to do it.

Module ④ Texts in Time

This module carries 30% of the final A2 mark and 15% of the final A Level mark. The marks are divided amongst the Assessment Objectives like this:

── ASSESSMENT OBJECTIVES ──

AO1 communicate clearly the knowledge, understanding and insight appropriate to literary study, using appropriate terminology and accurate and coherent written expression
(6% of the final A2 mark; 3% of the final A Level mark)

AO2ii respond with knowledge and understanding to literary texts of different types and periods, exploring and commenting on relationships and comparisons between literary texts
(5% of the final A2 mark; 2.5% of the final A Level mark)

AO3 show detailed understanding of the ways in which writers' choices of form, structure and language shape meanings
(6% of the final A2 mark; 3% of the final A Level mark)

AO4 articulate independent opinions and judgements, informed by different interpretations of literary texts by other readers
(7% of the final A2 mark; 3.5% of the final A Level mark)

AO5ii evaluate the significance of cultural, historical and other contextual influences on literary texts and study
(6% of the final A2 mark; 3% of the final A Level mark)

All of the Assessment Objectives are tested in this module, and they are allocated to period/genre in the following ways:

- Both Section A, Drama Pre-1770 and Section B Poetry Pre-1900 target Assessment Objectives 1, 2 and 3.

- Section A targets the additional dominant AO4.

- Section B targets the additional dominant AO5ii.

The main emphasis for your studies will be the dominant Assessment Objective for each period/genre, although you should pay attention to the other Assessment Objectives as well.

Content

This module meets the core syllabus requirements for Drama Pre-1770 and Poetry Pre-1900.

The examination

The question paper is split into two sections: Section A, Drama Pre-1770, and Section B, Poetry Pre-1900. You need to answer one question from each section. The questions are weighted equally, and marks are scaled to achieve the final mark. You are *not* allowed to take your texts into the examination for this paper.

How your work is assessed

The examiner will make an initial appraisal of your answer by making a judgement on your response to the dominant Assessment Objective for each section (AO4 for Section A, and AO5ii for Section B). Then your response to the other three Assessment Objectives will be assessed. This will, in general, confirm your initial mark, but may raise or lower it.

This module is designed to revise and build upon the work you did and the skills you acquired in AS Level Module 3, Texts in Context. It might be helpful to remind yourself of the work you did for this earlier module, and of the critical vocabulary you have already acquired. You do not need to work through the whole of Section A, Drama Pre-1770, as you will concentrate only on the text which you are studying. Nor do you need to work through the whole of Section B, Poetry Pre-1900, as again you will be studying one text only. However, it could be helpful to read through all the questions for Module 4 in this book to appreciate the different ways in which the Romantic context may be presented in these tasks.

Assessment Objective 4

This objective is more complex at A2 Level than it was at AS Level. You will need to be aware that:

- texts are open to multiple interpretations
- interpretations can change over time
- different readers bring different individual, social and cultural experiences to the reading of texts.

In the examination you will be assessed equally in two areas:

1 your grasp/consideration of the critical views which may be offered in a question

2 your own individual response to and judgement on your text.

This means that you must have a thorough knowledge and understanding of your chosen play, be flexible enough to take on board other readers' experiences of the play, and be confident enough to express and justify your own responses to the play and to interpretations offered by others. In doing this, you will also fulfil Assessment Objectives 1, 2 and 3.

In the Specimen Units offered for AQA Specification A, there are seven different ways in which AO4 appears in the examination questions:

1 You are given two opposing critical views and asked to discuss these and other views. This creates an opportunity to offer your own opinions.

2 You are offered two opposing critical views and asked to explore these, and the play, further.

3 You are offered one critical view and asked if you agree or disagree, or have further views to add.

4 You are offered two critical views to evaluate, with a request for additional opinions.

5 You are offered one critical view to assess and asked if there are other ideas to consider as well.

6 You are offered two critical views and asked if you agree with one/both/neither.

7 You are given two critical views from different historical periods and asked how far you agree with these, and what other views there might be.

The examples given in the Specimen Units are not exhaustive, and there will be other ways of testing AO4:

- you may be given two similar or related views from different critics to support or to argue against

- you could be offered two critical views from different social/cultural groups and asked to evaluate these, and perhaps explore further the views offered.

What is important is that in all cases you carry out two tasks:

- assess the critical view(s) offered

- offer your own judgement/opinion as requested.

For each play below, two sample tasks will be offered as a framework. Each of these will be based on key critical issues of the text. You may then develop these fully in your own time. In addition to these models, several further tasks will also be suggested, with an activity as a starting point, for you to work on yourself. These will also be based on central critical issues related to the text.

Othello by William Shakespeare

In *Othello* you see how Shakespeare explores the nature of the love between Othello and Desdemona, how people should or should not behave in society, and wider, universal matters of morality and religion.

In this section you will look at six different critical perspectives on *Othello*:

1 Whether *Othello* is anything more than an account of a personal tragedy.

2 The nature of audience response to the dramatic effects within the play.

3 Whether Desdemona is a victim or a temptress.

4 Whether Othello himself is a noble man.

5 Whether Iago is a devil, or just a jealous, scheming individual.

6 The idea that everything that is beautiful will decay and destroy itself.

1 *Othello* – a personal tragedy?

One critic has suggested that *Othello* lacks universal significance and is merely a story of terrible individual catastrophe. But another has written: 'Othello *is* the human soul as it strives to be and Iago *is* that which corrodes or subverts it from within.'

Examine each view and then indicate your own opinion of the play.

Try building your answer in three stages:

1 Consider the first criticism, that *Othello* is not a great tragedy because it is restricted to the personal problems of an individual.

2 Consider the second opinion that on the other hand there is a wide and universal look at the moral state of *all* mankind in this play.

3 You must be confident enough in your grasp of the text to present a viewpoint of your own. You could offer:

- agreement with one viewpoint or the other
- a compromise between both viewpoints
- outright rejection of these ideas
- a discussion of a viewpoint of your own.

Here are suggestions for a response to this question, but remember that all interpretations are personal or subjective, that there is no single correct reading of any text, and that you should treat these points as a framework and expand on it in your own time.

In reply to the first critical comment, consider:

- the settings of the play
- the events of the play
- the characters of Iago and Othello generally.

Set against this would be a response to the second critical view:

- Here you could focus on the imagery and the language used by individual characters.

The settings of the play

ACTIVITY 1

1 Make a list of the sequence of settings in *Othello*. What do you notice about these?

2 Work out the significance of the movement from Venice, the thriving seaport and centre of civilisation, to Cyprus, to a castle in Cyprus, to rooms in the castle, to a bedchamber, to the bed in this room. Does this suggest that *Othello* is a personal and domestic tragedy? Could Shakespeare have had any other reasons for making the settings progressively more domestic and intimate?

The events of the play

ACTIVITY 2

1 Summarise the events of the play.

2 What are the motivations behind these events?

3 Could these events be described as domestic, personal or trivial?

4 Could you see these events in another way?

Some consideration of Iago and Othello

To support a reading that this is a personal tragedy for Iago, without universal significance, consider Iago's motivation in the following speech in Act 1, Scene 1:

> One Michael Cassio, a Florentine –
> A fellow almost damned in a fair wife –
> That never set a squadron in the field,
> [. . .]
> He in good time must his Lieutenant be,
> And I – God bless the mark! his Moorship's Ancient.   (lines 20–33)

ACTIVITY 3

1 What do you think Iago feels here? Why might he appear to be so put out?

2 What are all the reasons for his jealousy of Cassio?

3 What else do you learn about Iago here?

Iago eventually has another reason for disliking Othello, as you may see by reading Act 1, Scene 3, line 380 ('I hate the Moor [. . .]').

ACTIVITY 4

1 What do you think is Iago's second reason for hating Othello?

2 Where else is this idea repeated in the play?

3 Do you think that Iago's reasons are genuine or not?

4 What does Iago have to say about reputation in Act 3, Scene 3?

At times we are given a negative view of Othello. Look at the first scene of the play:

> [. . .] that your fair daughter,
> At this odd-even and dull watch o' th' night,
> Transported with no worse nor better guard
> But with a knave of common hire, a gondolier,
> To the gross clasps of a lascivious Moor: (lines 123–127)

ACTIVITY 5

1 Has Othello treated Desdemona with proper respect, as the daughter of a wealthy Venetian? Does Othello, perhaps, have different attitudes and customs? Has he understood the social conventions of Venice?

2 Why does Shakespeare offer a contrast between 'fair' and 'Moor'?

3 Why does Shakespeare use the plural 'clasps'? What aspect of their relationship is stressed? What might this tell you about Iago's attitude?

ACTIVITY 6

Now look at the choice Othello makes when he is tempted by Iago in Act 3, Scene 3. Throughout the scene you see Othello changing his mind, until after the Cassio episode he declares:

All my fond love thus do I blow to heaven:
'Tis gone.
Arise, black vengeance, from thy hollow cell!   (lines 442–444)

1 Why is Othello so easily swayed? Is he simply jealous?

2 Could it be that he does not know his wife at all? Or that he is not intelligent enough to understand her?

Finally, look closely at the characters within the play and their status. The Duke is noble, but what is his part in the play? Look at the status, or place in the **social hierarchy,** of Othello, Desdemona and Iago.

For all these reasons you could claim that the play is a domestic, personal tragedy. But there is also the other view, that the play is a universal demonstration of a battle between good and evil. Here you could offer as supporting evidence, the language used in the play, particularly the imagery.

Language and imagery

Iago is repeatedly linked to the devil:

[. . .] Divinity of hell!
When devils will the blackest sins put on,
They do suggest at first with heavenly shows
As I do now. [. . .]

(Act 2, Scene 3, lines 340–343)

ACTIVITY 7

1 How does Iago align himself with the devil here?

2 How is an opposition set up between heaven and hell?

3 List and explore other **diabolical** references in Iago's words. Could he be a **vice figure** or devil as in a **morality play**?

   (It might help to remind yourself of the discussion of *Dr Faustus* as a morality play in *AS English Literature for AQA A*, page 95.)

On the other hand, *Desdemona* is often associated with heaven (Act 2, Scene 1 or Act 5, Scene 2):

> Then heaven
> Have mercy on me! (lines 33–34)

ACTIVITY 8

1 How is Desdemona related to Christian virtue here?

2 Carefully list and explore religious references in Desdemona's other speeches. Do you see any negative aspects of Desdemona?

Many critics have commented on the change in Othello's language from the poetic imagery at the beginning of the play, to the point where he takes on Iago's language (as in Act 3, Scene 3, above). At the end of the play (Act 5, Scene 2) Othello realises what has happened and says:

> Will you, I pray, demand that demi-devil
> Why he hath thus ensnared my soul and body? (lines 298–299)

ACTIVITY 9

1 What sort of understanding do you think Othello has reached by this point?

2 How could it relate to a battle of good and evil over a man's soul?

In *Othello* you can see evidence of the **seven deadly sins**: pride, covetousness, lust, gluttony (or drunkenness, as in the case of Cassio, for example), anger, envy, sloth.

ACTIVITY 10

Work out the ways in which these sins appear in *Othello*.

Other critics believe that when Iago ensnares Othello because of Desdemona, it is a reworking of Adam and Eve's **Fall from Paradise**:

> Now, by heaven,
> My blood begins my safer guides to rule,
> And passion, having my best judgement collied,
> Assays to lead the way. [. . .]
>
> (Act 2, Scene 3, lines 198–201)

ACTIVITY 11

1 What exactly is Othello suggesting here?

2 Can you see any opposition between 'safe guidance' and 'passion'?

3 Think about the story of the Fall from Paradise – Adam fell into Satan's trap when he gave in to his passion for Eve. Is there any link with *Othello*?

These are the two critical positions for you to think about and choose between when considering this particular perspective on *Othello*. You must indicate your choice, and explain your response, or reject both and add another viewpoint.

2 The audience's response to the drama in *Othello*

It has been suggested that part of the greatness of *Othello* lies in the relentless and sustained grip on the emotions of the audience. What do you think is great about the dramatic art of *Othello*?

In response to this you could consider several aspects of the play:

- settings
- plot
- use of character
- use of language
- treatment of time.

Settings

You could refer to the notes about settings you made for the previous question.

ACTIVITY 12

1 What reason could Shakespeare have for narrowing down the settings to smaller and smaller spaces?

2 Is the audience distanced from, or drawn into, the bedroom scene?

3 Is the relationship between audience and actors here intimate or distant?

Plot

ACTIVITY 13

Look at the sequence of events you worked out in Activity 2. Is the plot simple? Is there a sub-plot? What are the effects of this?

Use of character

ACTIVITY 14

1 Look at the first scene again.

- How does Shakespeare build up to the introduction of Othello?

- Does the audience have certain expectations about Othello?

- How does his noble language affect you? Are you forced to rethink?

2 How many important speaking characters are there in the play?

3 What effect is produced by having so few?

Use of language

One of the language effects which increases the tension of the play is the use of repetition.

ACTIVITY 15

Remind yourself of two scenes: that between Iago and Roderigo in Act 1, Scene 2, with the repeated refrain 'put money in thy purse', and the confrontation between Othello and Emilia in Act 5, Scene 2 with the repeated 'husband'.

1 Why do you think Shakespeare uses this repetition?

2 How does it help to build up tension or affect the pace of the verse?

3 How does the prose style of the first of these scenes reflect the theme?

4 Why does Shakespeare split the lines between the two speakers here?

Treatment of time

The action in *Othello* appears to move very quickly, with the action in Cyprus taking place in just thirty-six hours; this is known as the 'short time'. But Shakespeare has to present the idea that certain events, such as the journey from Venice to Cyprus, the interval in which Cassio is suspected of flirting with Desdemona, must naturally take longer than this – the 'long time'. Critics call this Shakespeare's use of 'double time'. Here are two examples:

> BIANCA   What! Keep a week away? Seven days and nights?
>
> (Act 3, Scene 4, line 169)
>
> EMILIA   My wayward husband hath a hundred times
>   Wooed me to steal it; [. . .]
>
> (Act 3, Scene 3, lines 289–290)

ACTIVITY 16

Make a list of the other places in the play where 'double time' can be seen.

1 Why do you think Shakespeare uses this technique?

2 Are you aware as you watch the play that this is happening?

3 How could it help to keep the tension high?

In addition to these points, you may add some of your own. Or you could disagree with the premise, and argue that there is no suspense.

3 Desdemona – a victim or a temptress?

One critic has suggested that Desdemona suffers at the hands of a patriarchal, male-dominated society. Another thinks that she is a temptress. How far do you agree with one or other of these viewpoints?

ACTIVITY 17

Consider Desdemona's increasing isolation; and also the failure of her language as she uses song to express herself.

4 Is Othello a noble man?

Is Othello the 'noble Moor', or is he full of pride and egotism and without self-knowledge? Do you agree with any of these assessments or do you have a completely different opinion of Othello?

ACTIVITY 18

Trace Othello's early use of poetic language up to the temptation scene with Iago, then his decline into Iago's language, until he returns to his original manner of speech near the end of the play.

1 Is Othello's fault gullibility? Or is he an outsider to Venetian society?

2 Could this be part of the reason that he is presented as a black Moor?

5 Is Iago a devil?

Is Iago a devil as some critics suggest, or just a low-minded military man, as others believe? Evaluate these views, adding your own if you wish.

ACTIVITY 19

Iago seems to be caught out by his own plans, to be afraid at Othello's words 'Villain, be sure thou prove my love a whor'e; (Act 3, Scene 3, line 356)

Does he lose control of events in the last act of the play?

6 All beauty must destroy itself eventually

A leading critic believes that Shakespeare expressed the view (later shared by Keats) that in *Othello* all beauty and happiness carries within it the seeds of its own destruction. Do you agree with this? Think of evidence from the play to support this view.

ACTIVITY 20

> [. . .] If it were now to die,
>
> OTHELLO   'Twere now to be most happy; [. . .]
>
> (Act 2, Scene 1, lines 183–184)
>
> DESDEMONA But that our loves
> and comforts should increase,
> Even as our days do grow.
>
> (Act 2, Scene 1, lines 188–189)

1 How perfect is their love at first? How well do they know each other?

2 How do one's ideas about love differ from the other's?

Now you have considered these six different perspectives on *Othello*, you can carry on to use this framework to explore other aspects of the play which interest you.

Measure For Measure by William Shakespeare

In the development of *Measure for Measure* and in its conclusion – when a reformed society based on sound principles of law and justice is established after a period of chaos – the play may be classed as a comedy. However, some critics call *Measure for Measure* one of Shakespeare's 'problem plays'. This may be partly because of the extreme cruelty evident at times, which could suggest that the play may be read as **tragicomedy**, and partly because the play varies in its methods of presentation between realistic and non-realistic methods. You should not quibble if certain events or situations seem unlikely, but rather accept that they are there for specific dramatic purposes. If you accept the conventions of the play and 'suspend your disbelief', you can see many possible critical perspectives to explore.

The six critical perspectives to be considered for the study of *Measure for Measure* are:

1 Is there an enquiry into the nature of just government?

2 A consideration of the links between morality and self-knowledge.

3 How far can *Measure for Measure* be considered a comedy?

4 What are the dramatic effects of interlinking two social classes?

5 Some considerations of the effects of the language of the play.

6 In what ways is *Measure for Measure* one of the 'problem plays'?

1 Is there an enquiry into the nature of just government?

An enquiry into the society of the play will enable you to think about issues relevant both to the time when the play was written and also, more broadly, to any society. More specifically, it might help you to consider the way society is organised and to reflect on the limits of legal justice.

But Shakespeare is not simply writing about how the law operates; he is more interested in that uncertain line between legal justice and moral justice. This leads naturally into considerations of what it means to rule both justly *and* wisely in the best interests of people generally.

Here you are being asked to consider one of the key ideas of the play, that amongst other concerns there is some consideration about what constitutes just and wise government. This is a central interpretation of the play, and it is worth your while spending some time on this perspective.

To develop this enquiry, you could consider three characters here: Angelo, Escalus and the Duke. You might well discover that each character has a different view of how to govern.

Angelo

The Duke makes Angelo his deputy in his absence and Angelo starts off by reviving an old law relating to fornication. The result of this is that Claudio is condemned to die. The Duke knows Angelo's character (Act 1, Scene 3):

> [. . .]   Lord Angelo is precise,
> Stands at a guard with envy, scarce confesses
> That his blood flows, or that his appetite
> Is more to bread than stone. [. . .]   (lines 50–53)

Angelo believes that 'we must not make a scarecrow of the law'.

ACTIVITY 1

1   What sort of a person is Angelo? What are his attitudes?

2   What is the significance of the word 'precise', both here and in Act 3, Scene 1?

3   Might it suggest that Angelo is an absolutist, seeing things in black and white, and not allowing for grey areas?

It would be helpful here to read through the two dramatic confrontations between Angelo and Isabella in Act 2, Scenes 2 and 4. You might ask yourself whether Angelo has fallen into a trap through his view of justice.

ACTIVITY 2

1   Should Angelo take into account an individual case such as Claudio's?

2   If he were to give in to Isabella, and pardon Claudio, would he still be impartial in carrying out the law?

3   If he were to go ahead and execute Claudio, would he be inhumane?

4   Does this suggest that there is a problem in his type of justice?

Escalus

Escalus is exactly the opposite. In Act 2, Scene 1, he is asked by his constable, Elbow, to arrest Pompey for being a bawd. Angelo leaves him to take the case, and Escalus comments to Elbow:

> Truly, officer, because he hath some offences in him that thou wouldst discover, if thou couldst, let him continue in his courses [. . .]
> [. . .]
> So, for this time, Pompey, fare you well.   (lines 177–239)

ACTIVITY 3

1 What do you make of Escalus's view of justice?

2 Does he take too much notice of the individual?

3 Might he undermine the idea of the necessity of rigorous laws?

The Duke

Perhaps the Duke is not completely blameless in his rule of Vienna. Perhaps he has let the law drift, and not made his presence strongly felt? Do you think this is why Lucio refers to him twice as the 'dark' Duke (Act 2, Scene 2 and Act 4, Scene 3)? Might there be another reason?

He has seen the lawlessness of Vienna: '. . . I have seen corruption boil and bubble / Till it o'errun the stew' (Act 5, Scene 1). Perhaps he has let the law drift because he knows that it may be too harsh if applied to the letter. Perhaps he wishes to establish a balanced form of justice tempered by mercy.

Overall, the Duke might be seen to represent both justice and mercy in the sentences he hands out in Act 5, Scene 1, where he 'punishes' Angelo, Claudio and Lucio.

ACTIVITY 4

1 What are these punishments? Are they 'negative' punishments, or are they designed to reform the 'sinners'?

2 Was Pompey's earlier punishment negative or redemptive?

Perhaps there is a justice in which the law works through wisdom and mercy, to reform and not just to punish. To take this idea further you could compare the sort of justice meted out by Angelo and Escalus to that of the balanced judgement of the Duke.

2 A consideration of the links between morality and self-knowledge

A consideration of the nature of justice in the play alone does not really get to the heart of the moral issues that Shakespeare was exploring in *Measure for Measure*. Similarly, whereas a consideration of the laws about pregnancy outside marriage gives some idea of the nature of the society Shakespeare chose to write about, a study of the morality evident in the play might show more about the issues that people are faced with in their daily lives.

Here you will consider how far self-knowledge is linked to morality. You may choose to think about which characters learn about themselves, and so are able to tackle their own moral flaws, and how such characters are seen. Of course, not all characters gain self-knowledge, and you might like to work out which characters appear to come to terms with their weaknesses, and which do not.

To consider this perspective, you might explore the moral qualities of Angelo, Isabella and Claudio.

Angelo

You read on page 14 a description of Angelo by the Duke. Other characters in this play, such as Justice, think that Angelo is 'severe' (Act 2, Scene 1). Angelo himself thinks that he is faultless:

> When I, that censure him, do so offend,
> Let mine own judgement pattern out my death   (lines 29–30)

ACTIVITY 5

1 What do you think of Angelo's attitude here? Is it rather smug?

2 Does the audience know at this stage that Angelo has had a love affair?

To consider the ways in which Angelo gains self-knowledge, and therefore can improve himself, you could consider two areas:

- his 'espousal' to Mariana
- his dealings with Isabella.

Angelo's 'espousal' to Mariana

The Duke is aware of this relationship, which he reveals in his plan to Mariana – 'he is your husband on a pre-contract' (Act 4, Scene 1) – so legally and morally he sees that Angelo is flawed. In Act 3, Scene 1, the Duke explains why she was abandoned by Angelo before the marriage agreement was finalised:

> [. . .] between which time of the contract and limit of the solemnity, her brother Frederick was wrecked at sea, having in that perished vessel the dowry of his sister. [. . .]   (lines 216–219)

ACTIVITY 6

1 Angelo was legally entitled to break his espousal, but do you think he acted morally?

2 What do you think his motives were? What might this suggest?

3 When you compare Angelo's actions to those of Claudio, who was also 'espoused', who do you think is the better man? Is there any irony here?

Angelo's dealings with Isabella

Angelo is presented as more than just a hypocrite, as you can see in his dealings with Isabella. In Act 2, Scene 4, he offers to waive Claudio's death penalty on condition that she:

> [. . .] to redeem him
> Give up your body to such sweet uncleanness
> As she that he hath stained?
> [. . .]
> Might there not be a charity in sin
> To save this brother's life?
>
> (Act 2, Scene 4, lines 53–64)

ACTIVITY 7

1 What do you think of Angelo now?

2 Why do you think Shakespeare uses words such as 'redeem', 'charity', and 'sin'?

Then Angelo gives the matter another twist. He plans to deceive Isabella after he has slept with her by ordering her brother's execution – in case Claudio might 'have ta'en revenge' (Act 4, Scene 4).

Isabella

When you first see Isabella she is about to become a novice nun. Even at this stage you can see that she is an extremist, who wishes 'a more strict restraint' on nuns (Act 1, Scene 4).

Shakespeare ensures that, as with Escalus and Angelo, the moral principles of Isabella are put to the test. You may see this in her two confrontations with Angelo in Act 2, Scenes 2 and 4, where she, too, faces an impossible choice. In the first confrontation, she works through four stages:

1 Claudio should condemn the fault but not her brother (from line 34).

2 She then makes a plea for tolerance for all sinners (from line 88).

3 She now moves to the idea of mercy in law, asking Angelo to 'show some pity' (from line 100).

4 When all these pleas fail, she attacks all human authority: 'man . . . like an angry ape plays such fantastic tricks before high heaven.'

ACTIVITY 8

Pick out the different stages of Isabella's argument, and Angelo's counter-arguments, as you read through the scene.

In the second confrontation, in Act 2, Scene 4, Isabella responds to the deadly choice of either sleeping with Angelo and so saving her brother's life, or keeping her virtue and letting him die:

> Th'impression of keen whips I'd wear as rubies,
> And strip myself to death as to a bed
> That long I have been sick for, ere I'd yield
> My body up to shame.   (lines 101–104)

ACTIVITY 9

1   Why does Shakespeare give Isabella such **sensuous** language here?

2   What do you make of her choices – that she must let her brother die or give up her virginity?

3   Is that choice consistent with the Christian ideas of love and sacrifice to which she claims she wishes to adhere as a nun?

4   Should she break her own pledge as a nun and lose her chastity?

Claudio

Claudio has rather different weaknesses. Technically, he has offended state and moral law by sleeping with Juliet before they were married, but Claudio has other moral difficulties, as you may see in the scene with the Duke in prison (Act 3, Scene 1). Claudio may be seen to waver in his responses to the Duke. However, when the Duke offers the advice 'Be absolute for death', Claudio seems heartened and resolute:

> [. . .] humbly thank you.
> To sue to live, I find I seek to die,
> And, seeking death, find life. Let it come on.   (lines 41–43)

But then Isabella reveals Angelo's offer, and when Claudio thinks about the terrors of death, his resolution fails:

> [. . .] Death is a fearful thing.
> [. . .]
> Ay, but to die, and go we know not where,   (lines 119–121)

ACTIVITY 10

1 How do you respond to Claudio at this point?

2 Might it be thought that just as Angelo was too absolute in his morality, so here Claudio wavers too much? That he is not resolute enough?

The Duke may be seen as the moral ideal, with the themes of morality and justice being drawn together in one of his speeches (Act 3, Scene 2):

He who the sword of heaven will bear
Should be as holy as severe,
[. . .]
Twice treble shame on Angelo,   (lines 249–257)

ACTIVITY 11

1 How does Shakespeare link morality and justice here?

2 Why might the Duke be made to refer to 'the sword of heaven'?

To complete this enquiry you could:

• assess how each character has gained moral self-knowledge through experiencing 'new' and difficult situations, and

• measure each character against the 'ideal' standard of the Duke.

3 The context of genre: *Measure for Measure* as a comedy

While they were watching *Measure for Measure*, contemporary audiences would probably have been thinking about similar plays they had seen, and would thus have been particularly alert to what Shakespeare was doing in his play. So a consideration of the play as a comedy would enable you to highlight some of those things in the play that an audience would find particularly striking. The audiences of Shakespeare's day would be well aware that a comedy was a play in which no one died, so they would have been prompted to think especially hard about the cruelty surrounding the report that Claudio had been killed.

As you read in the introduction to this text, the idea of comedy in *Measure for Measure* is a tricky matter. There is much cruelty, but there is also a good case to argue that the play conforms to the scheme of social comedy. Of course you may feel that the cruelty outweighs the comic sense, or causes uneasiness about the outcomes, and you are perfectly free to express this opinion. However, it is sensible at this stage to explore the ways in which the play might be classed as social comedy.

It has been suggested that in this distinctive form of social comedy there are three stages:

1 it opens with an unsettled society governed by a harsh or irrational law

2 there is then a temporary loss of identity

3 there is the discovery of a new identity and reconciliation.

This structure seems to suit the development of *Measure for Measure*.

An unsettled society governed by a harsh or irrational law

At the beginning of the play, you can see the result of reviving the old law about fornication in Claudio's arrest. In Act 1, Scene 3, the Duke says:

> We have strict statutes and most biting laws,
> The needful bits and curbs to headstrong weeds,
> Which for this fourteen years we have let slip;   (lines 19–21)

A temporary loss of identity

In exploring the first two contexts you have already identified the confusion in both events and moral attitudes.

ACTIVITY 12

Do you think that this society is unsettled? Why might this be?

The discovery of a new identity and a reconciliation

You could explore the ending of the play to see how the processes of self-discovery and reconciliation are achieved. You have already discussed 'punishment' and reconciliation in Activity 4 (page 15), so to complete the exploration of this context, you might 'flesh out' the full evidence under these three headings: 'Of an unsettled society', 'Discovery of a new identity' and 'Reconciliation'.

You might think about what the characters including Claudio, Angelo and even the Duke learn about themselves, and find the lines when the characters admit to these discoveries directly or indirectly. Then explore how social and personal harmony is established in this society at the end of the play guided by the Duke's decrees.

4 What are the dramatic effects of interlinking two social classes?

Some critics feel that *Measure for Measure* is a fractured play in that the two social classes in the play do not gel dramatically. If you consider the play's themes, you could argue that there are close links between both sets of characters.

To explore this perspective you might consider how the lower-class characters counterpoint or illuminate the issues related to the higher-class characters. You can look at Pompey, Lucio and Barnardine.

ACTIVITY 13

Pompey and his attitude to law

1 Does Pompey seem to talk good sense at times, for example when he points out the folly of closing all the brothels in the dukedom?

2 Might he be seen as a character of common sense?

3 Why is he made to make Escalus look foolish?

4 How is his behaviour reflected by those of a higher class?

5 Does he provide humour in the play?

6 How does his punishment fit into the final mood of the play? You might remember that the Duke is skilled in making the punishment fit the crime. Being forced to change his trade is perhaps a light outcome for Pompey. Can you see the aptness and the irony in the new 'profession' Pompey is forced to accept?

Lucio

7 Does Lucio seem at first to represent and parallel the Duke?

8 Does he, too, seem to exhibit common sense? What effects does this have?

9 Is he treated more harshly as the play goes on?

10 How does this affect the mood of the play?

11 How does his punishment fit into the final moral scheme of the play?

Barnardine

12 Does Barnardine deny the Duke's right of dispensing law to every citizen when he refuses to be executed?

13 What effect does this have on your perception of the Duke?

5 Some considerations of the effects of the play's language

Most critics believe that the language of the play is carefully controlled, and that if you look at the **registers** used by certain characters, you will find an indication of the themes of the play. This is a central enquiry in exploring the various readings of the play, as meanings are generated through the language and poetry of the play.

To consider this perspective you could explore two of the different registers evident in *Measure for Measure*. You may well conclude that there are two central registers operating in the play, each carrying certain values:

- the register linked to moral virtue, established by such words as 'redeem, grace, charity'; this register introduces the theme of morality and virtue

- the register linked to the title of the play, *Measure for Measure*, in other words language linked to weighing, testing, balancing; this register brings together the ideas of morality and justice.

ACTIVITY 14

1   How might the register to do with grace and Christian virtue interlink with that of testing?

2   Might they come together in the idea of Christian mercy?

3   Might this be part of the exploration of the nature of justice in the play?

4   Might the Old Testament idea of justice – of testing and weighing a person's deserts and then meting out punishment – need to be balanced with a New Testament concept of Christian grace in order to achieve a new sort of justice based also on mercy?

6 Why is *Measure for Measure* considered to be one of the 'problem plays'?

A modern audience, perhaps influenced by feminist ideas, would react strongly to the ending of the play. A consideration of the play as a comedy may have helped you to think in particular about whether the ending is a happy one. But there is no clear answer to this; Shakespeare leaves the audience to decide for themselves whether Isabella and the Duke are going to live 'happily ever after'. Thinking about *Measure for Measure* as one of Shakespeare's 'problem plays' (again, a type of genre) means that you can compare it with 'darker' plays, such as *Hamlet*, or *The Merchant of Venice*, and therefore concentrate on features very different from those you might have looked at had you been comparing it with other comedies.

Again, there was a reference to this point in the introduction to this section. There are real difficulties for a reader in coming to terms with and understanding the purpose of the harsh situations and evident cruelty within the play. You might feel rather hostile to the apparently high-handed cruelty of the Duke, so the best tactic is to face up to this problem and explore the issues which disturb you. The next activity raises some possible issues.

ACTIVITY 15

1   Which issues are too serious for comedy?

2   Is the Duke right to abuse Isabella and pretend that her brother is dead?

3   Is Angelo's seduction of Isabella – a nun – appropriate for comedy?

4   Is Claudio's attempt to prostitute Isabella in order to save his own life a proper subject for comedy?

5   Does the constant threat of death which hangs over several characters seem right for comedy?

6   Is the ending of the play completely convincing?

7   Might this play, with its dark and complex themes and its threats of death, be best defined as a tragicomedy – a blend of two genres?

Do you think that the different types of characterisation might cause an audience some difficulty? To answer this, work through the next activity.

ACTIVITY 16

1   Does Shakespeare present some characters, such as Angelo, Isabella and Claudio, with any psychological realism?

2   Is the Duke a difficult character to assess because he is not fully rounded, but indeed part realistic and part a **stock** 'type' issuing moral statements?

3   Does he hold up the pace of the play with his long speeches?

You might think about whether you are being asked to suspend disbelief and accept these presentations of character and situation without quibbling too much about the way in which Shakespeare has chosen to present certain ideas.

Conclusion

You have now worked through six critical perspectives on *Measure for Measure*. Using this model framework, you can now go on to address other readings on your own, such as the links Shakespeare appears to suggest between self-knowledge, mercy, compassion, morality and justice. In this way you will be working on some of the positive aspects of this complex text.

The Winter's Tale by William Shakespeare

The Winter's Tale was written in 1610 or 1611, in which year it was first put on at the Globe. Later the play was performed to celebrate the marriage of the princess Elizabeth to the Elector Palatine in 1612 or 1613. *The Winter's Tale* is one of Shakespeare's late plays known as **romances**. Many critics believe that Shakespeare's stagecraft and dramatic skills were at their highest at this point, and the plays carried not just a depth, but a complexity of possible readings. Critics offer many varied interpretations of this play such as:

- an exploration of myth
- a Christian parable
- a debate about the values of Court and Countryside
- a debate about the values of Nature versus Art, or Nature versus Nurture.

You will no doubt find more interpretations of your own to add to these as you explore this challenging play.

The six critical perspectives to be considered for the study of *The Winter's Tale* are:

1 *The Winter's Tale* as a romance.

2 Natural and human cycles in *The Winter's Tale*.

3 The debate between Court and Countryside.

4 Shakespeare's use of language in *The Winter's Tale*.

5 The dramatic effectiveness of *The Winter's Tale*.

6 *The Winter's Tale* as social comedy.

1 *The Winter's Tale* as a romance

Most critics describe this play as a romance. How would you define this term if you were asked to do so in an exam? To help you, you could consider that the romance originated in French courtly literature and became anglicised by writers such as Spencer and Shakespeare. There are several characteristics of Romance that you could point out:

- a necessity on the part of the audience to suspend disbelief
- the use of myth within the tale
- a fortunate or happy outcome.

How would you demonstrate these characteristics? Here are some examples from the play to start you off in your exploration.

1 *The suspension of disbelief*

In the course of the play, situations arise which are logically impossible. Often, there is the involvement of magic as Shakespeare brings home to the audience a moral truth or series of moral truths. Here just two of these will be considered: the presence of Time as a Chorus, and the resurrection of the statue in the last scene of the play.

Time as Chorus

After the drama of the first two acts, centred on the unjust actions of Leontes, and the third act with the farcical trial of Hermione, Shakespeare ends this sequence with the discovery of the child by the Shepherd. He then creates a pause for the audience with the presentation on stage of Time as the Chorus who explains his own role:

> [. . .] Impute it not a crime
> To me or my swift passage that I slide
> O'er sixteen years, [. . .]
> [. . .]
> [. . .] Your patience this allowing,
> I turn my glass, and give my scene such growing
> As you had slept between. Leontes leaving –   (Act 4, Scene 1, lines 4–17)

ACTIVITY 1

What do you think is going on here? What sort of character is Time? What functions might he serve here? You might consider these questions:

1 How is Time used as an economical way of showing passing years and events in a long play?

2 Does he help the audience to forget their resentment at Leontes?

3 Think of the image of the turned glass: the action of the sand seems exactly the same as before. Can you think of any similarities or parallels between what you have seen and are about to see in the next two acts?

Time continues to introduce the audience to events about to unfold. This then is typical of Romance: an illusion or non-realistic situation is created for several dramatic purposes and allows for the moral of the play to be developed.

The resurrection of Hermione in the statue scene

Again, this scene draws on magic and illusion. Shakespeare has left the audience unaware of Hermione's continued existence, although in Act 5, Scene 1, Paulina drops clues, for example at lines 67 and 82, and in Act 5, Scene 3, lines 60–1. Someone seeing the play for the first time, however, will probably not pick this up. Instead, the 'resurrection' is a magical device. Leontes is amazed at the likeness in the statue, but comments:

> [. . .] But yet, Paulina,
> Hermione was not so much wrinkled, nothing
> So agèd as this seems.
>
> (Act 5, Scene 3, lines 27–29)

However, he is overjoyed to find his wife living:

> [. . .] Thou hast found mine –
> But how is to be questioned: for I saw her,
> As I thought, dead; and have in vain said many
> A prayer upon her grave. [. . .]   (Act 5, Scene 3, lines 138–141)

ACTIVITY 2

At last the oracle of Apollo, from Act 3, Scene 1, between Cleomenes and Dion, is fulfilled. Here again Shakespeare uses magic and illusion to serve his dramatic purposes. What effects are achieved here? You might think about these questions:

1 What are the dramatic effects on an unsuspecting audience?

2 Do you find the scene moving?

3 Do you find yourself forgetting about the magic and thinking about the renewed relationship between Leontes and Hermione?

4 Are there any moral purposes served here? Think about Leontes's repentance, his prayers and request for forgiveness.

5 How does Shakespeare himself break the illusion: why do you think he does this?

Both of these scenes show how magic or illusion is used in Romance for many purposes, including that of presenting a moral for the audience. You might continue to discuss the effects of Shakespeare deliberately reminding the audience that they are watching a play, as in the Time scene, yet at the same time continuing to play with illusion and reality. Is this taking a great risk?

2 The use of myth within The Winter's Tale

The use of myth is another characteristic of Romance; many critics believe that Romance has primitive or folklore roots, and that this is why myth is a key element.

There are at least two central Greek myths drawn upon here: the myth of Persephone and Hades and the myth of Alcestis. Persephone was abducted from her mother by Hades and taken to the underworld, to be saved in what was represented as Spring. What are the links between Perdita and Persephone in events and seasons? In another myth Alcestis gave her life so that her husband could live: can you see the links with Hermione and Leontes? (You should spend some time investigating these myths.) But as you will see, these are loose links; it is more worthwhile to think about the ways in which Shakespeare adapts these myths to suit his own purposes.

3 A fortunate or happy outcome

The ending of this play gives great strength to this romance. Death is the worst of all accidents or evil situations; here, the most untimely, disastrous event of all, the death of a beloved caused by jealousy, is reversed and redeemed. You might think of Paulina's words at Act 5, Scene 3, lines 94–95:

> [. . .] It is required
> You do awake your faith.[. . .]

ACTIVITY 3

Think about the implications of the simple, moving words quoted above:

1 How does the word 'faith' pick up other themes and ideas at this part of the play?

2 In this section on Romance you have thought about the use of magic and illusion: might Shakespeare be making a plea to *you* the audience? What might this plea suggest? How might this relate to the Time scene and the statue scene?

So why does Shakespeare create illusions in this way? Could it be to place you, the audience, in the same situation as the characters on stage – a little confused, surprised, shocked, needing to think about things? Do you think, therefore, that his dramatic art has worked some magic on you too?

2 Natural and human cycles in *The Winter's Tale*

Most critics agree that there is a cycle of winter–spring–summer, and possibly autumn in *The Winter's Tale*. It is a cycle which may be seen to work on several levels.

The natural level

Mamillius establishes the season for the audience: 'A sad tale's best for winter' (Act 2, Scene 1, line 25). Then immediately after the Time interlude, Autolycus introduces the theme of spring in his song: 'When daffodils begin to peer (Act 4, Scene 2, line 53). Perdita introduces high summer when she speaks of the 'Whitsun pastorals' (Act 4, Scene 4, line 134). However, there is a deeper significance to the pattern than this.

Human cycles: the emotional patterning

Mamillius's tale is suggestive:

There was a man – [. . .]
Dwelt by a churchyard – I will tell it softly:

(Act 2, Scene 1, lines 29–30)

ACTIVITY 4

Think about the brief description of the man here: what might be suggested?

1 Is there a sense of isolation in his dwelling?

2 Why might he choose to dwell alone?

3 Why might there be a reference to a church?

4 Who might this refer to in the play?

To make this clearer, think about what you know of Leontes in the first part of the play. Look at his words to Camillo:

[. . .] Ha'not seen, Camillo –
[. . .]
My wife is slippery? If thou wilt confess –
                              [. . .] – then say
My wife's a hobby-horse, deserves a name
As rank as any flax-wench that puts to
Before her troth-plight: say't and justify't. (Act 1, Scene 2, lines 267–278)

ACTIVITY 5

If you remember that this is the language of a king, of a man who very recently appeared to adore his wife, his queen, what do you think is going on here? What do you think it suggests about Leontes's state of mind? You might consider:

1 the coarseness of the language, with the blatant sexual references

2 the punctuation creating disordered, erratic speech patterning

3 what actions Leontes is about to take concerning his family, and the immediate outcomes of these actions.

Perhaps Shakespeare's rhythmic pattern of the seasons may be applied to patterns of human emotions as Leontes faces a barren winter of evil, unjust, jealous thoughts. You might look here at Paulina's words, addressed to Leontes when she describes his wretched state: '[. . .] and still winter/ In storm perpetual' (Act 3, Scene 2, lines 210–11).

As you have seen, spring was signalled by Autolycus's song:

> When daffodils begin to peer
> With heigh, the doxy over the dale,
> Why, then comes in the sweet o'the year,
> For the red blood reigns in the winter's pale.   (Act 4, Scene 3, lines 1–4)

ACTIVITY 6

Here you may see explicit references to the 'spring' of the emotions.

1 What do you make of the contrast between the 'pale' of winter and the 'sweet' of spring?

2 Why are there sexual references such as 'the doxy over the dale' and the 'red blood'?

3 What sort of springtime is being suggested?

Perdita is used to develop this rhythmical patterning of the seasons in the famous flower scene of Act 4, Scene 4. She has reminded Polixenes and Camillo that they are winter creatures:

> For you there's rosemary and rue; these keep
> Seeming and savour all the winter long:
> Grace and remembrance be to you both,
>
>   (Act 4, Scene 4, lines 74–76)

Polixenes himself points out that these are 'flowers of winter' (Act 4, Scene 4, line 79).

ACTIVITY 7

Why have these flowers been selected for these two gentlemen? You might think about these questions:

1 What events have these men been involved in?

2 What is Polixenes about to do amidst the spring festivities?

3 What might remembrance bring about in the hearts and souls of men who have sinned? Might they 'remember' then 'repent', then find the 'grace' to which Perdita refers? In this sense, can you see a similar patterning to that of the seasons? In *The Winter's Tale* 'grace' has two meanings. The first is the secular or non-religious meaning of the courtly behaviour of a noble gentleman. The second is the religious meaning of 'grace' as the inspiring and strengthening influence which comes from God to help people act virtuously.

Perdita wishes she had 'some flowers o'th'spring' (line 114), and this has a special significance to the young girl who represents the very spring of life and love. She reveals her feelings through her references to flowers for the young shepherdesses who are of the same age. She wishes to give them flowers:

> That wear upon your virgin branches yet
> Your maidenheads growing. [. . .]
> [. . .]
>   [. . .] pale primroses
> That die unmarried ere they can behold
> Bright Phoebus in his strength – a malady
> Most incident to maids; [. . .]
>
>   (Act 4, Scene 4, lines 115–125)

Perdita says that she 'lacks' such flowers.

ACTIVITY 8

What are the suggestions presented in the register of this language? You might think about:

1   the sequence of words – 'maidenheads', 'unmarried' and 'malady'

2   how the idea of the 'pale primroses', delicate flowers without vigour, is linked to this grouping of words

3   what 'bright Phoebus', the powerful sun god might represent in his force and vigour

4   how, therefore, these young shepherdesses might be seen as in their 'spring'.

Perdita, however, is also aware of what summer might be, when she describes a lover whom she'll 'strew' with flowers, not like a 'corse':

> No, like a bank for Love to lie and play on,
> Not like a corse; or if, not to be buried,
> But quick and in mine arms. Come, take your flowers.
> Methinks I play as I have seen them do
> In Whitsun pastorals: [. . .]
>
>   (Act 4, Scene 4, lines 130–134)

ACTIVITY 9

Is this then, the Whitsun, or high summer of the seasons and emotions, and of human life? What is it that Perdita envisages here? Again, you might look at the register:

1 'Love', 'play', 'quick and in my arms': what is Perdita implying here?

2 What might be the natural sequence, then, for these young maids?

However, there is no movement towards this final stage in the play yet. Shakespeare has yet to complicate the scheme of the seasons by a belated 'frost'; think about what Polixenes is about to do, and think of the consequences of this. You will realise that Shakespeare prevents the final stage of harmony and marriage until all have repented, been forgiven and found harmony together. Perhaps the re-established love between Leontes and the 'wrinkled' Hermione represents the final season of the autumnal love of middle age. Do you think this could be the case?

3 The debate between Court and Countryside

Critics tend to disagree about this aspect of the play. Some assert that there actually is such a debate about the values of Court versus those of the pastoral or country characters. Others say that because of the ending of the play, where the pastoral characters are seen as gentlemen, there is no such distinction. You will make some sort of decision about that in the course of your studies.

You might well take the middle road, and decide that the values of courtly life need to be reinvigorated by the influence of the country characters: Leontes has killed a son, and tried to kill his daughter and imprisoned his wife; Polixenes also banishes his son. But look at the Shepherd and his values: he calls the baby he finds 'fairy gold' and acts in charity and love, setting a wonderful example to his son, the Clown. The Clown also buries Antigonus, which the Shepherd calls 'a good deed'. Who do you think has the better morals – Court or Country?

You might respond to this set of ideas by looking at Hermione's speeches at the court, when she is defending herself against her husband, in Act 3, Scene 2, lines 42, 46 and 50, for example. She emphasises 'grace' and repeats the word 'honour'. When Leontes realises his error, he picks up her word 'honour' (Act 3, Scene 2, line 164). The progress of the play traces Leontes's development towards achieving this very 'honour' and 'grace', and Perdita picks up this register in the pastoral scenes, talking to Florizel. The conversation is important if you wish to discuss this theme as Perdita seems to echo her mother's register when she chides Florizel for loving her:

O, pardon that I name them: your high self,
The gracious mark o'th'land, you have obscured
With a swain's wearing, and me, poor lowly maid
Most goddess-like pranked up. [. . .]   (Act 4, Scene 4, lines 7–10)

Florizel responds:

                              [. . .] I bless the time
When my good falcon made her flight across
Thy father's ground.   (Act 4, Scene 4, lines 14–16)

Perdita again rebuffs him:

                              [. . .] Now Jove afford you cause!
To me the difference forges dread; [. . .]
[. . .]
How would he [your father] look to see his work, so noble,
Vilely bound up? [. . .]   (Act 4, Scene 4, lines 16–22)

After Florizel tries to persuade her by giving a bad example of gods lowering their states to become 'beasts' to achieve their desires (line 27) Perdita makes a clear statement: 'you must change this purpose/ Or I my life' (lines 38–9).

ACTIVITY 10

This is an important conversation in a strange situation, and there is a lot going on here. To unpick this, you might consider these questions:

1 What point is Perdita making about their relationship?

2 Who is the realist here about unequal love? Is it the inexperienced Perdita, or the more experienced Florizel? Therefore, who is the idealist?

Look at this discussion again, in the light of the debate between the critics: is Shakespeare suggesting that the pastoral scenes present a perfection of life which the court does not? What do you think? If the rustic life were perfect, then Perdita would not have to change. But there seems to be a suggestion that courtly virtues cannot be fulfilled in the pastoral life. Does Shakespeare imply that some of the virtues held by the country characters, such as vitality and vigour, love, charity and honour to one's family, need to be imported into the court to improve and strengthen that life?

On the other hand, there could be a great irony here. Perdita thinks that she is too humble for Florizel in her 'borrowed flaunts' (line 22); but perhaps the youth is right when he says that 'all your acts are queens' (line 146)? Is goodness of character something inside us all irrespective of social status?

4 Shakespeare's use of language in *The Winter's Tale*

Many critics comment on the complexity of the language that Shakespeare uses in this play. If you understand how the language works to create character and to introduce themes or ideas, you will have found a way into discussing various interpretations of the play. Two examples will be explored here, the first being Leontes's speech to his son:

> Go play, boy, play: thy mother plays, and I
> Play too – but so disgraced a part, whose issue
> Will hiss me to my grave. [. . .]
> [. . .] Go play, boy, play [. . .]
> (Act 1, Scene 2, lines 187–190)

How does this language work? Shakespeare works here by accumulating meanings. The innocent child's play becomes the sexually provocative 'play' of sexual flirtation. This play in turn becomes the role Leontes is forced to play as a cuckold. And overall there is the reminder that Leontes is playing as he is an actor. This is how meanings are generated through language. To complete the sequence Perdita picks up the word 'play' (as you have seen in Activity 9 above), and restores a healthy association to this word. Hers is the innocence and naturalness of real love.

At the same time, Leontes's register is made to change during this speech. It becomes coarser and harsher – note the words 'sluiced' and 'fished'. Why might this be? And at the same time Leontes is made to appeal to the men in the audience, to enlist them on his side, as the 'tenth of mankind' have unfaithful wives.

These are some of the ways in which Shakespeare uses language to present character, increase tension and to develop ideas.

The second example is a speech from the last scene of the play, again by Leontes, when he touches the statue:

> O, thus she stood,
> Even with such life of majesty – warm life,
> As now it coldly stands – when I first wooed her!
> I am ashamed. Does not the stone rebuke me
> For being more stone than it? O royal piece!
> There's magic in thy majesty, [. . .]
>
> (Act 5, Scene 3, lines 34–39)

A few lines later more oppositions are established: blood/stone; statue/moving/ veins/blood.

Following the first example, you will be able to work through this one yourself, noting a couple of things in particular. The first is the initial word-play: 'warm/stone' and 'statue/life'.

ACTIVITY 11

1 What purposes does this pattern serve?

2 How does it work in the light of the play as a whole?

3 How does it prepare for the final great revelation?

4 How does this apparent simplicity of language prepare for such a complex and miraculous denouement?

Finally, if you consider that these two speeches are by the same character, at different ends of the play, you will see how the whole development of the play is reflected.

You will now be able to carry on and consider the language of other characters in a similar way.

5 The dramatic effectiveness of *The Winter's Tale*

All critics agree that this play is highly effective on stage and that the theatrical effects are superb. Here are some suggestions on how to respond to a question asking you how far you agree with this view. It is generally agreed that the play has a tripartite structure: (1) the tragic first three acts centred around the jealousy and subsequent 'sinning' of Leontes; (2) the festivity of the very long pastoral fourth act; and (3) the highly symbolic drama of the fifth act drawing all together – as if by magic.

You have already looked at the use of Time as Chorus and the statue scene in the first section of this chapter. You have just considered the dramatic language of the play. It might be worthwhile looking at the pastoral scenes of Act 4. In this section, Shakespeare cleverly binds together many different elements of the drama. He pushes the play forward, but at the same time elaborates upon many of the major issues in another direction; this is called the **spatial** development of the ideas. So, how does this happen?

There are at least ten different interests presented on stage in this act:

1 the debate between Polixenes and Perdita about nature and art

2 Perdita's flower passages

3 Florizel's declarations of love to Perdita

4 her honest and sensible replies

5 the old Shepherd's reminiscences over his wife and family life

6 the idle flirting and courting of the holiday season

7 Autolycus introducing a whole new theme, then cheating the courtly people

8 Polixenes lapsing into a similar sin to that of Leontes

9 the Shepherd and his son and friend acting as Chorus on events

10 the sheep-shearing, together with three songs and two dances in the festive mood.

The stage is full of people of different types, doing different things with some serious mood changes. There is huge energy expended. Of course, the question you ask is how does this work as a whole?

ACTIVITY 12

As you watch this act there is something going on wherever you look. The spectacle demands your full attention. What sort of things might Shakespeare be doing here? You might think about these points:

1 How does Shakespeare set up a comparison between the people of Court and Country; e.g. Polixenes and the Shepherd?

2 How does Shakespeare set up a system of checks and balances so that you don't make any simple judgements? For example, as you have seen, Perdita demonstrates how country virtues on their own are not sufficient for courtly life.

3 Autolycus can be seen as a minor character, yet what sort of major change does his song indicate?

4 How can he be both energetic, likeable, and yet a thief?

5 Why might Shakespeare insist that this scene is set in holiday time? Are the major characters enjoying a time out for several reasons?

6 During the course of this long act, have you remembered Leontes? Has the 'infection' of his mood been lifted from you? Are you ready yet to share in the feeling of forgiveness?

These are just some of the purposes behind this act. Of course, there are more, and this would be an ideal starting point for group work. You could select individual topics, develop each and bring them together in a forum.

6 *The Winter's Tale* as social comedy

One question you may well be asked is how, despite the tragedy, Shakespeare establishes a mood of comedy at the end of the play. You could think here about what Northrop Frye has said about the typical development of Shakespearean comedy.

Frye suggests that there are three different phases: a period of unsettlement caused by a harsh or unjust law; a period of confusion; the establishment finally of reconciliation and a new society.

You will be able to link these phases to details of the play quite readily. Think about Leontes's false judgement of his wife, her imprisonment and the death of his son, and the banishment of his daughter. Then there are the pastoral scenes in which characters are not what they seem or think, and struggle to find identity. Finally there is the forgiveness, reconciliation and newly established harmony. How exactly is each phase represented on stage?

ACTIVITY 13

You will probably find agreement with Northrop Frye, but remember that this is strictly not a comedy but a romance, so think about the ways in which Shakespeare varies the formula. Here are some questions you might think about:

1 Usually in social comedy Shakespeare excludes the character(s) causing the difficulties. Does this happen here? Why?

2 Usually there are different levels of society evident even at the reconciliation; what happens to the characters at the end of this play? What status do the pastoral characters such as Shepherd and Clown have at the end of the play? Why?

Here are some conclusions which you might consider:

3 Is Shakespeare bringing about yet another reconciliation of ideas as well as situations? Think about the debate between nature and nurture (Activity 10): whether humans are naturally good or need to be taught goodness. Perdita makes it clear that she believes her pastoral simplicity is not enough to qualify her to be Florizel's wife.

4 But at the end of the play the Shepherd and the Clown become 'brothers' to the nobles, to be seen as honourable gentlemen. So what do you think this might imply?

5 Might this 'transformation' complete the earlier argument to suggest that in fact the choice between goodness and evil is one we must each make for ourselves?

6 Perhaps that is how the total reconciliation is brought about – by our recognition of this? Is this total reconciliation a difference between romance and comedy? What are your views on this?

7 Finally you might consider the universality of this play: is it a play for all humans at all seasons of their life? Might this be why the ending of the play incorporates *all* in a final glorious harmony? Might Leontes therefore be a sort of 'everyman' representing a parable for all of us, as well as an individual? Is he a man who made a bad decision?

This concludes this section on *The Winter's Tale*, and you will now be able to explore further issues on your own. Here is an idea to start you off:

ACTIVITY 14

You could begin by exploring the play as a Christian parable, a reading which many critics agree upon. You might begin by looking at Hermione's, Paulina's and Perdita's words about goodness, honour and grace. Then you might explore Leontes's (and also Polixenes's) fall from grace into sin, the **expiation** or **penance** served for this sin, and their redemption and forgiveness, leading to future happiness.

Edward II by Christopher Marlowe

Edward II is written in a much plainer style than Marlowe's earlier plays, one that is much more muted in tone. His drama had moved from the presentation of powerful heroic characters to the depiction of the personal struggle of a rather weak individual who is subjected to intense pressures by the inheritance of the crown.

The six critical perspectives to be considered for the study of *Edward II* are:

1 The nature of kingship in *Edward II*.

2 Considerations of moral issues within the play.

3 A critical reading: *Edward II* as a morality play.

4 The role of religion in *Edward II*.

5 A critical reading: *Edward II* as a tragedy.

6 Some aspects of the significance of the language in *Edward II*.

1 The historical context: kingship in *Edward II*

An Elizabethan audience would probably have seen many plays that dealt with the subject of kingship. They would probably have known, for example,

Shakespeare's *Richard II*, which was performed at about the same time. They would also have been aware that Elizabeth I had no heir and that the issue of who would succeed her was beginning to preoccupy the Court. So a consideration of the meanings within the play can bring you close to some of the issues which may seem remote at the beginning of the twenty-first century, but which were of passionate interest to people of all social classes at the time the play was written and first performed.

Marlowe's consideration of kingship differs in many ways from that of other Elizabethan writers. Generally, the Elizabethans accepted the theory of the **divine right of kings**, according to which God chose the king independently of the wishes of the nation's subjects, this right to rule being passed down through generations.

In *Edward II*, Marlowe seems to explore what it is that gives a king the right to rule, but the ideas he offers may not be concerned with divine right. Here are some of the questions which you may ask yourself in exploring this interpretation of the play:

What sort of a king is Edward II?

At the start of the play Scene 1, Edward is introduced through Gaveston's words:

> 'My father is deceased; come Gaveston,
> and share the kingdom with thy dearest friend.'
> Ah, words that make me surfeit with delight!
> What greater bliss can hap to Gaveston,
> Than live and be the favourite of a king?   (lines 1–5)

ACTIVITY 1

1 What might Edward's priorities be when he takes over the kingdom?

2 Do you think that a king should have favourites?

3 What do you make of Gaveston's attitude here?

The Barons believe that Edward neglects his kingdom because of his relationship with Gaveston, and demand that he renounce his friend. Edward replies:

> I cannot brook these haughty menaces:
> Am I a king and must be overruled?   (lines 133–134)

ACTIVITY 2

What is Edward's attitude to the Barons and to his own powers?

Shortly afterwards (Scene 4), Mortimer makes a clear threat that if the King does not give up his favourite, the Pope will have to –

Curse him if he refuse, and then may we
Depose him and elect another king.   (lines 54–55)

ACTIVITY 3

1 Why should the Pope oppose Edward's wishes?

2 Who is now seen to have the right to elect the king?

Edward, however, is seen to be reconciled with the Barons when he appears to make peace with his Queen, Isabella, and most of the Barons offer loyalty:

EDWARD: Once more receive my hand, and let this be
               A second marriage 'twixt thyself and me.
               [. . .]
LANCASTER: This salutation overjoys my heart.
               [. . .]
WARWICK: Slay me, my lord, when I offend your grace.   (lines 335–350)

ACTIVITY 4

1 Why do you think Edward makes peace with Isabella?

2 Do you think he has 'won over' the Barons at this point?

In the course of the ensuing battles, Edward, supported by the Spencers, crowns himself afresh in what is a very dramatic moment, saying (Scene 11):

[*Kneeling*] By earth, the common mother of us all,
By heaven and all the moving orbs thereof,
By this right hand and by my father's sword,
And all the honours 'longing to my crown,
I will have heads and lives for him [. . .]   (lines 128–132)

ACTIVITY 5

1 This is like Edward's coronation service; what are his motives in repeating this service here?

2 Why does Marlowe use such noble language, and refer to 'heaven'?

3 Are Edward's motives here worthy of a king?

The decline of Edward II as a king

In Scene 17, Isabella explains how Edward might be regarded:

> Misgoverned kings are cause of all this wrack;
> And Edward, thou art one among them all,
> Whose looseness hath betrayed thy land to spoil
> And made the channels overflow with blood.   (lines 9–12)

ACTIVITY 6

1 What problems might a weak king cause?

2 Do you think that the description 'a weak king' might apply to Edward?

3 Do you trust Isabella?

Edward cannot help his affections for his favourites. In the course of the play you see Edward arrested, imprisoned, degraded, tortured and finally killed. He therefore sees the reversal of his ideas about kingship and of his earlier hopes. When Lightborn comes to kill him (Scene 24), Edward says:

> Know that I am a king – O, at that name,
> I feel a hell of grief. Where is my crown?
> Gone, gone. And do I remain alive?   (lines 88–90)

ACTIVITY 7

1 Do you see a reversal in Edward's language from that quoted before (Activity 5)?

2 Why does Marlowe use the word 'hell'?

3 Is there anything in life left for Edward if he is not a king?

Here are some questions you might consider in order to think about *Edward II* as a play about kingship (remembering that this is just one reading of a complex play):

- Who is seen to have a right to elect kings? Is it God?

- What do you think might be the qualities of a good ruler?

- How does Edward match up to these qualities?

2 Considerations of moral issues within the play

Consideration of the morality within the play could make you aware of the ethical issues that are important in any period – those of justice, loyalty, dishonesty, judging character against behaviour, and so on. But ideas, attitudes and values about crucial moral issues are often very different now from what they were in the sixteenth century. Important examples include attitudes to homosexuality and the role and status of wives. A consideration of moral issues in *Edward II* alerts us to the fact that while some issues are universal, attitudes and values relating to them may change profoundly during time and across cultures. In other words, you are considering how readings of a play may vary over time, and addressing AO4.

It also raises specific questions about the extent to which you think Marlowe might be arguing for change, and about what kinds of things he wanted to change.

To consider this perspective you could look at two areas:

1 the moral framework of the play

2 how other characters fit into the moral scheme of the play.

The moral framework of the play

You have already seen in the discussion of kingship how the right of electing a king shifted from being the responsibility of God to being that of man.

At the end of the play (Scene 25), Mortimer Junior speaks what might be regarded as the 'moral' of the play:

Base Fortune, now I see that in thy wheel
There is a point to which, when men aspire,
They tumble headlong down; [. . .] (lines 59–61)

ACTIVITY 8

1 Is there any reference to God or morality here?

2 Does Mortimer Junior suggest that life is ruled by fate and chance?

The new king, Edward III, makes reference to 'grief and innocence', but probably does not draw any further moral conclusion. Marlowe often made comments about his own atheism, such as 'The only beginning of religion was to keep men in awe.' Do you think that it is possible that he deliberately offered a play in which there are no moral rules stemming from divine law?

How other characters fit into the moral scheme of the play

The characters to be considered here are Gaveston, Mortimer Junior and Isabella (but you could consider others for your own study).

Gaveston

You have already looked at Gaveston's words when he asked what 'greater bliss' there could be than to be a king's 'favourite' (Activity 1).

Later in Scene 1, Gaveston arranges entertainment for the King, saying that he:

> May draw the pliant King which way I please.
> Music and poetry is his delight;   (lines 52–53)

ACTIVITY 9

1 What do these words suggest about Gaveston? Might he be cunning?

2 Might he be seen as manipulative, aware of the King's weaknesses?

3 Is he governed by any concern for the King's well-being?

Do you think that Gaveston is a manipulator? A **Machiavellian** figure? Niccolo Machiavelli (1469–1527) was an Italian writer and statesman who advocated the use of ruthless means to secure and retain political power. The adjective *Machiavellian* is used to describe a person who practises duplicity and scheming in order to win political power.

- Remember the King's words about why he loves Gaveston: 'Because he loves me more than all the world' (Scene 4).

- Do you think Gaveston is rather shrewd in his analysis of the King?

Mortimer Junior

Mortimer Junior might have some justification for being angry with the King. But does this anger justify his ambition to plot with Isabella and overthrow the King? In Scene 18, his feelings are made clear:

> [*Aside to* ISABELLA] I like not this relenting mood in Edmund;
> [. . .]
> Your King hath wronged your country and himself,
> And we must seek to right it as we may.   (lines 47–77)

ACTIVITY 10

1 What do you make of Mortimer Junior's aside to Isabella?

2 Is he interested in reaching a peaceful solution?

When you consider his final words (which you looked at in Activity 8), you might consider whether Mortimer Junior had any moral purposes at all, or whether ultimately he, like Gaveston, was just out to better himself.

Isabella

In the scene where Edward makes peace with Isabella (Activity 4), you might feel sorry for her. But think about what happens in Scene 8, where Isabella and Mortimer join forces:

> MORTIMER JUNIOR: Madam, I cannot stay to answer you;
>   But think of Mortimer as he deserves.
> ISABELLA: So well hast thou deserved, sweet Mortimer,
>   As Isabel could live with thee forever.   (lines 58–61)

ACTIVITY 11

1 How do you respond to Isabella now? Do you still feel sympathy?

2 Do you think that she, too, might be self-interested?

3 Is she out for revenge?

To take this reading further, you might consider if there are any moral rules established in the play. You could ask yourself whether any of them think of anything other than themselves. Do you think there might be some real love shown by Edward and his two lovers, who are both finally willing to die for him?

3 A critical reading: *Edward II* as a morality play

A consideration of the effects of the use of two literary genres – both of which raise questions relating to the meanings of the play – will alert you to very different aspects of the play. Comparison with morality plays, for example, encourages you to think about good and evil, particularly in a religious context.

The **episodic** structure of the play also conforms to the morality-play structure. (Consideration of the play as tragedy follows on page 45.)

Morality plays were popular in the Middle Ages, dramatising mankind's journey through life, with all its temptations. Moral qualities of evil and goodness were presented on stage, and there were 'good' and 'bad' angels. The **mystery plays** developed a similar theme using stories from the Bible, playing out the whole of mankind's story from the Fall to redemption through the birth of Jesus Christ.

There might be echoes of the morality and mystery plays in the presentation of Lightborn in *Edward II*. When the audience first sees Lightborn (Scene 23), he describes his 'apprenticeship':

> 'Tis not the first time I have killed a man.
> I learned in Naples how to poison flowers,
> To strangle with a lawn thrust through the throat,
> To pierce the windpipe with a needle's point,   (lines 29–32)

ACTIVITY 12

How might Lightborn be seen as a Machiavellian figure (see Activity 9)?

This speech might establish Lightborn as a villain, but there are references that link him, as a character, with morality plays. His name is taken from the name of a Devil in the Chester Cycle of mystery plays. The name 'Lightborn' is Lucifer, the name of the Devil, anglicised. In his scenes in the dungeon with Edward, certain significant references are made (Scene 24):

> This dungeon where they keep me is the sink
> Wherein the filth of all the castle falls.
> [. . .]
> My mind's distempered and my body's numbed,
> And whether I have limbs or no, I know not.   (lines 55–64)

ACTIVITY 13

Look at the language register here and in the dungeon scenes – darkness, rats, damp, dungeon, deprivation of the senses, Lightborn as Lucifer: might Marlowe be suggesting that Edward is in hell on earth? To explore this idea further, you might consider whether Marlowe created a drama with some suggestion of a Christian framework, but without drawing a Christian moral.

4 The role of religion in *Edward II*

To explore this topic you could reorder material you assembled in Activities 12 and 13 above, and interweave the material from the second perspective – considerations of moral issues within the play (see page 41).

ACTIVITY 14

1 Might the morality-play elements imply a religious reading?

2 Are there the suggestions of Lightborn as a devil, and of damnation?

3 Might Edward be seen to endure the tortures of hell on earth?

4 Do you think Marlowe suggests that there are consequences for mankind's wrongdoing, other than punishment here on earth?

5 Is there in the play any sense of reward or punishment in an afterlife?

6 Are there any 'judges' for Edward, other than his fellow men?

7 What might Mortimer Junior's words about the 'Wheel of Fortune', at the end of the play, suggest about certain views of mankind's destiny?

8 Is the 'Wheel of Fortune' a Christian concept?

5 A critical reading: *Edward II* as a tragedy

Consideration of *Edward II* as a tragedy allows you to compare this play with quite different ones and so focus on what happens to the main character at the end of the play, and also on how different audiences and individuals might respond to the main character (AO4). Many aspects *of Edward II* correspond to the concerns and structure of a tragedy.

To assess this perspective you could consider three types of tragedy:

1 the tragedy of a king's fall from grace: Edward

2 the tragedy implicit in the concept of the 'Wheel of Fortune': how a person may apparently achieve wealth or fame, and then suddenly lose everything

3 the personal tragedy of Edward himself.

ACTIVITY 15

To consider a king's fall from grace, think about the following:

1 What does Marlowe suggest about the divine right of kings?

2 Should a man be entitled to rule because he is from a certain family?

3 Alternatively, should he have particular qualities that entitle him to rule?

6 Some aspects of the significance of the language in *Edward II*

To assess this perspective, think about the plainness of the language of this play, unusual for a drama of its time, and very unusual for Marlowe. There is a limited use of 'elevated' language, so when it appears in this play, you need to consider Marlowe's reasons for including it. You have seen the use of noble language in Activity 5 above (page 40).

- Why does Marlowe make Edward speak in this noble way here? How does this language affect your response to Edward?

- Why do you think the language is generally so plain? (You might think about what Marlowe could be suggesting about a 'new' sort of king.)

- Is he a king in an age that is less heroic than that presented in other dramas of the period?

- Might he be a non-heroic king for a non-heroic age?

You might also consider Isabella's lofty speech to the troops (Scene 17). Mortimer Junior cuts the speech down:

> Nay Madam, if you be a warrior,
> Ye must not grow so passionate in speeches.   (lines 14–15)

ACTIVITY 16

1 How does this language affect your response to Isabella? Does it change your sympathies for her?

2 What might Marlowe be implying in Mortimer Junior's rebuff to Isabella?

3 Might Mortimer Junior be a better politician and tactician than Isabella is, aware of the needs of the troops? Aware of how language must be adapted to suit situations?

Conclusion

You have now worked through six perspectives relating to *Edward II*. Using this model framework, you can go on to address other readings on your own, perhaps beginning by considering *Edward II* as a history play, exploring Edward's conflict with the Barons.

The Duchess of Malfi by John Webster

The Duchess of Malfi falls within the genre of revenge plays. The Elizabethan/Jacobean audience had mixed views about revenge, and an ambiguous attitude towards those who extracted it. While it was acceptable to avenge the murder of a blood-relative, or a very brutal murder, it was still an offence in the eyes of God to kill a fellow human being. Hence the Elizabethan/Jacobean audience's fear and distrust of the ideas of Niccolo Machiavelli (1469–1527) – the Italian writer and statesman who advocated the use of ruthless means to secure and retain political power.

Revenge plays had certain characteristics: there would be one or more revengers; they were often set in Italy or Spain; there was often a discontented character who acted as commentator; there was intrigue, poisoning, violent actions and death; disguise was often used to create confusion; and there was a violent final scene. If you are asked to consider *The Duchess of Malfi* as a revenge play, these are the features you should discuss.

Below, you will look at six different critical perspectives on *The Duchess of Malfi*:

1 Whether there is evidence of a firm social and moral viewpoint.

2 How far the men are ruled by their intelligence or by their passions.

3 Whether it is only by their actions that characteristics are revealed.

4 How you respond to Bosola.

5 Whether there is any light in the darkness of the play.

6 Whether Webster presents his characters with pity or contempt.

1 The social and moral viewpoint

It has been commented that in *The Duchess of Malfi* there is a readily identifiable social and moral viewpoint against which to judge each of the characters. How far do you agree with this judgement?

To answer this, you need to decide whether the statement is true, and/or offer another viewpoint. You could begin by looking at the speech of three of the characters: Antonio, Bosola and the Duchess.

Antonio

In Act 1, Scene 2, Antonio speaks about Ferdinand and the Cardinal, and then the Duchess:

> [. . .] and verily I believe them:
> For the devil speaks in them.
> But for their sister, the right noble duchess,
> [. . .]
> There speaketh so divine a continence,
> As cuts off all lascivious, and vain hope.   (lines 107–122)

ACTIVITY 1

1 Pick out the references that show the contrast between the brothers and the Duchess.

2 What do you understand about the Duchess from this speech?

3 At this point, what is Antonio's relationship to the Duchess?

Bosola

Many critics see Bosola as a reliable commentator. In Act 1, Scene 1, he describes the state of the nation under the rule of the brothers:

> He, and his brother, are like plum trees, that grow
> crooked over standing pools, they are rich, and o'erladen
> with fruit, but none but crows, pies, and caterpillars feed
> on them. [. . .]   (lines 49–52)

ACTIVITY 2

1 What is Bosola saying here about the brothers and their method of rule?

2 What images are used to create the effect? Where else are similar images used in the play?

3 How reliable a commentator do you think Bosola is?

The Duchess

The Duchess is fearless in the face of death, and critics point to her 'diamond' speech to show her contempt for her executioners (Act 4, Scene 2). She continues:

> Yet stay, heaven gates are not so highly arch'd
> As princes' palaces: they that enter there
> Must go upon their knees. [*Kneels*]   (lines 228–230)

ACTIVITY 3

1 What is the Duchess's attitude to her brothers?

2 What is her attitude to death? Does this suggest her goodness?

3 How do you respond to the Duchess at the moment of her death?

If you take the speeches of Antonio and Bosola above, and the words and actions of the Duchess, you might agree that a social and moral judgement is being made. But many critics argue that Webster is not at all clear-cut in his attitude to traditional Christian attitudes to death.

The Cardinal says, 'I am puzzl'd in a question about hell' (Act 5, Scene 5) and when he dies Bosola, despite his goodness in avenging the death of the Duchess, says:

> [. . .] Oh, this gloomy world,
> In what a shadow, or deep pit of darkness
> Doth, womanish, and fearful, mankind live?
> [. . .]
> Mine is another voyage.
>
> (lines 99–104)

ACTIVITY 4

1 Why is the Cardinal, a Churchman, puzzled about hell?

2 If the play reflects traditional Christian beliefs, why does Bosola speak like this?

3 Do you think that there is any traditional Christian consolation at the end of the play?

2 Are men ruled by their intelligence or their passions?

One critic believes that in Jacobean drama the men are ruled by either their intelligence or their passions. Other critics argue that it is the absence of a motive that makes the Duchess's murder so terrifying. What do you think about the brothers and their motivation?

Assess the first statement, and then relate it to the second, finally expressing your own opinion.

This time you could examine the three characters: Ferdinand, the Cardinal and Bosola. You could argue that Ferdinand is ruled by passion, the Cardinal by intelligence, and Bosola by a combination of the two.

Ferdinand

Ferdinand speaks to the Cardinal about the birth of his sister's child in Act 2, Scene 5:

> I have this night digg'd up a mandrake.
> [. . .]
> And I am grown mad with't.
> [. . .]
> Read there, a sister damn'd, she's loose, i'th'hilts':
> [. . .]
> Till I know who leaps my sister I'll not stir. (lines 1–78)

ACTIVITY 5

1 How does Ferdinand react to the news of the birth?

2 What sort of language does he use here and elsewhere in this scene?

3 Look for this combination of horror, violence and sex in Ferdinand's other speeches. What does it tell you about Ferdinand's state of mind and his obsessions?

4 Would you say that Ferdinand is ruled by intelligence or the passions?

The Cardinal

The Cardinal reacts sharply to Ferdinand's lack of control (Act 2, Scene 5):

> CARD.   How idly shows this rage! which carries you,
>   As men convey'd by witches, through the air
>   On violent whirlwinds: this intemperate noise
>   [. . .]
>
> FERD.   [. . .] Have not you
>   My palsy?
>
> CARD.   Yes, I can be angry
>   Without this rupture;
>   [. . .]
>   [. . .] chide yourself: (lines 50–59)

ACTIVITY 6

1 What differences can you see in the temperaments of the two brothers?

2 Who do you think is the more controlled of the two? And the more dangerous?

3 What do you learn about the Cardinal's values here?

4 Would you say that the Cardinal is ruled by his intelligence?

Bosola

It could be claimed that initially Bosola is governed by a sort of passion. In Act 1, Scene 2, he speaks heatedly to Ferdinand:

> I would have you curse yourself now, that your bounty,
> Which makes men truly noble, e'er should make
> Me a villain: [. . .]
>
> (lines 192–194)

ACTIVITY 7

1 What is Bosola's relationship to the brothers? How does he serve them?

2 To what degree is he driven by the need for payment?

3 How aware is he of his own motives and wickedness?

4 Would you say he was ruled by both passion for money *and* by intelligence? How do these two passions dictate his actions later in the play?

Now turn to the second part of the question, and the comment that 'it is the absence of a motive that makes the Duchess's murder so terrifying.'

Many critics say that it is difficult to pin down the motives of the brothers. Early on in Act 1, Scene 2, the Cardinal hints at a motive when he talks to the Duchess about her marrying again:

> No, nor any thing without the addition, Honour,
> Sway your high blood.   (lines 217–218)

Later he says (Act 2, Scene 5):

> [. . .] Shall our blood?
> The royal blood of Aragon and Castile,
> Be thus attainted?   (lines 21–23)

ACTIVITY 8

1 What are the Cardinal's declared motives?

2 Look at his speech in Act 2, Scene 5. How important are appearances to him?

3 Do you think that he might have any other motives?

Ferdinand is often considered to be more complex. You have already looked at his passion for his sister, which he frequently declares, for example when he talks of 'her delicate skin', and adds 'Damn her! that body of hers', in Act 4, Scene 1.

ACTIVITY 9

What might these comments suggest about the nature of Ferdinand's feelings?

There is also another possible motive revealed in the exchange between Ferdinand and the Cardinal (Act 2, Scene 5):

> [. . .] I could kill her now,
> In you, or in myself, for I do think
> It is some sin in us, Heaven doth revenge
> By her.
>   (lines 64–67)

ACTIVITY 10

1 What effect does the Duchess have on Ferdinand?

2 Might the Duchess's goodness make the brothers aware of their own evil and of their punishment to come?

Both motives seem to come together in Ferdinand's last speech (Act 5, Scene 5):

> My sister, oh! my sister, there's the cause on't,
> *Whether we fall by ambition, blood, or lust,*
> *Like diamonds we are cut with our own dust.*
>   (lines 70–72)

ACTIVITY 11

1 Is it being suggested here that Ferdinand is his own worst enemy?

2 Does Webster deliberately make Ferdinand's motivation ambiguous and complex? Why?

Finally, you must make your own assessment of the characters of Ferdinand, the Cardinal and Bosola, and whether you think there are clear motives behind their actions. Consider as well the possibility that Webster makes his characters complex and ambiguous to deliberately unsettle or confuse the audience.

3 Characters are revealed only by their actions

It has been said that in *The Duchess of Malfi* 'it is only in action that men are truly themselves'. Do you agree with this assessment?

You have already looked at the difficulty of relating words to deeds with regard to the motives of Ferdinand and the Cardinal. It might also be useful to consider Antonio, whom many critics find hard to assess. Begin with Bosola's words to him in Act 3, Scene 5:

> [. . .] This proclaims your breeding.
> Every small thing draws a base mind to fear;
> As the adamant draws iron: fare you well sir,
> You shall shortly hear from's.
>
> (lines 51–54)

ACTIVITY 12

Do you agree with Bosola's judgement of Antonio?

4 How do you respond to Bosola?

'Bosola is no mechanical villain; instead he is a misfit, a man of rather worthier talents forced into a degrading position, and with a brutal philosophy, making the most of it by the thoroughness with which he plays his part.' Do you agree with this assessment of Bosola? Find evidence in the play to support your view of him.

You have already considered Bosola's need for money. Now you could look at his speech after the death of the Duchess in Act 4, Scene 2:

> [. . .] My estate is sunk
> Below the degree of fear: where were
> These penitent fountains while she was living?
> Oh, they were frozen up: here is a sight
> As direful to my soul as is the sword
> Unto a wretch hath slain his father. Come,
> I'll bear thee hence,
> And execute thy last will; that's deliver
> Thy body to the reverent dispose
> Of some good women: that the cruel tyrant
> Shall not deny me. Then I'll post to Milan,
> Where somewhat I will speedily enact
> Worth my dejection.
>
> (lines 357–369)

ACTIVITY 13

Do you agree with critics who claim that the most important change in Bosola is the growth of his pity and admiration for the Duchess?

5 Is there any light in the darkness of the play?

It has been claimed that 'if you look into the deepest darkness of the play, there is a flash of light.' Do you agree with this optimistic view of *The Duchess of Malfi*?

You could begin by looking at two areas of the play which might give some hope to the audience. One is Bosola's 'conversion' into a bringer of goodness and destroyer of the evil brothers and their court, referred to (page 49). It may also be helpful to consider the Duchess herself as a source of light in the play, for example in her playfulness in the wooing of Antonio in Act 1, Scene 2.

However, her death scene (Act 4, Scene 2) is the scene which most critics would point to as evidence of her strength and majesty: 'I am Duchess of Malfi still'.

ACTIVITY 14

1 What opinion do you form of the Duchess here and in the scene as a whole?

2 How do her words and actions reflect upon her brothers?

6 Does Webster present his characters with pity or contempt?

It has been suggested that 'Webster has a kind of pity for all of his characters, an attitude towards good and bad alike [. . .]'. Do you agree with the interpretation – or does Webster treat some characters with contempt?

You could start by looking at the Cardinal, possibly one of the most evil characters. Look at the Cardinal's fear and confusion in Act 5, Scene 5:

When I look into the fish-ponds, in my garden,
Methinks I see a thing, arm'd with a rake
That seems to strike at me. [. . .]   (lines 5–7)

ACTIVITY 15

1 What has happened to the usually confident Cardinal here? What has he seen?

2 Do you think Webster could be playing on the audience's pity in his presentation of the old man's confusion here?

Now that you have explored the six critical perspectives here, you can use this framework to explore other aspects of the play, perhaps beginning with Webster's presentation of the Duchess herself, and her moving speech before her death, beginning 'Not a whit: [. . .]' (Act 4, Scene 2, line 211). Do you think, as some critics do, that Webster was in love with his own creation?

The Alchemist by Ben Jonson

The Alchemist was probably written and performed in 1610. It is one of Ben Jonson's satirical comedies in which he tried, by exposing the greed and hypocrisy of society, to shame his audience into change for the better. Jonson modernised the medieval idea of the **humours** by portraying his characters with one dominant characteristic. In *The Alchemist* this characteristic is a desire for change as the 'gulls' or foolish, greedy characters seek to improve their situations through **alchemy**. Some critics believe that this is Jonson's best play, claiming that the flawless plot entertains and satisfies audiences who enjoy the sight of the catchers being caught in the final act. Other critics attack Jonson on four grounds: (1) the weakness of the two-dimensional characters; (2) weakness of plot; (3) language which is impenetrable and clumsy; and (4) a lack of theatricality. Finally, there is a dispute about whether the play has a moral purpose because what seems to be celebrated is not so much morality as the triumphant display of witty ingenuity.

The six different critical perspectives on *The Alchemist* to be discussed here are:

1 What is the significance of the image of alchemy?

2 How effective is Jonson's method of creating character?

3 Is this the perfect plot?

4 The theatricality of the play.

5 An exploration of Jonson's use of language in *The Alchemist*.

6 How far is Ben Jonson concerned to teach a moral lesson in *The Alchemist?*

1 What is the significance of the image of alchemy?

Here you are being asked to talk about the central image of the play, to show how important it is to the unity of ideas and presentation. In Jonson's time people believed that it really was possible to change base metals into precious gold if only the right formula could be discovered. The experiment into such change was known as alchemy. Ben Jonson took the literal meaning of an alchemist pretending to bring about such change and developed the idea to a metaphorical level, a desire for social improvement through change. So in this play there is both a literal and metaphorical sense of alchemy presented on stage.

Alchemy is presented on stage through the continuous efforts of Subtle, whose central trick in the play is to masquerade as an alchemist. Jonson introduces the central theme at the beginning of the play with Face's words to his co-conspirator Subtle:

> When all your alchemy, and your algebra,
> Your minerals, vegetables, and animals,
> Your conjuring, cozening, and your dozens of trades,
> Could not relieve your corps [. . .]
> I ga' you countenance [. . .]   (Act 1, Scene 1, lines 38–43)

ACTIVITY 1

A consideration of this speech will reveal quite a lot about Jonson's methods and purposes. You might think about these questions:

1 How is alchemy used as an image: can you find both a literal use of the word here, and also a metaphorical sense of social change?

2 What do you think about the very dense, packed lines: how would these be delivered on stage? Do you expect the action to be as fast-paced?

3 How does Jonson point out the immorality of this sort of alchemy?

4 Can you see any irony here? Has scientific alchemy been seen to work? How do you think any plans based (as Face points out) on previous failures will turn out?

If you bear this activity in mind it should prove helpful as you study this text.

Metaphorically, alchemy lies at the heart of the play, representing a desire for transformation in society. All of the victims, the 'gulls', seek to better themselves.

Hence, Subtle speaks of Sir Epicure Mammon's ambitions:

> This is the day, I am to perfect for him
> The *magisterium*, our great work, the stone;
> And yield it, made, into his hands: of which,
> He has, this month, talked, as he were possessed.
> And, now, he's dealing pieces on't, away.   (Act 1, Scene 4, lines 13–17)

Subtle describes Mammon's visits of promise to people such as lepers, housewives with their fear of the plague, beggars, bawds, concluding:

> He will make
> Nature ashamed of her long sleep [. . .]
> If his dream last, he'll turn the age, to gold.   (Act 1, Scene 4, lines 25–29)

ACTIVITY 2

1 What sort of ambitions does Jonson suggest in Mammon's works?

2 What qualities does Mammon show in his ambitions?

3 How does Jonson suggest that there are flaws in Mammon's ambitions?

4 How does the punctuation, with its frequent brief pauses, help to show the scope of Mammon's plans?

Sir Epicure Mammon, whose name suggests that he wants too much of a good thing, is at least generous in his desires initially. You might now think about the other characters in the play: *all* desire social transformation.

Dapper wants a spirit to help him cheat at gambling. But think of his entrance in the first act. Arriving late, he explains why:

And I had lent my watch last night, to one
That dines, today, at the sheriff's: and so was robbed
Of my pass-time.   (Act 1, Scene 2, lines 6–8)

ACTIVITY 3

What do you make of Dapper's words? You might consider:

1 What has happened to the would-be conman?

2 Are his social ambitions therefore reasonable?

3 How does Jonson use irony here?

Jonson presents a similar picture for the audience in Kastril, who explains his desired transformation:

To carry a business, manage a quarrel, fairly,
Upon fit terms [. . .]   (Act 3, Scene 4, lines 18–19)

But then Kastril explains how he will use this desired change to become an 'angry boy':

And I would fain be one of 'em, and go down
And practice I' the country.   (Act 3, Scene 4, lines 24–25)

ACTIVITY 4

Can you see how Jonson presents Kastril in a similar way to Dapper? You might think about the following:

1 Look at Jonson's reference to the country: in his period, city-dwellers laughed at people from the country as country bumpkins.

2 So, as what sort of a man is Dapper presented?

3 How appropriate is his social ambition?

4 Do you think he will be easy to 'con'?

Now you might work out what it is that each of the other victims wants: Drugger, Ananias and Tribulation. The conspirators are also transformed. You might work out how and when each change occurs. Subtle becomes the alchemist; Face goes through four transformations: his drudge, 'Lungs', the captain and Jeremy; and Dol becomes a lady, prompting Face to say:

> (Why, this is yet
> A kind of modern happiness, to have
> Dol Common for a great lady.)
>
> (Act 4, Scene 1, lines 22–24)

ACTIVITY 5

1 How does Jonson show the falseness of such transformations here?

2 In what role is Face acting at this moment in the play?

3 How effective do you think Jonson's use of irony is here and when applied to the ambitions of the other gulls?

The idea of transformation is also important in the language Jonson uses in this play. This will be considered as the fifth critical perspective on this text (page 63).

2 How effective is Jonson's method of creating character?

Many critics think that the portrayal of character is a weakness in Jonson's plays; you may be asked to offer your opinion on this. You may agree, or you may argue, as T. S. Eliot did, that the characters become important symbols and help to create the play's universality.

All the characters in this play have a common motive: to become in some ways upwardly mobile, and seek social improvement. The problem arises that these characters are not developed beyond their one need: it is their sole motive, and the only distinctive feature about each is exactly what sort of change they desire. What critics object to is the fact that there is no internal life displayed for each character beyond this, and therefore no development of character is available.

How then might Jonson give vitality to such characters? You are given an indication as soon as the play begins, and the three conspirators are on stage together. A quarrel breaks out between Face, who has organised the use of his master's house, and Subtle, who has the master role of alchemist to play:

> FACE: You might talk softlier, rascal.
> SUBTLE: No, you scarab,
> I'll thunder you, in pieces. I will teach you
> How to beware, to tempt a fury again
> That carries tempest in his hand, and voice.
> FACE: The place has made you valiant.
> SUBTLE: No, your clothes
> [. . .]
> DOL: Gentlemen, what mean you?
> Will you mar all? (Act 1, Scene 1, lines 59–81)

ACTIVITY 6

How is Jonson maintaining interest in his characters here? You might think about:

1 What is their relationship to each other at this stage of the play?

2 What sort of alliance has been formed?

3 How secure is this relationship?

4 What might be Dol's role here?

You might deduce that whilst Jonson's characters do not change internally, their relationship to each other changes constantly; it becomes a dynamic force within the play. So, as part of the audience, you wonder if this unholy alliance will hold out, and become intrigued by the changes.

It would be worthwhile for you to track all the changes. For example:

• What happens when Dame Pliant is introduced in Act 4, Scene 2? Might this bring the rivalry between the two men to a head?

• What happens to the triple alliance when they face threats of being found out on Lovewit's return in Act 5, Scenes 1–5? Do they care a jot about each other?

You may conclude that because of the group dynamics the characterisation is lively and often very funny as it drives the plot along.

3 Is this the perfect plot?

Some critics suggest that there is no plot at all in *The Alchemist* – just a series of comic situations. You may be asked to express your views on this. It seems to be relatively easy to combat this criticism.

The plot of the play is simple, but absolutely logical. Three conspirators plot to gull several victims; the audience watches as each appears on stage, and appointments are made for their return, when the conspirators hope to make their financial killings (Acts 1 and 2). This plan crumbles; the conspirators fail to realise that, because of greedy anxiety, the victims arrive too early or at the wrong time. At this stage the audience becomes aware that the plan will fail, and settle down to enjoy watching the conspirators caught in their own trap (Acts 3–4) and finally gain their 'just' desserts in Act 5.

ACTIVITY 7

It would be helpful for you to make a detailed record of the victims' appearances and appointments, and then the times when they arrive. This will give you a very clear grasp of how the plot is constructed.

4 The theatricality of the play

Some critics also suggest that the play lacks dramatic effectiveness. But again, you might well decide that this is rather unjust. After all, when this play is performed it is usually very well received. How would you argue for Jonson's skills as a dramatist? Here are some suggestions which might start off your exploration.

Ben Jonson's use of setting

Jonson creates something of an illusion in establishing the setting of his play. The audience is very aware that the town, with its various dangers, is nearby; and Lovewit has fled from the threat of plague. There is also the real threat of punishment for the conspirators. For example, when Ananias arrives, Kastril says rather fearfully, 'Is he the Constable?' (Act 4, Scene 7, line 44). You will find other references to this throughout the play. Also, Subtle is made to explain clearly the actual layout of Drugger's ideal shop:

> [. . .] just,
> At corner of a street: (here's the plot on't.)
> And I would know, by art, sir, of your worship,
> Which way I should make my door, by necromancy.
> And, where my shelves. And, which should be for boxes.
> And, which for pots.
>
> (Act 1, Scene 3, lines 8–12)

ACTIVITY 8

Jonson is achieving several effects in this speech. You might consider:

1 What sort of shop is created here? It is a vivid picture – you can almost see it. How does this work set against the claustrophobic, minimal setting?

2 How does Jonson use punctuation and repetition here to give you a glimpse into Drugger's character: what sort of man do you think he is?

You realise however, that although Jonson presents a picture of city life, all the scenes with the conspirators are set within the limits of Lovewit's house. They are confined and claustrophobic, with all the action occurring between nine o'clock in the morning and three in the afternoon.

ACTIVITY 9

What do you think Jonson's purposes were in creating this claustrophobia? Think about the effect on the plot of the play. You, as the audience are living with the conspirators in that confined space. So, what happens when the perfectly timed appointments for the gulls start to go wrong? Or when Face and Subtle make mistakes in timing? Look at their responses to something unexpected, such as at the arrival of Surly in disguise. There are the complications when people arrive early, as does Sir Epicure Mammon. How is Dol forced to act? What happens to Dapper? Tension inevitably builds.

You have looked at how the settings have mattered to the plot, how with relentless logic, the spotlight has been thrown on the ingenuity of the characters to avoid trouble facing up to the implications of their crimes. Do you think that the claustrophobia of the setting has a great effect on the dramatic effectiveness?

Ben Jonson's use of comic effects

You might conclude that the comedy rests on split-second timing, a series of mishaps punctuated by the knocking at the door as you are somehow in the middle of this confusion. Did you, along with the other characters, forget about Dapper with his gingerbread gag, when Face cries out, 'Our clerk within, that I forgot!' (Act 5, Scene 3, line 63)? Or that Lovewit might arrive unexpectedly, as he does at the start of Act 5?

Would it be fair to claim that the flawless comic plot creates great suspense based on the imminent breakdown of the conspirators' plans, and that it is really funny to watch the characters' frantic efforts to forestall the inevitable discovery?

One example of the play's dramatic effectiveness is when Sir Epicure Mammon arrives unexpectedly. Dol has been preparing to be the Queen of the Fairies for Dapper, when Sir Epicure Mammon unexpectedly arrives. Face is horrified:

FACE: God's lid, we never thought of him, till now.
        Where is he?
DOL: Here, hard by. He's at the door.

(Act 3, Scene 5, lines 51–52)

ACTIVITY 10

1 Reading or watching the play, how do you react now?

2 Do you feel any suspense?

3 Are you engaged with the show of ingenuity and made to wonder how they will get out of this one?

4 Jonson offers a suitably off-the-wall strategy as Subtle takes over and explains to Dapper:

> She, now, is set
> At dinner, in her own bed; and she has sent you,
> From her own private trencher, a dead mouse,
> And a piece of gingerbread, to be merry withal,

(Act 3, Scene 5, lines 63–66)

Does Jonson expect us to believe in the plot here?

5 Do you believe in these characters as real people now – or are you aware only of the exercise of ingenuity?

6 Why are the dramatic characters willing to believe such patently absurd stories?

7 In terms of dramatic plotting, how is Jonson about to use the 'piece of gingerbread'?

8 The dramatic movement of the play rests on its own absurd logic. Do you think that this absurdity is perhaps matched by the absurd desires of the characters themselves?

Apart from the almost **slapstick** humour, Jonson creates some very lively theatrical effects. There is constant arguing, quarrelling, rushing around; in contrast to the confined setting, there is a lot of movement, actual and verbal in *The Alchemist*. There is also the ongoing stage business of the alchemist at his task. This is a smelly, noisy business, and here is a typically noisy moment as Subtle works on his experiment and reassures Mammon:

SUBTLE: So the reward will prove.
A great crack and noise within
How now! Ay me.
God, and all saints be good to us. What's that?
[*Enter* FACE]
FACE: O sir, we are defeated! All the works
Are flown *in fumo*; every glass is burst.
Furnace and all rent down!

(Act 4, Scene 5, lines 55–58)

ACTIVITY 11

This is a terrific moment on stage: what effects might Jonson achieve here? You might think about the following:

1 What are the effects on the audience of the sudden shock of the loud noises?

2 Consider the effectiveness of the way in which Jonson provides the commentary to match the explosion: why might he do this?

3 In terms of characterisation, look at the dynamics between the characters: what might this tell you about the conspirators at this point?

4 Why might Face use the Latin phrase?

5 What might the explosion of the experimental equipment suggest about the character's worldly ambitions? How is this effect used metaphorically?

This last prompt naturally leads on to the last aspect of the play to which critics object – the language used.

5 An exploration of Jonson's use of language in *The Alchemist*

Some critics object to Jonson's use of language on two grounds: that it is clumsy, and that at times it becomes inaccessible. However, if you chose to defend Jonson's practice it would be easy to do so, as it could be argued that this is one of the most effective elements of the play.

Each character is given his/her own language code, and this provides insight into attitudes and desires. Here is an example from one of Sir Epicure Mammon's speeches as he prepares to seduce Dol:

Now, Epicure,
Heighten thyself, talk to her, all in gold;
Rain unto her as many showers, as Jove did drops
Unto his Danae:[. . .]

(Act 4, Scene 1, lines 24–27)

ACTIVITY 12

This extract reveals a lot about the way in which Jonson makes the language work. You might think about: the sort of code established for Mammon, and what this language suggests:

1 Look at the grandeur of Mammon's language here: what might it suggest about his ambitions?

2 How does he use metaphor? Look at the register and sound patterning: how do these enforce the sense?

3 Look at the way in which language itself becomes tied to the central image of alchemy: how is this link expressly made? How does language become linked to character?

Finally, you might make a list of all the characters and define the separate language code of each. Then you will be able to assess how language develops character and helps to achieve thematic purposes.

Some critics also suggest that the language can be impenetrable. It would be possible for you to suggest that this is indeed the case, because that is exactly what Jonson intended!

It would be helpful for you to look up the biblical story of the Tower of Babel, in which a group of men decide to build a tower so high that it reaches God in heaven. God is so offended by the vanity of the scheme that he curses the builders, making every one speak in a different language so that it is impossible for the work to continue. It could be argued that Jonson uses echoes of this parable in *The Alchemist*.

You will have seen that all of the characters use language for their own purposes: the conspirators to cheat, harass and bully; Subtle and Face use quasi-chemical jargon; Surly uses bits of Spanish; Kastril thinks this is French, and tries to respond; Dapper attempts to offer some Turkish; Dol has a different language as Face points out:

Firk, like a flounder; kiss, like a scallop, close:
And tickle him with thy mother-tongue. His great
Verdagoship has not a jot of language:
So much the easier to be cozened, my Dolly.

(Act 3, Scene 3, lines 69–72)

ACTIVITY 13

In the brief extract above you might be able to deduce quite a lot about Jonson's use of language in this play. You might think about:

1 What is Dol's natural language? Is there a general truth in the power of this natural, rather than assumed language?

2 Are you able to see how Jonson suggests that access to the right language code is essential to 'improve' oneself in society?

Language, then, is a useful tool for all the characters in the play, if it can be mastered. But some of the language used in this scene might suggest something else, 'Ti, ti', chants Face (Act 3, Scene 5, line 33) and Subtle picks up this nonsense-language: 'Ti, ti, do, ti, ti, ti, do, ti, da'. Is it possible that language, if abused, can achieve exactly the opposite effect from usual? Is it now a vehicle of non-communication? How might this echo the social theme of ambition?

In Act 4, Scene 5, Jonson echoes this word-play when Surly disguises himself as a Spaniard, but he finds an even harsher use for his dramatic language in the next scene, in which Dol has her 'fit of talking' and speaks nonsensically of Egyptian and classical history, and of those intending:

> To come from Salem, and from Athens
> And teach the people of Great Britain –
> [. . .]
> To speak the tongue of Eber, and Javan –
>
> (Act 4, Scene 5, lines 14–16)

ACTIVITY 14

Can you see what is happening here? The word 'tongue' might give you a clue? In the miracle of **Pentecost** a rushing wind came from heaven and the Holy Spirit allowed the Apostles to speak in tongues, and have some understanding of God. How does Jonson parody this 'miracle'? You might think about:

1 What happens next between all of those characters on stage?

2 What happens next in the loud sound effects?

3 What is the conspirators' immediate purpose?

Ben Jonson seems to have played around with language very cleverly. He has undermined the very purposes of language, suggesting the flaws and breakdown of society, and creating some very comic effects. Do you think that he has had some success here?

6 The idea of morality in *The Alchemist*

Once again, critics are divided in their responses to Ben Jonson's purposes behind this play. In his Prologue, the author himself claimed that he aimed to instruct his audience:

> But, when the wholesome remedies are sweet,
> And, in their working, gain, and profit meet,
> He hopes to find no spirit much diseased,
> But will, with such fair correctives be pleased.
>
> (Prologue, lines 15–18)

ACTIVITY 15

How does Jonson achieve this aim of instruction?

1 You might think about the positive register of this extract.

2 Exactly how will Jonson's 'cure' work?

3 Can you see any ironies in the references to 'gain' and 'profit'?

The nature of the society of the play

In Activity 2 you looked at the ambitions of the characters. To assess the image Jonson conveys of this society, have another look at their ambitions, and you will find that you will be able to rank them morally. Most of them want to achieve something. Mammon is probably to be placed at the top of the pile – at least he wants to improve the lot of other humans. Clearly, Ben Jonson places Puritans at the very bottom of the group. Do you think they want change? Or just more of the same – money! In fact the Puritans agree to the casting of fake money, which is 'revealed' to the 'holy Synod' as 'most lawful' (Act 4, Scene 7, lines 75–78). But the Puritans have a worse fault than greed, as you may see in the following extracts. Subtle is used to bring out their hypocrisy, showing the audience their double standards when he talks of changing base metals to gold:

> SUBTLE: Or changing
> His parcel gilt, to massy gold. You cannot
> But raise your friends. Withal, to be of power
> To pay an army, in the field, to buy
> The King of France, out of his realms; or Spain,
> Out of his Indies: what can you not do,
> Against lords spiritual, or temporal,
> That shall oppone you?
>
> TRIBULATION: Verily, 'tis true.
> We may be temporal lords, ourselves, I take it.
>
> (Act 3, Scene 2, lines 44–52)

ACTIVITY 16

How is the hypocrisy of the Puritans revealed in their desires and in their language? Do their desires seem spiritual? You will find many other examples of their 'sins' each time they appear onstage.

Ben Jonson has presented a society which at the end of the play crumbles from twin crimes of greed and hypocrisy. So what is the outcome? It is probably not what you would expect from a 'moral' play'. In fact, being dismissed, Surly grumbles:

> Must I needs cheat myself,
> With that same foolish vice of honesty!
>
> (Act 5, Scene 5, lines 83–84)

ACTIVITY 17

Do you think that there is really something strange in these words? You might consider:

1 How vices and virtues have been reversed.

2 How this portrays a morally rotten society.

3 Why, despite this, we feel no pity for Surly.

4 How Jonson has alienated us from this character, who is actually the only sane and moral person in the play.

The idea of justice in The Alchemist

There is a big build-up to Lovewit's return, over two whole scenes, focused on neighbours' accounts of the goings-on as Lovewit returns (Act 5, Scenes 1 and 2). The audience and characters fear doom, but what actually happens? Firstly, as you have just seen, Jonson gets rid of Surly, who realises that he has been outwitted, so he can't bring about justice. Then, one by one, the characters are exited from the stage. Lovewit has caught them all out by offering compensation if they will make a formal appeal to magistrates.

Lovewit explains his attitude:

> That master
> That had received such happiness by a servant,
> In such a widow, and with so much wealth,
> Were very ungrateful, if he would not be
> A little indulgent to that servant's wit,
> And help his fortune
>
> (Act 5, Scene 5, lines 146–151)

ACTIVITY 18

What do you think of the ending to this play? You might ask yourself:

1 What qualities are suggested as important to a good society here?

2 Why does Face alone survive?

3 What is implied by Lovewit's name?

4 What sort of justice is this?

At the end of a comedy by Shakespeare, the 'bad' characters would have been removed from society and a new, just society would be established. But Ben Jonson works in a different way. He would claim that he has done enough by putting vice and folly on stage, and letting his audience learn from what they have seen, and laugh along the way.

This concludes your study of the six critical perspectives on *The Alchemist*. Now you may continue to use the model framework to explore other aspects of the play, perhaps by thinking about Ben Jonson's views on religion, using Activities 16 and 17 as starting points.

Assessment Objective 5ii

The dominant Assessment Objective in this section of Module 4 is AO5ii.

Candidates will be expected to:

> evaluate the significance of cultural, historical and other contextual influences on literary texts and study.

At A2 Level, four types of context are specified:

- the context of period or era, including significant social, historical, political and cultural processes

- the context of the work in terms of the writer's biography or **milieu**

- the language context, including relevant episodes in the use and development of literary language, the question of **demotic**, colloquial or **dialect** styles

- the different contexts established by the work's reception over time, including the recognition that texts have different meanings and effects in different periods.

This module also tests – to a lesser extent – Assessment Objectives 1, 2 and 3. These objectives should be covered as you discuss ideas relating to the context.

Romanticism

All of the poets represented in this section of Module 4 are known as 'Romantic' poets. Romantic poets reacted against many aspects of eighteenth-century thought, including:

- Rationalism – the belief that the world is controlled by reason. The Romantic poets rejected certain ideas about the importance of reason, emphasising instead the importance of the imagination. Visions of society as a sort of machine, within which individuals have an allotted function, were also rejected.

- Classicism – the Romantics hated the well-structured formal language of eighteenth-century poetry. They preferred loose forms, expressing personal feelings.

- Organised religion – the Romantic poets were not necessarily anti-religious, but their religion was personal and subjective. Their view of religion was often unorthodox, at times embracing God-in-nature, or the **pantheism** of the ancient Greeks.

To counteract these earlier ideas, Wordsworth and Coleridge first defined their ideas in the *Lyrical Ballads* of 1798. The power of the imagination over reason was stressed. Nature was to be seen as evidence of a living God (the doctrine of pantheism). Experience was to be gained through the senses rather than reason. The language used was to be the everyday language of man.

But there was no collective sense about the Romantic movement. Each of the poets you will study here is an individual, sharing some, but not all of the characteristics of Romanticism and some, but not all of the ideas of the other writers labelled as Romantics. You will see that these poets sought what they believed were more appropriate ways of expressing these 'modern' attitudes.

At A2 Level you are required to explore the context as well as the text. This does not mean that you should spend excessive time studying context, but it is essential that you understand the links between the context and the text in the ideas and manner of expression of the writers. In this way you will 'evaluate the significance of the context'.

Example of a context

The French Revolution provided a historical and a political context for some of the poems of Blake, and for *The Prelude* (*Book Ninth* and *Book Tenth*) by Wordsworth, who lived in Paris during the Revolution. You should be aware that the experience of the French Revolution affected the ideas and expressions of the poetry but you do not need to know all the details of the Revolution itself. What you need to do is show awareness of how the poets' reactions to this event coloured their thoughts – what it was about the Revolution that sparked off particular responses, and how this context affected the poets' ideas and writing.

Finally, since all the poets in this section are Romantic poets, each time you write about the poetry you will be addressing the literary context, exploring some aspect of it, as well as any other particular context you may be investigating.

Method of exploring contexts

The method will be similar to that used in Section A on drama. For each poem, four contexts will be selected and illustrated in a sample response for you to develop in your own time. Another two contexts will be suggested for further exercises, with a starting point from which you can build an answer. You will look at how the context is apparent in the ideas of the poetry, and also how these ideas are expressed, because the method of expression is itself part of the Romantic literary context. The word 'primary' is used to describe the particular context explored in each of the sub-sections because, as you will see, there are almost always overlaps between contexts.

The Prelude (1805) *Book Ninth* and *Book Tenth* by William Wordsworth

To many readers, William Wordsworth defined and embodied in his writings the concepts behind Romantic poetry. *The Prelude* is generally regarded as an important statement about the ideals and purposes, and also the methods of writing Romantic poetry. Throughout, Wordsworth explores his relationship with nature and the crucial role it has played over the years in his development as a poet. However, in *Book Ninth* (years 1790–1) and *Book Tenth* (1792–3), known as 'the France' or 'the Revolution' books, Wordsworth considers the impact of the French Revolution on his mind and development as poet–philosopher. Writing the first *Prelude* in 1799, he recalls his fervent youthful support, the horror of the Reign of Terror, his subsequent crisis of identity, and his final return to his roots as he rediscovers the power of nature. The version which you are studying appeared in 1805, fifteen years after the first events of *Book Ninth*.

The six primary contexts to be considered here are:

1 The historical/political context.

2 The moral context.

3 The psychological context.

4 The literary context.

5 The philosophical context (1).

6 The philosophical context (2).

1 The historical/political context

To assess the significance of this context you might consider how the passing events of the French Revolution changed the course of both history and Wordsworth's life.

As an idealistic youth, Wordsworth firmly believed in the rightness of the French Revolution. He felt privileged to be born at a time when he could witness such an important political and historical event, and he makes his joy very clear:

> Bliss was it in that dawn to be alive
> But to be young was very heaven!

Like many young men of his generation, the noble aims of the French Revolution captivated this innocent youth; this is what drew Wordsworth on his first trip to France in 1790, with his friend Coleridge, whilst he was an undergraduate at Cambridge. When Wordsworth recalls these days, he seems to remember at first the pure aims to overthrow old tyrannies and re-establish equality:

> Of a Republic, where all stood thus far
> Upon equal ground, that they were brothers all
> [. . .]
> 　　　　　　subservience from the first
> To God and Nature's single sovereignty,

> Familiar presences of awful Power
> And fellowship with venerable books
> To sanction the proud workings of the soul,
> And mountain liberty.
>
> (*Book Ninth*, 230–242)

Wordsworth repeats the important phrase 'to build liberty' (*Book Ninth*, 367).

ACTIVITY 1

What claims does Wordsworth make here for the aims and events of the French Revolution? How does he present these aspects? You might think about:

1 How does Wordsworth apply his own principles to this event?

2 How does he make the revolution seem just by his choice of register, using words such as 'God', 'Nature', 'sovereignty', 'awful', 'venerable', 'sanction', 'liberty'?

3 What sort of language is Wordsworth using here?

As events are recalled, Wordsworth's trust and hope seem to overwhelm him, until he reaches a point of decision:

> and I gradually withdrew
> Into a noisier world; and thus did soon
> Become a Patriot [. . .]
>
> (*Book Ninth*, 123–125)

ACTIVITY 2

There is some strange language being used here; you might look at these lines and think about:

1 Is the linking of the ideas of 'withdrawing' with a 'noisier' world a contradiction? What do you think Wordsworth is implying here?

2 What might he mean by his use of the single word 'patriot'?

3 What do you think might be happening to Wordsworth's loyalties now?

2 The moral context

To assess the significance of this context, you may consider how the collapse of morality in France had such a huge impact on Wordsworth's moral and philosophical qualities.

Sadly, this jubilation appears not to have lasted long: *Book Ninth* spans the years 1791–2, and *Book Tenth*, 1792–3. All too soon in this short period of his life Wordsworth appears to have become alienated and disillusioned. What caused this? Wordsworth seems to place the blame on the **Reign of Terror,** when all noble principles gave way to a bloodbath. Wordsworth describes his responses very strongly as he becomes very disturbed:

> And in such a way I wrought upon myself,
> Until I seem'd to hear a voice that cried,
> To the whole City, 'Sleep no more.'
>
> (*Book Tenth,* 75–77)

ACTIVITY 3

1 Do you recognise a quotation from Macbeth, where the two murderers, Macbeth and his wife, become so deep in sin that they cannot sleep? How might this metaphor be effective in describing the aftermath of the revolution?

2 How does Wordsworth link his feeling to those of other innocent French citizens?

3 Wordsworth needs to work through his responses. Do you think that he had to revisit his old haunts but also his old frame of mind? Why might he need to do this? What help could this revisiting be?

He is increasingly appalled at the 'domestic carnage' (*Book Tenth,* 329), and describes it in detail:

> [. . .] The old man from the chimney-nook
> The Maiden from the bosom of her Love,
> The Mother from the Cradle of her Babe,
> The Warrior from the Field, all perish'd, all,
>
> (*Book Tenth,* 330–333)

ACTIVITY 4

How does Wordsworth use language to create effects in this extract? Consider:

1 How does the list format affect you?

2 What sort of people does he describe?

3 What do these things tell you about the Reign of Terror?

Clearly the sights are shocking, and have a profound effect on Wordsworth. He comments:

> This threw me first out of the pale of love;
> Sour'd and corrupted upwards to the source
>
> (*Book Tenth*, 760–761)

And the effects developed, becoming stronger and stronger:

> No shock
> Given to my moral nature had I known
>
> (*Book Tenth*, 233–234)

At this stage, you might think about Wordsworth's frame of mind: how would you describe it? Think of a language register including such words as 'alienated', 'lost' and 'estranged': what could these words imply psychologically?

3 The psychological context

To assess the significance of this context you might think about the temporary identity crisis Wordsworth faces here, and how the revolution affected him so deeply.

No doubt you will have decided that Wordsworth is having some sort of breakdown. Perhaps he is going through an identity crisis – what do you think? A man in tune with nature; seduced into city life; the French Revolution is betrayed by the Reign of Terror – what do you think is Wordsworth's way out of this mess?

First of all, by revisiting the past, Wordsworth has to pinpoint what went wrong. Wordsworth was lost, bewildered, suffering a:

> 'stride at once/ Into another region.'
>
> (*Book Tenth*, 240–241)

He says he felt:

> [. . .] a sense
> Of treachery and desertion in the place
> The holiest that I knew of, my own soul.
>
> (*Book Tenth*, 378–380)

ACTIVITY 5

Do you think this is an important moment, an important admission for Wordsworth? You might think about how he tries to make the horror of the sense of loss clear:

1 How does Wordsworth create effects here by using two opposite registers: what does this imply?

2 Why does Wordsworth use the dash in the third line?

3 Why might Wordsworth write 'soul' and not 'mind'?

Then comes realisation, and Wordsworth might be seen to be on the way to rediscovering his former self. He has left France, cannot go back because of the dangers, and retraces both his thoughts and his footsteps in his beloved Lake District:

> [. . .] I pursued my way
> Along that very Shore which I had skimm'd
> In former times [. . .]
>
> (*Book Tenth*, 558–560)

Then Wordsworth makes clear the power that will heal him:

> In all conditions of society,
> Communion more direct and intimate
> With nature, and the inner strength she has,
>   [. . .] To Nature then
> Power had reverted [. . .]
>
> (*Book Tenth*, 605–610)

ACTIVITY 6

How has Wordsworth presented the idea of recovery and revival in these two extracts? You might think about:

1 How does he use the idea of retracing and revisiting the past as important in his poetic development?

2 What had he sacrificed in his city life in France?

3 Exactly how and where does he announce his recovery?

4 Why does he use a capital letter for 'Nature'?

Wordsworth seems finally to have come to terms with what went wrong in his poetical and moral life, and realises significantly that he lost the safety in his judgements, as he became 'indulgent oft-times to the worst desires' (*Book Tenth*, 740), so he finally admits his 'erring' wisdom and thinks of what he has learned. In *Book Tenth*, lines 882–887, do you think that this admission shows a clear insight into his previous situation and also his route to recovering his identity and direction?

4 The literary context

To assess this context you might think of how the language register, for example the use of images in these books, reveals Wordsworth's true loyalties at this time of confusion.

Wordsworth realised where his true destiny lay: he believes that he was 'In brief, a child of nature' (*Book Tenth*, 752).

At this point you might think about how Wordsworth has underpinned this section by stressing the power of nature. To this end, you can see that many of the images used throughout the book, despite the urban landscape of France, were drawn directly from nature:

> As oftentimes a River [. . .]
> Turns, and will measure back his course, far back,
> Towards the very regions which he cross'd
> In his first outset; so have we long time
> Made motions retrograde, in like pursuit
> Detain'd [. . .]
>
> (*Book Ninth*, 1–9)

ACTIVITY 7

Throughout *The Prelude* Wordsworth uses several images to suggest the course of his wanderings through his younger memories. The structure of the book, as you will have already seen, is not chronological. Instead, Wordsworth describes his route. How do you think he presents this route? You might consider:

1 How does he use the image of a river here?

2 What does this suggest about the journey he has been making?

3 What does it suggest about the wisdom of his journey and of his method?

You will see natural images used elsewhere to denote positive qualities, for example in the description of the good man Michael Beaupuis (or Beaupoy) whom Wordsworth compares to 'aromatic flowers on alpine turf' (*Book Ninth*, 304). How does this metaphor suggest certain qualities about this much-admired man?

On the other hand, Wordsworth also uses images drawn from nature to suggest that things can go wrong, as he explains the condition of France:

The soil of common ground was at that time
Too hot to tread upon.

(*Book Ninth*, 169–170)

ACTIVITY 8

How does Wordsworth show disruption here? You might think about:

1 What is the natural image underpinning this description?

2 How effective is this image in conveying the dangers of the age?

5 The philosophical context (1)

To assess the significance of this context you might consider how this particular pattern of thought forms part of the whole structure of the two books which you are studying.

So far you have explored Wordsworth's state of mind, the crisis of identity which he faced and then overcame. How has his pattern of thinking helped him through his crisis? There are two key aspects of the way he thought which you might look at here. The first is the precise way in which contemplation of nature, and of his own relationship to nature, has helped him to develop as a philosopher–poet. This idea is probably most clearly expressed in *Book Second*:

                              so wide appears
The vacancy between me and those days,
Which yet have such self-presence in my mind
That, sometimes, when I think of it I seem
Two consciousnesses, conscious of myself
And of some other Being.

(*Book Second*, lines 28–33)

ACTIVITY 9

Here Wordsworth explains one of the key elements of his philosophy. It is quite a difficult concept, but as it is central to your understanding of *The Prelude*, it might be worthwhile to unpick this theory. Therefore, think about:

1 What does he mean by 'Two consciousnesses'? Think of what Wordsworth is doing: he is, in the *present* looking at himself as he was in the *past*. So, how might it be that there are two images of the man himself present in his writings?

2 Can you now work out how there are two responses to the events in France present in *Book Ninth* and *Book Tenth*?

When you are able to think this idea through, you will have worked out one of the key elements of Wordsworth's philosophy which underpins his writing.

Wordsworth might be seen to take the idea of the two consciousnesses further. As you read through these books and see Wordsworth's horrified response to events in France and what happened to him because of them, gradually it becomes clear to the reader, as it did to Wordsworth, that he was not entirely lost, had not been deserted by his former guide. After he left France, and came back to the Lake District to rediscover himself, he was helped very much by his sister Dorothy, and made the discovery which was to be his salvation:

> She, in the midst of all, preserv'd me still
> A Poet, made me seek beneath that name
> My office upon earth, and nowhere else,
>
> (*Book Tenth*, 917–920)

Nature 'revived the feelings of my earlier life' (*Book Tenth*, 924).

ACTIVITY 10

To complete this enquiry, you might consider:

1 How do you think Wordsworth has been 'rescued'?

2 What important aspect of his life and his thinking has re-established itself?

3 Do the images of nature found throughout these two books suggest a presence which has never left him?

4 By looking at his former life, before France, was he able to get to the real problem?

So, with his 'two consciousnesses' working in harmony, Wordsworth has cleared the ground for continuing *The Prelude* with order restored, and a clear way ahead for *Book Eleventh* and *Book Twelfth*.

6 The philosophical context (2)

To assess the significance of this context, as with the previous context, you might explore this aspect of Wordsworth's pattern of thinking as one of the lynchpins of his philosophical methods.

This second key principle for you to explore is described clearly in *The Prelude*: it is the way in which certain crucial events or moments stay in our mind, and, when revisited, enable us to form valid conclusions about our own development. This is how Wordsworth explains this notion:

> There are in our existence spots of time,
> Which with distinct pre-eminence retain
> A vivifying Virtue [. . .]
>
> (*Book Eleventh*, 258–260)

Most critics agree that this is another principle which underpins Wordsworth's writing. How does this principle operate?

ACTIVITY 11

Think about the idea of 'spots of time', and consider:

1 How these may be distinct memories.

2 How Wordsworth may have sifted through his experiences to isolate key moments which made a change in him.

3 Whether that is why these moments/experiences are described as having 'distinct' pre-eminence.

4 The powers Wordsworth might claim for these 'spots of time'.

Can you see this second philosophical principle evident in *Book Ninth* and *Book Tenth*? Think about how Wordsworth treats the events of the French Revolution and of the Reign of Terror. What is his method? Is it inclusive, or would you say that he selects certain details to make his points?

Similarly with his feelings and emotions: is the account inclusive, or does he select certain moments of intense feeling and almost 'freeze' them for contemplation?

In France, on his visit to the old revolutionary sites, Wordsworth also steps through miniature spots of time as he treads through 'the Field of Mars', 'Mont Martyr' and the 'Dome of Geneviève' (*Book Ninth*, 43–46).

ACTIVITY 12

1 How do you think Wordsworth first selects these 'spots'?

2 Why list those particular places?

3 How are these spots linked to his journey of discovery?

Perhaps you might conclude that the 'two consciousnesses' theory, when linked with the idea of 'the spots of time', reveals what happened to Wordsworth during the course of the Revolution, but also how he came to make the crucial movement onward towards self-discovery and 'salvation', and towards the ability to pick up and complete his life's journey.

Remember, you have been exploring one particular reading of the contexts related to *The Prelude*; there are many other contexts to be considered as you work through your course of study.

This concludes your study of six contexts from *The Prelude*, and you may now continue to explore others. You could begin by looking at the autobiographical context of the Vaudracour and Julia tale from *Book Ninth*, beginning at line 556. You could relate this to Wordsworth's love affair with Annette Vallon in France in 1792. They had a child later that year, Anne-Caroline, but Wordsworth had to leave them because of his poverty. How close are the details to that of Wordsworth's own life? Where are the similarities emotionally if not physically? What is the relationship between autobiography and romance?

Songs of Innocence and *Songs of Experience* by William Blake

In his poetry, William Blake explores the relationship between individuals and society. In his *Songs of Innocence* there are harmonious relationships between human beings, and between humans and God, resulting in a mutual trust and happiness in an open society. But Blake is honest about the times in which he lived. He saw, for example, the hopes for the French Revolution crushed by the first Terrors of 1792. He witnessed poverty and exploitation in London, and the oppression caused by the Industrial Revolution. In a radical way, he reworked the **pastoral** conventions from the first songs to create his *Songs of Experience*. In these poems, he asks how man can survive in a grimly oppressive society. He suggests that the answer might be by learning some sort of wisdom from experience. The irony, of course, is that this wisdom, like the Fall from Eden, must be bought at the cost of a certain naive innocence. In his poems Blake produces a series of myths in order to explore the 'new' human condition, to replace the 'outworn' myths of the Bible.

The seven primary contexts to be considered here are:

1 The literary context.

2 The social context of childhood.

3 The **socialist** political context.

4 The political context.

5 The context of society and human relationships.

6 The psychological context.

7 The philosophical context of Blake as a **visionary** and prophetic Romantic poet.

1 Blake's Introduction to the Songs: the literary context

Critics see Blake in two ways: (1) as very much a man of his times, a strongly engaged social reformer who knows from his own work as an artisan all about the condition of the people in the city of London where he lives and works; (2) as an inheritor of tradition, a poet who seeks to create new myths as a means of hope for his failing contemporary society. You can see both of these aspects in his *Introduction* to the *Songs of Innocence and of Experience* in the following extracts:

> Piping down the valleys wild
> Piping songs of pleasant glee
> On a cloud I saw a child,
> And he laughing said to me:
>
> 'Pipe a song about a lamb.'

How might these lines act as an introduction to the *Songs of Innocence*? You will notice aspects of this poem which become features of these *Songs* overall:

- there is the insistence on joy ('glee')
- there is the sound of the child laughing and the simple, lilting rhythm of laughter enforced by repetition
- the sound is 'piping', not harsh or troublesome
- the relationship is interactive and harmonious
- there is an indirect reference to religion in 'lamb', but *no* sense of a formal religious doctrine.

If you consider this extract so that you are sure of these aspects of ideas and style, you will be well prepared to explore the *Songs of Innocence*.

However, look at the last two verses from the 'Introduction' and you will see a change when the poet actually begins to write:

> So he vanished from my sight.
> And I plucked a hollow reed,
> And I made a rural pen,
> And I stained the water clear,

ACTIVITY 1

Here there is a very different tone to the poem. As soon as the poet within begins to write, the child vanishes. What happens here? You might think about:

1 How has the language register changed: 'hollow', 'stained'?

2 How has the act of writing, linked to the 'plucked' of the reed, changed the nature of the poet's vision?

3 Why does the joy and light of the beginning, rather like *Songs of Innocence*, yield to the darkness of *Songs of Experience*?

To follow this introduction, there will be a consideration of Blake as mythmaker in *Songs of Innocence*, and then as social reformer in *Songs of Experience*.

2 The social context of childhood

You might start by considering what Blake uses childhood to symbolise, and how his language develops the contextual ideas. To begin, read the first stanza of 'The Lamb', and then work through the activity questions below:

> Little Lamb who made thee?
>   Dost thou know who made thee?
> Gave thee life and bid thee feed
> By the stream and o'er the mead;
> Gave thee clothing of delight,
> Softest clothing wooly bright;
> Gave thee such a tender voice,
> Making all the vales rejoice.
>   Little Lamb who made thee?
>   Dost thou know who made thee?

ACTIVITY 2

How does the presentation develop this context?

1 Look at the simplicity of the language. Does it resemble the language of a child?

2 Look at the rhymes of soft vowel sounds. What effect does this have?

3 Why does Blake use repetition in this poem?

4 Are the questions answered in the second stanza?

You may well have decided that this is the happy language of an innocent child; but also you may realise that the child acts as a mediator for you, asks questions for you, and you actually imaginatively become one with the child, sharing reassuring answers.

What sort of world is Blake writing about here? When you read the second stanza you begin to wonder if Blake is creating his own myth for mankind, a myth of happiness and joy in an innocent world of security, joy, peace and great harmony. Therefore can you see any similarities to descriptions of the Garden of Eden before mankind committed the first sin? You might take these ideas further and consider the following points.

ACTIVITY 3

1 In conveying in the poem the imaginative honesty of a child, what do you think Blake is saying about the state of adulthood?

2 How do you think the innocence of the child relates to the innocence of man before the Fall from Eden?

3 How does this world compare with the diseased contemporary society implied in *Songs of Experience*? Could man ever return to the state of earlier innocence?

Do you think Blake has written about the child to express a real sense of joy in a harmonious, caring world because as a child, there will be no sense of the shades of death and despair of which more experienced humans are aware? Is the innocence intact because there are no shades of sin, social or moral? You will find these characteristics in many of the other poems from the *Songs of Innocence*, perhaps beginning with 'Laughing Song'.

However, whilst you may share the joy of the childish vision temporarily as an adult, you are aware of the shades of death which life brings, and that is the sad development leading to the in *Songs of Experience*.

3 The socialist political context

Blake was horrified by social conditions in London, and expressed views which today could be called 'socialist'. Many critics see 'London' as the complete **antithesis** to the *Songs of Innocence* as it is a complete expression of the horrific failing within society. It is a poem which Blake sees as universal, written on behalf of all underprivileged people, a true song of revolution in a place where there is no true liberty. For this reason Blake writes that 'In every cry of every man,/ In every infant's cry of fear,/ In every voice' he hears the cry of despair, certainly not a *Song* any more.

Inspired by the French Revolution and the overthrow of tyranny for the sake of individual liberty, Blake is appalled at his own society; he sees a society in which all institutions, both legal and religious, seem to oppress the poor.

Everything is 'chartered'; there is no moral, intellectual or social freedom: the poor are little more than worthless and endure absolute misery. You will find that the tone and concerns of this poem are repeated throughout the *Songs of Experience*.

Here are two stanzas from 'London' in which Blake exemplifies the 'mind-forged manacles' of the society of his day. Amongst other explanations, these manacles may have been created by powerful people such as the wealthy mill owners, but perhaps also by philosophers who justified this sort of society.

> How the chimney-sweeper's cry
> Every black'ning church appalls,
> And the hapless soldier's sigh
> Runs in blood down palace walls.
>
> But most through midnight streets I hear
> How the youthful harlot's curse
> Blasts the new-born infant's tear
> And blights with plagues the marriage hearse

ACTIVITY 4

1 How many different groups of people are involved in this poem?

2 Is there a sense of great deprivation in this poem? Do the groups of people mentioned here have any rights?

3 What is Blake's attitude to the authority of kings? And to the Church?

At this point, read the second and third stanzas, and move on to the next part of the reading of this complex poem.

ACTIVITY 5

See how the presentation develops this context: this is important because Blake creates some clever and subtle effects in this poem. First, work your way into the poem by thinking about:

1 Why does Blake call the streets 'chartered'?

2 What effects are created by the use of the first person as the speaker?

3 What is the register: look at verbs, such as 'cry', 'sigh', 'curse', 'tear', and adjectives, such as 'black'ning', 'hapless', 'youthful'?

4 How have songs become cries and sighs?

5 How do these effects help to create the sense of oppression of the individual?

Blake makes language work in a special way here. The clue lies in the first stanza, with the 'marks' which the poet will 'mark in every face . . . weakness, woe'. Are these marks the labels which society has put upon each impoverished individual? Think about the 'cry' of the 'chimney-sweepers': this links to the 'weep weep weep weep' of the other song, 'The Chimney Sweeper'. In London then, these poor children were forced to ply their trade through the streets; the cry of 'Sweep' became the 'cry' of broken children. Can you see how society has forced these poor people into trade that makes them weep with despair? Their 'mark' as a sweep indicates their social and spiritual wretchedness.

There are three more images which you should look at as, in them, Blake uses language in the same mobile, fluid way:

1 the phrase 'Every black'ning church appalls'

2 the 'hapless soldier's sigh/Runs in blood down palace walls'

3 the rhyme between 'harlot's curse/marriage hearse'.

ACTIVITY 6

Look carefully at each of these examples within the poem. Then think about:

1 In the first example, look at the word-play on 'appalls': there is an echo of a funeral pall, as well as the literal meaning of the word 'appall' – to make pale (normal spelling: appal). But the real question is whether the Church cares enough to be appalled by the poverty, or by the cries of suffering. What do you think?

2 In the second example, look at how the soldier's sigh becomes blood: is this the 'mark' of a soldier? Does he recognise that his mark is the stamp of death, to shed his blood for an uncaring Palace? Is that why he sighs?

3 In the third example, why does Blake rhyme 'harlot's curse' with 'marriage hearse'? Why does he substitute 'hearse' for 'bed'? Again, there is a song – the curses of the prostitutes as they roam the streets. There is also the curse of venereal disease. What other curses might there be, and how might this relate to marriage among the poor?

This is a special and subtle use of language which might well disguise great bitterness of tone: using this exercise as a model, you will be able to assess each of the *Songs of Experience* in this complex way.

4 The political context

After *Songs of Innocence* appeared in 1789, Blake published *The French Revolution* in 1791. He seemed to be both attracted to, and horrified by, events during the French Revolution, approving of the revolt against the authority of kings, but appalled by the anarchy the Revolution unleashed. It is generally believed that these attitudes are expressed in 'The Tiger'. Read the first two stanzas of 'The Tiger':

Tiger Tiger, burning bright,
In the forests of the night:
What immortal hand or eye
Could frame thy fearful symmetry?

In what distant deeps or skies,
Burnt the fire of thine eyes?
On what wings dare he aspire?
What the hand dare seize the fire?

ACTIVITY 7

1 What sort of universe is Blake describing here?

2 How does it compare to the universe portrayed in 'The Lamb'? Think about how things are described as man-made and machine-made.

3 Now read the whole poem. What overall impression do you get of this world? Is it full of kindness and goodness?

4 Why might the stars 'water Heaven with their tears'? Think again about the Fall from Eden and the sinful state of man.

5 Could Blake be suggesting something more complex? Is the world represented in 'The Lamb' really the ideal? Does man perhaps need to experience the darker world represented by 'The Tiger' as a transitional stage towards a better universe?

ACTIVITY 8

See how the presentation develops this context:

1 Look at the register of the language. How would you describe it?

2 Why are all the questions unanswered?

3 What is the purpose of these images of violent creation and terror?

4 Why is the language left grammatically incomplete?

5 What effect does the use of **incantatory** repetition have throughout the poem?

As you can see, other contexts have been drawn in, including the historical and social context of the Industrial Revolution.

ACTIVITY 9

1 What might the maker/forger of the tiger symbolise?

2 How might mechanical creation suggest the idea of the Industrial Revolution?

3 How does Blake view the power of men and machines?

4 Is Blake making a political statement here?

5 The context of society and human relationships

As well as making clear comments on the direction in which society is heading, Blake offers certain insights into the nature of human relationships, as seen in his poem 'The Sick Rose'. These observations are about relationships between people, their social sphere and their moral and spiritual contexts.

> O rose, thou art sick;
> The invisible worm
> That flies in the night,
> In the howling storm,
>
> Has found out thy bed
> Of crimson joy,
> And his dark secret love
> Does thy life destroy.

Relationships between people

ACTIVITY 10

1 Can 'rose' suggest that the poem might be about a woman?

2 Similarly, what does 'his dark secret love' suggest about male power?

3 Do you think the words 'worm' and 'bed' could have sexual meanings? If so, what kind of sickness could Blake be alluding to? Could this type of love 'destroy' the lovers?

Relationships between people, their social sphere and their moral and spiritual contexts

ACTIVITY 11

1 Taking a different approach, could the rose be said to represent England?

2 If so, what might the state of 'night' be referring to? Think about the social conditions of the time and about the Industrial Revolution.

3 What then is the implication for society's effect on the individual? Will it help its members or destroy them?

ACTIVITY 12

How the presentation develops this context:

Explore the series of images which Blake uses in this poem:

1 the rose, an image from gardens and a symbol of England

2 the worm, also associated with gardens; but in addition the old word for a dragon

3 the worm could be the serpent of Eden, as Blake again echoes the religious 'myth' of the Fall of Adam and Eve

4 'bed' and 'crimson' may suggest sexuality, especially female sexuality with a possible allusion to blood and menstruation

5 the archaic word 'thou' may remind you of biblical language, and the Fall from Eden, with its sexual overtones.

6 The psychological context

In the discussion of 'The Sick Rose' in Activity 10 you were given an example of a psychological/sexual reading of the poem. Now read 'A Poison Tree' – another poem by Blake – and work out how Blake creates a myth about jealousy with a psychological insight into the fragility of human friendships.

ACTIVITY 13

1 Begin by working out links between the poison tree of the poem, and the tree from the Garden of Eden.

  • What sort of fruit do both trees bear?

  • Is there any similarity between the outcome of the poem and what happens to Eve in the Garden of Eden? What are the differences?

2 How far do you think Blake is trying to rewrite the biblical myth?

Blake's engravings also form a context, in that he seemed to want to make the experiences conveyed by the poems as concrete as possible. Perhaps he was suggesting that experience should be considered in physical as well as abstract terms. He may also have felt that the expression of the experiences he wished to convey would be reinforced by using two mediums.

This study of contexts in Blake's poetry is not exhaustive. The biographical context is evident throughout many of the poems, since Blake lived in London and witnessed many of the events and situations he described.

Using this model framework, you can go on to explore other contexts related to Songs of Innocence and Songs of Experience, perhaps beginning with the philosophical context.

7 The philosophical context

To help with this context, read the poem 'To Tirzah', and then consider the following ideas:

ACTIVITY 14

1 Who or what is Tirzah?

2 Is there an echo of the Fall from Eden in the second and third stanzas?

3 Does Blake find a solution to the problems in the fourth stanza?

4 After the darkness of the *Songs of Experience*, has Blake found a way through the difficulties of physical and spiritual life for his contemporary society?

5 Unlike the myth in 'A Poison Tree', does 'To Tirzah' offer some hope? Or not?

The influence of Rousseau and Swedenborg

In his **Discourses**, published in 1750 and 1755 Jean-Jacques Rousseau explored the problems which he saw in his contemporary society, and Blake, who read these works picked up and developed these ideas in his poetry.

In the first of these works, Rousseau claimed that the spread of knowledge and culture actually helped to corrupt mankind, that in fact social inequality was the direct result.

These ideas were developed further in the second Discourse, as Rousseau went on to claim if man were to live close to nature, working to fulfil only genuine needs there would not be the problems of dissatisfaction and anger in modern society, where the poorer people are condemned to servitude in a system approved of by the State and the Church. He believed that it was possible to change institutions to bring this improvement about.

Blake had more direct contact with the ideas of Emanuel **Swedenborg**, as his close friend Flaxman was a disciple of Swedenborg. Blake shared these ideas in which God was seen as Man made Divine: that the purpose of creation was to allow man to grow close to God.

ACTIVITY 15

It might be helpful to look through the *Songs* to see how these ideas become apparent. For example, you might see the ideas of natural man in the *Songs of Innocence*, and of the social ills in the *Songs of Experience*. You will also be able to see Blake's unconventional ideas about religion, and the dislike for formal religious institutions in the *Songs*.

Blake's cosmology or his theory of the creation of the universe

Songs of Innocence were written in 1789, and *Songs of Experience* in 1794. In the years between these works, Blake began to develop his ideas about the creation of the world and the nature of human society which were to preoccupy him very much.

Briefly, Urizen was the Creator, a harsh and tyrannical ruler linked to the faculty of reason. One way in which Urizen subdued his subjects was to weave a web over them, which Blake identified as established religion. His great opponent was Los, who was shown with a fiery forge, and who represented creativity – poetic, artistic and sexual. There was also the son of Los, Orc who was the symbol of flaming rebellion and revolution. Los was slow to take action against Urizen at first, and then forged a great chain imprisoning the tyrant. However, Urizen realised that this chain was metaphorical, not physical, so he freed himself; obviously it was his power of reason which enabled him to realise this.

However, gathering strength, Los paired with Orc as poet/rebel and in one of the later poems was seen to overthrow the tyrannical archangel guarding Albion, or England, leading the way to a newer and freer society.

ACTIVITY 16

1 You will be able to see hints of Blake's cosmology in the *Songs of Experience*. Explore how this appears in 'London', with the 'mind-forged manacles', and in 'The Tiger' also with the iron forged bonds holding together a harsh, tyrannical and mechanical society.

2 How might the Los–Orc pairing help to free the oppressed poorer classes?

The poem 'To Tirzah' also carries echoes of Blake's cosmology. Valla was one of Blake's mythical figures who craved power and domination; she used her cruel daughter Tirzah to gain the power she desired. Creating sexuality, Valla created breasts and testes and so made man a slave to women because of sex, so that man was reduced to the status of a phallic worm.

ACTIVITY 17

Read the poem 'To Tirzah' and explore what Blake has to say about sexual love; then look again at 'The Sick Rose' to see perhaps some similar ideas presented.

Don Juan by Lord Byron

George Gordon, Lord Byron lived and worked during the Regency, a brief period in English history sandwiched between the decorum and tastefulness of the Augustan Age, typified by the poetry of Pope, and the Victorian Age, with its inclinations towards prudery and sentimentality. The Regency period was a time of vitality, flamboyance and extravagance, and Byron typified all of these in both his life and his writing. As a result, readers were divided in response to his poetry. Many were shocked – even his first editor could not cope with it. Others saw his work as innovative, daring, fresh, but also idealistic. Byron began *Don Juan* in Venice in 1818, and was still writing the poem on his death, fighting for the Greek cause in 1824. The first four cantos exhibit all the characteristics of the whole poem, with a huge range of emotions and ideas presented by the narrator, a fine Regency gentleman himself.

The six contexts to be explored here are:

1 The language context: Romantic poetry and the use of **ottava rima**.

2 The literary, social and moral contexts: persona and role of the narrator.

3 The literary context: role of the 'hero'.

4 The moral and philosophical contexts: the quest for a golden age.

5 The social and moral contexts: ruthless men and scheming women.

6 The social and moral contexts: a **satire** on society.

1 The language context

Lord Byron was a Romantic poet; he believed in the power of the imagination over reason and in the power of a certain sort of youth to experience a truly complete life. But at the same time, he was deeply sceptical about the society he saw around him, hating the hypocrisy and cant of the age. In 1822 he wrote in a letter to his publisher:

> Don Juan will be known by and bye, for what it is intended – a Satire on the abuses of the present states of society, and not an eulogy of vice; it may be now and then voluptuous; I can't help that . . . No girl will ever be seduced by reading Don Juan – no, no.

So there was a problem for Byron: how could he find a poetic form which suited both of his visions? He seemed to wish to search for or idealise a certain sort of existence, but at the same time he wanted to write a moral poem tackling the flaws of the society of his age. His brilliant solution was to use an old poetic form known as *ottava rima*.

Byron decides to justify this strange choice of form to us, his readers. Firstly, he explains that the poem is not meant to be seen as a whole, it is unplanned, so will develop haphazardly. Then he made some account of the reasons for selecting an unusual form:

>   But the fact is that I have nothing planned,
> Unless it were to be a moment merry,
> A novel word in my vocabulary.
>
> To the kind reader of our sober clime
>   This way of writing will appear exotic.
> Pulci* was sire of the half-serious rhyme,
>   Who sang when chivalry was more quixotic,
> And revelled in the fancies of the time –
>   True knights, chaste dames, huge giants, kings despotic.
> But all these, save the last, being obsolete,
> I chose a modern subject as more meet.
>
> (Canto IV, stanzas 5–6)

[* Pulci was a medieval Italian writer of Romances.]

ACTIVITY 1

What reasons does Byron give here for the need for a modern poetic form? You might think about:

1 Who is Byron appealing to here?

2 What has he to say about the new conditions of the age?

3 What sort of sideswipes does he make against his own society?

4 What sort of poetic forms is he satirising when he starts Canto III with 'Hail Muse! – et cetera'?

You might conclude that the *ottava rima* form is a very effective choice. This form is written in eight-line stanzas, rhymed AB AB AB CC. It is a highly flexible form as you will see, and the use of the final couplet creates brilliant effects. These vary enormously: sometimes acting as summary; to contrast with the rest of the stanza; to de-sentimentalise; and to create downright funny effects. Here are some examples for you to explore. The first is a description of Julia:

Her glossy hair was clustered o'er a brow
  Bright with intelligence and fair and smooth.
Her eyebrow's shape was like the aerial bow,
  Her cheek all purple with the beam of youth,
Mounting at times to a transparent glow,
  As if her veins ran lightning. She in sooth
Possessed an air and grace by no means common;
Her stature tall – I hate a dumpy woman.

(Canto I, stanza 61)

ACTIVITY 2

Byron has begun this description of Julia in a very classical way, but then it all changes. What is going on here? You might think about:

1 How does Byron use traditional methods in the first five lines: what does he praise about Julia, and how does he praise her?

2 How does Byron use the senses?

3 What happens in the last line of the stanza?

4 Why does Byron undermine the first six lines in this way?

You have now seen the *ottava rima* couplet used for certain comic and serious effects. Here is a second example for you to think about. It comes from the account of the shipwreck, which shocked so many readers with its graphic description of cannibalism. Byron again uses the couplet for a variety of effects:

Which in their way that moment chanced to fall,
They would have eat her, olive branch and all.

(Canto II, stanza 95)

Asleep; they shook them by the hand and head
And tried to waken them, but found them dead.

(Canto II, stanza 98)

ACTIVITY 3

Think carefully about Byron's purposes and methods here. The poem had shocked many people, as Byron knew it would: whether death should be dealt with in such an unfeeling light-hearted way was a common complaint. What does he achieve in these couplets? You might consider:

1 Does he deliberately try to disarm readers with the sheer fun of these comments?

2 How does he undermine 'serious' literature by attacking false sentimentality?

3 Does he also poke fun at some biblical episodes, or our gullibility in accepting them as true?

2 The literary, social and moral contexts

The persona and role of the narrator will be considered under this heading, and it might be helpful for you to think about the effect of the narrator actually presenting the poem to us. You might think about the following ideas:

1 The narrator's role is that of observer, not participator. In this he might be seen to resemble the reader; we and the narrator both see events as they unfold.

2 But he is not an impartial observer: he actually selects for us what we are to see. Therefore we can only judge as he intends.

3 He also manipulates the events, never allowing us to see them from any other viewpoint but his own. In this sense he controls our viewpoint.

As you read through the four cantos, bear all of these points in mind so that you can reach a conclusion later.

However, you will realise that Byron does more than give the narrator a role; he also gives the narrator a persona. Here are some aspects of this persona evident in the throwaway comments the narrator frequently makes. Firstly, he is presented as the typical Regency gentleman:

Let us have wine and woman, mirth and laughter,
Sermons and soda water the day after.

(Canto II, stanza 178)

I'm fond of fire and crickets and all that,
A lobster salad and champagne and chat.

(Canto I, stanza 135)

But at sixteen the conscience rarely gnaws
   So much as when we call our old debts in
At sixty years and draw the accounts of evil
And find a deuced balance with the devil.

(Canto I, stanza 167)

ACTIVITY 4

What sort of character has Byron created for his narrator here? You might think about:

1 What age does he attach to the narrator: why might Byron do this? Does he want you to believe in this character?

2 What things does he like and dislike?

3 How do these things form a parody of English life?

4 Importantly, is there any subtle criticism here? Think about the reference to religion, Sunday service, prayers near death: what is implied about English hypocrisy here?

5 Significantly, do you think Byron has managed to blend humour with genuine criticism here?

Elsewhere, the narrator directly engages with the audience. Do you perhaps begin to feel some intimacy with him, as though you were beginning to know him as a person? Look at the subtle comments he makes about Don Juan's affection for Julia, followed by some extracts which suggest the narrator's life beyond this poem:

If you think 'twas philosophy that this did,
I can't help thinking puberty assisted.

(Canto I, stanza 93)

'Tis in arranging all my friends' affairs
Not having, of my own, domestic cares.

(Canto I, stanza 23)

But scandal's my aversion. I protest
Against all evil speaking, even in jest.

(Canto I, stanza 51)

There is fun when he describes a girl from the company with whom Juan was being taken to slavery:

> Which might go far, but she don't dance with vigour,
> The more's the pity, with her face and figure.
>
> (Canto IV, stanza 85)

ACTIVITY 5

Byron is creating a profile of this man. What have you now learned about him? You might think about:

1 his commonsense attitude to love and lust

2 his hypocritical denial of gossip

3 the suggestion that he could be fussy and interfering

4 above all, whether Byron ever so gently makes this man condemn himself out of his own mouth.

Finally, the narrator drifts into digressions:

> But I'm digressing. What on earth has Nero
>   Or any such like sovereign buffoons
> To do with the transactions of my hero.
>
> (Canto III, stanza 110)

Byron has chosen to write a rambling account of a 'hero' as the main text, but what is the sub-text, do you think? What happens in the many digressions? What sort of satire does Byron slip in? For this reason, you might think about the relationship between Byron and the narrator.

At times, it is hard to deny that Byron is speaking directly to the reader, as when the narrator describes Cadiz:

> Alas, to dwell
> Upon such things would very near absorb
>   A canto. Then their feet and ankles – well,
> Thank heaven I've got no metaphor quite ready
> (And so, my sober Muse, come, let's be steady.
>
> (Canto II, stanza 6)

At another time the narrator apologises for a digression when he must 'leave Juan':

> Because the publisher declares in sooth,
> Through needles' eyes it easier for the camel is
> To pass than those two cantos into families.
>
> (Canto IV, stanza 97)

ACTIVITY 6

1 Can you tell here whether it is the narrator or Byron's voice coming through? All the references to the poem, the public reception, and the reader suggest that this is Byron's voice.

2 When the narrator is speaking in his allotted role with his relatively rounded persona, he is still serving Byron's purposes. So do you think it matters whether the voice is Byron indirectly or directly?

To round off this aspect of the poem you will be able to compose a clear, rounded profile of the narrator, and you will also be able to draw up a reasonable list of the purposes he serves. At the bottom line, the narrator's use of the direct 'you' to the reader, his tendency to wander from the subject, might be seen as an invitation to you, as readers, to participate in the fun, but also to evaluate what you have read. It might seem to you that the narrator is the central figure, and all the other characters, including the hero Don Juan are just his puppets (or Byron's!).

3 The literary context

Under this heading, we will consider Don Juan as hero. Although the poem is called *Don Juan,* and although there is a central figure presented, you might well decide that to call him 'hero' might be overstating the case. Don Juan the character rarely speaks, and is moved to action by circumstances rather than any inner swashbuckling tendency. At the beginning of the poem Byron says: 'I want a hero . . . I'll therefore take our ancient friend Don Juan – / We have all seen him in the pantomime / Sent to the devil before his time.' Byron's hero seems to have been chosen casually. You might well feel that almost anyone would do for Byron. And while Byron's Don Juan is not 'sent to the devil', he hardly emerges from the pantomime in respect of character development. He seems incredibly immature, passive, and ineffectual: not quite the usual hero you would expect to go adventuring. However, perhaps Byron gives us a sly hint about why he created Don Juan:

> I want a hero, an uncommon want,
>   When every year and month sends forth a new one,
> Till after cloying the gazettes with cant,
>   The age discovers he is not the true one.
>
> (Canto I, stanza 1)

ACTIVITY 7

Think about what Byron might be suggesting here:

1 In what ways is there a pun on the word 'want'?

2 How is Byron mocking the customs and attitudes of his society?

3 Could it be that Byron has chosen an anti-hero for an unheroic age?

Don Juan is offered the typical education of the young man-about-town of his age – and of Byron's age:

He learned the arts of riding, fencing, gunnery,
And how to scale a fortress – or a nunnery.

(Canto I, stanza 38)

This was Don Juan's earliest scrape; but whether
  I shall proceed with his adventures is
Dependent on the public altogether.

(Canto I, stanza 199)

ACTIVITY 8

Again, Byron cannot resist poking fun at his society, and offers a few clues about his purposes. You might consider:

1 What sort of education is the young man receiving?

2 What sort of morality is implied?

3 What does Byron gain by his use of **bathos** in the second line of the extracts?

4 Are you meant to see Don Juan as a hero-figure at all, given the nature of his scrapes?

5 How does Byron make an appeal to his readers?

All in all, you might well conclude that Don Juan is an extraordinary, or rather, very ordinary hero who seems to be ideally suited for Byron's complex and varied purposes.

4 The moral and philosophical contexts: the quest for a golden age

Many critics believe that Byron in some ways sought for an ideal, a possible golden age of youth, purity and innocence, so it is an idea which you might consider.

To prepare the way for his presentation of the relationship between Don Juan and Haidee, Byron first shows you, the reader, a vision of the lovesick Juan as he is on the boat leaving his 'beloved' Julia. Don Juan is presented as being apparently desperate with love, but Byron describes what happens as he reads Julia's letter where she claims that she has:

'A mind diseased no remedy can physic'
(Here the ship gave a lurch, and he grew seasick.)　　　(Canto II, stanza 19)

And again:

'Beloved Julia, hear me still beseeching!'
(Here he grew inarticulate with retching.)　　　(Canto II, stanza 20)

ACTIVITY 9

What do you think Byron's purposes are here? You might think about:

1　the use of bathos in the last line of the couplet

2　how this makes you respond to Don Juan as a lovesick youth

3　what this might make you feel about the quality of their love.

There is a very different type of representation when the love affair between Don Juan and Haidee is evident. Byron describes Haidee as very beautiful:

Her hair, I said, was auburn, but her eyes
　Were black as death, their lashes the same hue,
Of downcast length, in whose silk shadow lies
　Deepest attraction [. . .]

(Canto II, stanza 117)

Byron might also be suggesting that Haidee is undemanding, untypical of any of the women presented so far in *Don Juan*:

[. . .] She had never heard
Of plight and promises to be a spouse,
  Or perils by a loving maid incurred.

She loved and was belovèd, she adored
  And she was worshipped after nature's fashion.
Their intense souls, into each other poured,
  If souls could die, had perished in that passion,

(Canto II, stanzas 190–191)

ACTIVITY 10

You might put together some of these images of Haidee, and consider in the first extract:

1 What qualities does Byron attribute to Haidee?

2 Is this description **sensual** or spiritual?

3 Why are there some negative aspects, such as the references to death, the dark, delicate colours, the use of the word 'downcast'?

Then in the following extracts:

4 What is Byron implying through his references to her undemanding nature?

5 How, therefore, does she compare to Don Juan's first love, Julia?

6 What is he suggesting about male–female relationships generally?

Later, we have a full-length vision of Haidee in her 'orange silk full Turkish trousers' (Canto III, stanza 72): still a strangely neutral, almost non-sexual image. Byron goes on to define their love with the same lack of sexuality and sensuality:

All these were theirs, for they were children still
  And children still they should have ever been.
They were not made in the real world to fill
  A busy character in the dull scene,

(Canto IV, stanza 15)

ACTIVITY 11

How do you think Byron 'places' their love? Is it the usual love of man and woman? What qualities mark their feelings for each other? Is it the sort of love that exists in real society? Even the reference to the unborn child is fleeting:

She died, but not alone; she held within
  A second principle of life, which might
Have dawned a fair and sinless child of sin,

(Canto IV, stanza 70)

Perhaps there are several interpretations for you to think about here:

1 Does the satire made on Don Juan's and Julia's love affect the way you view all the love affairs which Byron presents?

2 Is the love between Haidee and Don Juan presented as the ideal?

3 Is this sort of love even possible in the society in which Byron lives?

4 In the strange lack of defined female sexuality, might the lover be seen equally as a young man in his qualities?

5 Is there a preference for spiritual rather than physical love, the ideal innocent love of a golden age?

You might think about all of these ideas and form your own judgements as you become familiar with this complicated text.

5 The social and moral contexts: men and women

Having looked at the sort of love idealised between Haidee and Don Juan, you might compare this with the behaviour of the other male and female characters in the poem.

In *Don Juan* Byron generally seems to present men as ruthless and power-obsessed, and women as cunning and scheming. Neither seems to offer reasonable examples of caring moral behaviour.

First of all, the men:

Don Jóse, like a lineal son of Eve,
Went plucking various fruit without her leave.

(Canto I, stanza 18)

Then Byron turns his attention to Lambro: is he an evil man, Byron asks you? Perhaps he gives you an answer if you reply 'yes':

You're wrong. He was the mildest mannered man
  That ever scuttled ship or cut a throat.
With such true breeding of a gentleman,
  You never could divine his real thought.

(Canto III, stanza 41)

However, women generally seem to fare no better in Byron's treatment of them. Donna Inez and Donna Julia are both presented harshly at times:

> For Inez called some druggists and physicians
>   And tried to prove her loving lord was mad,
> But as he had some lucid intermissions,
>   She next decided he was only bad.
>
> (Canto I, stanza 27)

> During this inquisition Julia's tongue
>   Was not asleep
> [. . .]
> Is it for this that General Count O'Reilly,
> Who took Algiers, declares I used him vilely?
> 'Did not the Italian *Musico* Cazzani
>   Sing at my heart six months at least in vain?
>
> (Canto I, stanzas 145–149)

ACTIVITY 12

Work through these extracts and assess what points you think Byron is making about both sexes. You might think about:

1 What criticisms of men are offered?

2 What criticisms of women are offered?

3 Are we offered stereotypical views of each sex?

4 How does Byron makes his satire effective, for example in his use of irony?

5 What sort of moral criticism is Byron making about society here?

6 The social and moral contexts: a satire on society

Byron peppers his poem with scathing criticism, usually satirical, of the behaviour, attitudes and morality of his contemporary English society. The satirist is an observer of contemporary life, who tries by gentle or by savage criticism of what he believes to be faulty in people or customs to bring about a change, or at least to shock those people who unquestioningly accept the follies and vices of the age. Byron passes satirical comment on many aspects of domestic and public life. He paints an overall picture of a 'busy' society:

This is the age of oddities let loose,
  Where different talents find their different marts
[. . .]
What opposite discoveries we have seen,
  Signs of true genius and of empty pockets!
One makes new noses, one a guillotine,
  One breaks your bones, one sets them in their sockets
[. . .]
The goal is gained, we die you know – and then?

(Canto I, stanzas 128–133)

ACTIVITY 13

Have a good look at what aspects of his contemporary society Byron criticises here. You might ask yourself:

1 What sorts of activities are satirised?

2 What sort of attitudes are presented?

3 How does Byron attack the materialism of the age?

4 How does Byron attack the lack of spirituality of the age?

5 What sort of devices does he use to do so, such as bathos?

You will be able to compile the targets of Byron's satire, and the methods he uses to make this so effective. Here are a couple more examples for you to think about. He attacks the mercenary attitude of Catholicism:

They won't lay out their money on the dead.
It costs three francs for every mass that's said.

(Canto II, stanza 55)

There is an attack on the hypocrisy within contemporary marriages:

For no one cares for matrimonial cooings;
  There's nothing wrong in a connubial kiss.
Think you, if Laura had been Petrarch's wife,
He would have written sonnets all his life?

(Canto III, stanza 8)

And he extends the mockery to the English nation as a whole:

We know too they are very fond of war,
  A pleasure, like all pleasures rather dear;
So were the Cretans, from which I infer
That beef and battles both were owing to her.

(Canto II, stanza 156)

ACTIVITY 14

Have a look through all of these extracts: if Byron's main targets were hypocrisy and extreme perspectives, how does he address these vices here? You might consider:

1 Exactly how does the mockery of Catholicism and marriage work?

2 What do these views suggest about the morality and spirituality of the age?

3 Why is Byron so keen to deflate the usual claims of the heroic nature of our British ancestry?

4 Is he trying to force people to look at themselves afresh?

Finally, you might decide that when Byron deliberately shows that his nation is unheroic, you are going full circle in this section. If the age is unheroic, do you feel the need for a heroic main character? If the age is unheroic, do you think therefore that Byron is wise to choose a form which suits the modern age and allows for such severe, if very funny, criticism?

This concludes your study of *Don Juan* in this section. Now that you have worked through the six contexts above, you will be able to go on to explore others on your own, perhaps beginning by looking at other targets of Lord Byron's satire. You might explore the literary satire in which scorn is poured on Coleridge, 'Bob' Southey, and above all, Wordsworth, of whose work Byron writes:

A drowsy frowzy poem called the *Excursion*
Writ in a manner which is my aversion.

(Canto III, stanza 94)

Selected Bibliography

General textbooks

Cambridge Companion to English Literature, 1500–1600 (Cambridge University Press, 2000)

The New Pelican Guide to English Literature, ed. Boris Ford: *The Age of Shakespeare* (Penguin, revised and expanded edn 1982)

Drama

William Shakespeare – *plays*

General reading

Themes and Conventions of Elizabethan Tragedy, M. C. Bradbrook (Cambridge University Press, 1969)

The Problem Plays of Shakespeare: a study of Julius Caesar, Measure for Measure, Anthony and Cleopatra, Ernest Schantzer (Routledge & Kegan Paul, 1965)

The Wheel of Fire, G. Wilson Knight (Routledge & Kegan Paul, 1930 repr. 1959)

Shakespeare's Language, Frank Kermode (Penguin, 2001)

A Companion to Shakespeare's Works, ed. Richard Dutton and Jean Howard (Blackwell, 2003)

Othello

Othello, ed. Kenneth Muir (Penguin, 1968)

Aspects of Othello, eds. Muir and Edwards (Cambridge University Press, 1981)

Othello: A casebook, John Wain (Macmillan, 1971)

Shakespeare's Tragic Sequence, Kenneth Muir (Hutchinson University Library, 1972)

Measure for Measure

Measure for Measure, ed. J. M. Nosworthy (Penguin, 1995)

The Problem of Measure for Measure, R. Myles (Vision Press, 1976)

Themes and Conventions of Elizabethan Tragedy, M. C. Bradbrook (Cambridge University Press, 1980)

The Problem Plays of Shakespeare, Ernest Schanzer (Routledge & Kegan Paul, 1965)

The Wheel of Fire, G. Wilson Knight (University Paperbacks, 1960)

Aspects of Shakespeare's Problem Plays, eds. Kenneth Muir and Stanley Wells (Cambridge University Press, 1982)

Shakespeare's Problem Plays, E. M. W. Tillyard (Chatto & Windus, 1957)

The Moral Universe of Shakespeare's Problem Plays, Vivian Thomas (Rowman & Littlefield, 1987)

The Winter's Tale

The Winter's Tale, ed. Ernest Schanzer (Penguin, 1986)

Things Supernatural and Causeless: Shakespearean Romance, Marco Mincoff (University of Delaware Press, 1992)

Shakespeare: The Four Romances, Robert M. Adams (W. W. Norton & Co., 1989)

Shakespeare's Other Language, Ruth Nevo (Routledge, 1987)

Shakespeare and the Comedy of Forgiveness, R. G. Hunter (Columbia University Press, 1965)

A Natural Perspective, Northrop Frye (Columbia University Press, 1965)

Christopher Marlowe – *Edward II*

Edward II ed. Martin Wiggins and Robert Lindsey (New Mermaids, 2003)

Themes and Conventions of Elizabethan Tragedy, M. C. Bradbrook (Cambridge University Press, 1980)

Marlowe: 'Tamburlaine the Great', 'Edward II' and 'The Jew of Malta', ed. J. R. Brown (Macmillan, 1982)

Christopher Marlowe: A Study of his Thought, Learning, and Character, P. H. Kocher (Russell & Russell, 1962)

The Overreacher, H. Levin (Faber & Faber, 1965)

Marlowe: A Critical Study, J. B. Steane (Cambridge University Press, 1970)

Christopher Marlowe and the Renaissance of Tragedy, Douglas Cole (Praeger, 1995)

John Webster – *The Duchess of Malfi*

The Duchess of Malfi ed. Elizabeth M. Brennan (New Mermaids, 1996)

The White Devil and the Duchess of Malfi: A casebook, ed. R. V. Holdsworth, (Macmillan, 1975)

The White Devil and The Duchess of Malfi, John D. Jump (Blackwell, 1970)

John Webster: A Critical Study, Clifford Leech (Hogarth Press, 1951)

Themes and Conventions of Elizabethan Tragedy, M. C. Bradbrook (Cambridge University Press, 1969)

Ben Jonson – *The Alchemist*

The Alchemist ed. Elizabeth Cook (New Mermaids, 1998)

Ben Jonson: his Crafts and Art, Rosalind Miles (London, 1990)

Ben Jonson, Dramatist, Anne Barton (Cambridge University Press, 1984)

Jacobean City Comedy, Brian Gibbons (1968, rev. edn Routledge, 1980)

The Jacobean Drama: an Interpretation, Una Ellis-Fermor (Methuen, 1969)

Jacobean Theatre, eds. John Russell Brown and Bernard Harris (Stratford-upon-Avon Studies, Arnold, 1969)

Poetry

William Wordsworth – *The Prelude*

The Prelude ed. Ernest De Selincourt (Oxford University Press, 1970)

The Prelude, 1799, 1805, 1850, eds. Johnathon Wordsworth, M. H. Abrams and Stephen Gill (Norton Critical Edition, 1979)

Wordsworth: A Casebook, eds. A. R. Jones and W. Tydeman (Macmillan, 1972)

Wordsworth, The Prelude: A Casebook, eds. W. J. Harvey and R. Gravil (Macmillan, 1972)

The Confessional Imagination: A Reading of Wordsworth's Prelude, Frank Demay Mac Connell (John Hopkins University Press, 1974)

William Blake – *Songs of Innocence* and *Songs of Experience*

Songs of Innocence and Experience ed. Richard Willmott (Oxford University Press, 1990)

William Blake, New Casebook, ed. David Putner (Macmillan, 1996)
The Romantic Imagination, John Spencer Hill (Macmillan, 1977)

English Romantic Poets: Modern essays in criticism, ed. M. H. Abrams (Oxford University Press, New York, 1975)

Natural Supernaturalism, Tradition and Revolution in Romantic Literature, M. H. Abrams (Oxford University Press, New York, 1971)

Lord Byron – *Don Juan*

Don Juan ed. T. G. Steffan, E. Steffan, and W. W. Pratt (Penguin Books, 2004)

Romanticism and Male Fantasy in 'Don Juan': A Marketable Vice, Charles Donolan (Macmillan Press / St Martins Press, London / New York, 2000)

Byron: Don Juan, Anne Barton (Cambridge University Press, 1992)

Lord Byron's 'Don Juan' (Modern Critical Interpretation Series), ed. Harold Bloom (Chelsea House, USA, 1991)

'Don Juan' and Regency England, Peter W. Graham, (University of Virginia, Charlottesville, 1990)

'Don Juan' and Other Poems, Bernard Beatty (Penguin Masterstudies, Penguin, London, 1987)

Byron's Don Juan and the Don Juan Legend, Moyra Haslett (Clarendon Press, 1977)

Module ⑤ Literary Connections

This module carries 30% of the final A2 mark and 15% of the final A Level mark. The marks are divided amongst the Assessment Objectives like this:

— ASSESSMENT OBJECTIVES —

AO1 communicate clearly the knowledge, understanding and insight appropriate to literary study, using appropriate terminology and accurate and coherent written expression
(5% of the final A2 mark; 2.5% of the final A Level mark)

AO2ii respond with knowledge and understanding to literary texts of different types and periods, exploring and commenting on relationships and comparisons between literary texts
(13% of the final A2 mark; 6.5% of the final A Level mark)

AO3 show detailed understanding of the ways in which writers' choices of form, structure and language shape meanings
(6% of the final A2 mark; 3% of the final A Level mark)

AO4 articulate independent opinions and judgements, informed by different interpretations of literary texts by other readers
(6% of the final A2 mark; 3% of the final A Level mark)

The purpose of this module

The aim of this module is to provide you with the opportunity to focus on the ways in which texts relate to each other, by comparing two texts. As you can see from the list of Assessment Objectives above, AO2ii is very important here. This means that whichever texts you use for this module, and however you tackle the module, you must keep the requirement to explore comparisons at the centre of your work.

There are two ways to use this module, as a coursework unit or as a written exam unit. Whichever you choose, one of the texts has to be a prose text. If you take the coursework unit, you can choose any texts you like, as long as at least one of them is prose, and both are suitable for A Level study. The choices have to be approved by AQA, however. If you opt for the written unit, you have to choose one of the options of paired texts set for the exam.

Whichever way you use the module, the important thing is to find and explore the relationships and comparisons between the texts. The first section will therefore look at ways in which you can start exploring comparisons. The second, third and fourth sections examine the two assessment methods.

Ways of looking at texts for comparison

Whether you are choosing your own texts for coursework or looking at set texts for the exam, it is important to identify at least two or three ways in which comparisons can be made, so that the individual texts are illuminated by the comparison. This is one of the central points of AO2ii: by looking at one text in the light of another, you come to understand more about it. A good way to think about similarities and differences between texts is to focus on the other Assessment Objectives. The ideas and related activities that follow are intended to offer you a wide range of possibilities for comparison.

Assessment Objective 3

show detailed understanding of the ways in which writers' choices of form, structure and language shape meanings

Form

Form is an interesting starting point for comparison, as you can think about the ways in which different forms deal with the same ideas. You could, for instance, compare the novel *Birdsong* by Sebastian Faulks and the war poetry of Wilfred Owen. These texts, or any two concerned with the First World War, would also prepare the way for Module 6, Reading for Meaning. The following activities begin by comparing form, but move on to other issues – you should try to do the same with your texts.

Below is a 'fragment' of a poem from *Wilfred Owen – The War Poems*:

FRAGMENT: CRAMPED IN THAT FUNNELLED HOLE

Cramped in that funnelled hole, they watched the dawn
Open a jagged rim around; a yawn
Of death's jaws, which had all but swallowed them
Stuck in the bottom of his throat of phlegm.

They were in one of many mouths of Hell
Not seen of seers in visions; only felt
As teeth of traps; when bones and the dead are smelt
Under the mud where long ago they fell
Mixed with the sour sharp odour of the shell.

In the following extract from *Birdsong*, Stephen, the main character in the novel, has taken refuge in a shellhole during an attack:

Stephen dropped his face into the earth and let it fill his mouth. He closed his eyes because he had seen enough. You are going to hell. Azaire's parting words filled his head. They were drilled in by the shattering noise around them.

Byrne somehow got the boy back into the shellhole. Stephen wished he hadn't. He was clearly going to die.

Harrington's sergeant was shouting for another charge and a dozen men responded. Stephen watched them reach the first line of wire before he realized that Byrne was with them. He was trying to force a way through the wire when he was caught off the ground, suspended, his boots shaking as his body was filled with bullets.

Stephen lay in the shellhole with the boy and the man who had died in the morning. For three hours until the sun began to weaken he watched the boy begging for water. He tried to close his ears to the plea. On one corpse there was still a bottle, but a bullet hole had let most of it leak away. What was left was a reddish brown, contaminated by earth and blood. Stephen poured it into the boy's beseeching mouth.

ACTIVITY 1

Compare the two extracts above, using these questions to help you.

1 The *forms* are clearly different. The extract from the novel is exactly that. How do you know it is not complete in itself? What information might you expect to have been given before this point in the novel?

2 The poem is a fragment – it was found after Owen's death, and thought to be incomplete. Can it stand by itself, though? How is it different from the prose extract in this respect, and why? Do you need to know anything else? Think about the writer's intentions.

3 Owen creates some effects in this poem using structures not available to Faulks. Look at the second line in each stanza, where the end of a line naturally creates a gap. You might look at the rhymes, too – again not found in the prose passage.

4 The ideas and situations – part of the *context* of the writing here – are clearly comparable. Think about the status and rank of the speakers, their attitudes, the time of day, the noise, or lack of it.

5 The *language* used by each writer is revealing. Throughout the poem, Owen uses the idea that the shellhole is like a mouth. Find where the idea begins and trace it through, noticing how he uses the metaphor to comment on the soldiers' situation.

6 Although the prose is not as packed with imagery as the poem – a difference resulting from form, perhaps – Faulks does use language to convey images, and to create emotive effects. Look at the first and last lines of the extract with this in mind.

7 Both writers use the senses extensively to involve the reader. Look at the way they use sight, hearing, touch and smell.

8 What is the attitude of each of the writers to the war, do you think? Notice that they both use the same key word to describe the nature of the experience.

If you had chosen this pair of texts, the prose extract here might have led you to read other poems by Wilfred Owen for comparison: 'Anthem for Doomed Youth'; for example, or 'Inspection'.

Here are two more pairs of extracts to work on:

Pair 1

The opening four lines of 'Dulce Et Decorum Est', also by Wilfred Owen:

Bent double, like old beggars under sacks,
Knock-kneed, coughing like hags, we cursed through sludge,
Till on the haunting flares we turned our backs
And towards our distant rest began to trudge.

And a different passage from *Birdsong*:

It was dark at last. The night poured down in waves from the ridge above them and the guns at last fell silent.

The earth began to move. To their right a man who had lain still since the first attack, eased himself upright, then fell again when his damaged leg would not take his weight. Other single men moved, and began to come up like worms from their shellholes, limping, crawling, dragging themselves out. Within minutes the hillside was seething with the movement of the wounded as they attempted to get themselves back to their line.

'Christ,' said Weir, 'I had no idea there were so many men out there.'

It was like a resurrection in a cemetery twelve miles long. Bent, agonized shapes loomed in multitudes on the churned earth, limping and dragging back to reclaim their life. It was as though the land were disgorging a generation of crippled sleepers, each one distinct but related to its twisted brothers as they teemed up from the reluctant earth.

Pair 2

The first fourteen and last five lines from 'Strange Meeting', by Wilfred Owen:

It seemed that out of battle I escaped
Down some profound dull tunnel, long since scooped
Through granites which titanic wars had groined.

Yet also there encumbered sleepers groaned,
Too fast in thought or death to be bestirred.
Then, as I probed them, one sprang up, and stared
With piteous recognition in fixed eyes,
Lifting distressful hands, as if to bless.
And by his smile, I knew that sullen hall, –
By his dead smile I knew we stood in Hell.

With a thousand pains that vision's face was grained;
Yet no blood reached there from the upper ground,
And no guns thumped, or down the flues made moan.
'Strange friend,' I said, 'here is no cause to mourn.'

[. . .]

'I am the enemy you killed, my friend.
I knew you in this dark: for so you frowned
Yesterday through me as you jabbed and killed.
I parried; but my hands were loath and cold.
Let us sleep now . . ..'

The following extract from *Birdsong* falls at the end of a chapter, and almost at the end of the account of First World War experience in the novel. Stephen is pulled from a blown-up tunnel by a German soldier, who has also been trapped underground:

He looked up and saw the legs of his rescuer. They were clothed in the German *feldgrau*, the colour of his darkest dream.

He staggered to his feet and his hand went to pull out his revolver, but there was nothing there, only the torn, drenched rags of his trousers.

He looked into the face of the man who stood in front of him and his fists went up from his sides like those of a farm boy about to fight.

At some deep level, far below anything his exhausted mind could reach, the conflicts of his soul dragged through him like waves grating on the packed shingle of a beach. The sound of his life calling to him on a distant road; the faces of the men who had been slaughtered, the closed eyes of Michael Weir in his coffin; his scalding hatred of the enemy, of Max and all the men who had brought him to this moment; the flesh and love of Isabelle, and the eyes of her sister.

Far beyond thought, the resolution came to him and he found his arms, still raised, beginning to spread and open.

Levi looked at this wild-eyed figure, half-demented, his brother's killer. For no reason he could tell, he found that he had opened his own arms in turn, and the two men fell upon each other's shoulders, weeping at the bitter strangeness of their human lives.

ACTIVITY 2

Pair 1:

1 Consider how the use of dialogue in the prose passage adds to the effect.

2 Compare the imagery used in the two extracts. Notice particularly how ideas are developed through imagery. For instance, look at 'old beggars under sacks' from 'Dulce Et Decorum Est' and 'like worms' from *Birdsong* and work out how the ideas are continued in the lines that follow.

3 Look for words and phrases in the two extracts which are the same or very similar. Why do both writers make these choices, do you think?

4 Compare the situations and the writers' attitudes.

The prose passage might also lead you to look at 'At a Calvary near the Ancre', by Wilfred Owen, if you had chosen this pair of texts.

Pair 2:

5 There is a lot to say about the effects of the different forms here. In the poem, look at the **half-rhymes** and how these add to the impact and the effect produced by the last line. The prose passage also has a finality about it – in what way does it read like an ending? Putting the two together, you can compare the different effects of form.

6 Both language and situations are similar here. Compare them closely. The similarities should reveal something about the attitudes and intentions of the writers.

7 What futures are suggested in each of these endings?

Now look at the section on Coursework on page 141, and you'll see how this sort of comparison can be applied to complete texts.

Structure

Structure can be an important factor in making comparisons between texts. For instance, four novels which all deal with war, but which differ significantly in structure, are *Birdsong*, Joseph Heller's *Catch-22*, Martin Amis's *Time's Arrow*, and J. G. Farrell's *The Siege of Krishnapur*. Although the central subject of each novel is war, there are some significant differences in the structures chosen by the writers to present it. Only *The Siege of Krishnapur* is a straightforward chronological narrative. Although *Birdsong* is chronological through the war episodes, there are significant leaps of time, and a late twentieth-century narrative is interwoven with the 1914–18 episodes. *Catch-22* offers characters' names rather than numbers as chapter headings, when that character is the focus of the chapter. Although there is time development, it has to be pieced together by the reader, and it returns to the same incident several times. *Time's Arrow* is chronological in the sense that it tells the story of the Holocaust backwards, each chapter starting at a point before the previous one.

If any two of these novels were chosen as texts to compare, a key element would be the effects of these choices of structure: how the writers 'shape meanings' from their choices, to echo the words of the Assessment Objective. The contexts could also be compared, as well as the writers' attitudes, which might be conveyed by language as well as structure. You could also think about which approach you found most effective, to enable you to address AO4.

Language

Language is a key point of focus when comparing texts. There are texts, for instance, where dialect is a significant factor. Irving Welsh's *Trainspotting*, for example, could be compared with Peter Roper's play *The Steamie*, also set in Glasgow, or with any of Roddy Doyle's 'Barrytown' novels. The social and cultural contexts are different in each. Language change across time could also be looked at, if two texts from very different time periods were studied. Nathaniel Hawthorne's *The Scarlet Letter*, for example, which deals with the consequences of adultery, could be compared with A. S. Byatt's *Possession*, which within itself has contrasting forms and different language registers to reflect language changes across time.

Activity 3 focuses on similarities and differences in language. In each text, the writer is showing significant moments in the lives of the central characters, and is trying to convey the nature of joy using a range of techniques.

In this extract from *Sons and Lovers*, by D. H. Lawrence, Miriam Leivers takes Paul Morel to see a bush which she admires.

He followed her across the nibbled pasture in the dusk. There was a coolness in the wood, a scent of leaves, of honeysuckle, and a twilight. The two walked in silence. Night came wonderfully there, among the throng of dark-trunks. He looked round, expectant.

She wanted to show him a certain wild-rose bush she had discovered. She knew it was wonderful. And yet, till he had seen it, she felt it had not come into her soul. Only he could make it her own, immortal. She was dissatisfied.

Dew was already on the paths. In the old-oak wood a mist was rising, and he hesitated, wondering whether one whiteness were a strand of fog or only campion-flowers pallid in a cloud.

By the time they came to the pine-trees Miriam was getting very eager and very intense. Her bush might be gone. She might not be able to find it; and she wanted it so much. Almost passionately she wanted to be with him when he stood before the flowers. They were going to have a communion together – something that thrilled her, something holy. He was walking beside her in silence. They were very near to each other. She trembled, and he listened, vaguely anxious.

Coming to the edge of the wood, they saw the sky in front, like mother-of-pearl, and the earth growing dark. Somewhere on the outermost branches of the pine-wood the honeysuckle was streaming scent.

'Where?' he asked.

'Down the middle path,' she murmured, quivering.

When they turned the corner of the path she stood still. In the wide walk between the pines, gazing rather frightened, she could distinguish nothing for some moments; the greying light robbed things of their colour. Then she saw her bush.

'Ah!' she cried, hastening forward.

It was very still. The tree was tall and straggling. It had thrown its briers over a hawthorn-bush, and its long streamers trailed thick right down to the grass, splashing the darkness everywhere with great split stars, pure white. In bosses of ivory and in large splashed stars the roses gleamed on the darkness of foliage and stems and grass. Paul and Miriam stood close together, silent, and watched. Point after point the steady roses shone out of them, seeming to kindle something in their souls. The dusk came like smoke around, and still did not put out the roses.

Paul looked into Miriam's eyes. She was pale and expectant with wonder, her lips were parted, and her dark eyes lay open to him. His look seemed to travel down into her. Her soul quivered. It was the communion she wanted. He turned aside, as if pained. He turned to the bush.

'They seems as if they walk like butterflies, and shake themselves,' he said.

She looked at her roses. They were white, some incurved and holy, others expanded in an ecstasy. The tree was dark as a shadow. She lifted her hand impulsively to the flowers; she went forward and touched them in worship.

'Let us go,' he said.

There was a cool scent of ivory roses – a white, virgin scent. Something made him feel anxious and imprisoned. The two walked in silence.

'Till Sunday,' he said quietly, and left her; and she walked home slowly, feeling her soul satisfied with the holiness of the night. He stumbled down the path. And as soon as he was out of the wood, in the free open meadow, where he could breathe, he started to run as fast as he could. It was like a delicious delirium in his veins.

In this extract from *To the Lighthouse* by Virginia Woolf, Mrs Ramsay is serving a meal to her guests, and feels that the coherence she had wanted has happened at last:

Everything seemed possible. Everything seemed right. Just now (but this cannot last, she thought, dissociating herself from the moment while they were all talking about boots) just now she had reached security; she hovered like a hawk suspended; like a flag floated in an element of joy which filled every nerve of her body fully and sweetly, not noisily, solemnly rather, for it arose, she thought, looking at them all eating there, from husband and children and friends; all of which rising in this profound stillness (she was helping William Bankes to one very small piece more and peered into the depths of the earthenware pot) seemed now for no special reason to stay there like a smoke, like a fume rising upwards, holding them safe together. Nothing need be said; nothing could be said. There it was, all round them. It partook, she felt, carefully helping Mr Bankes to a specially tender piece, of eternity; as she had already felt about something different once before that afternoon; there is a coherence in things, a stability; something, she meant, is immune from change, and shines out (she glanced at the window with its ripple of reflected lights) in the face of the flowing, the fleeting, the spectral, like a ruby; so that again tonight she had the feeling she had had once today already, of peace, of rest. Of such moments, she thought, the thing is made that remains for ever after. This would remain.

'Yes,' she assured William Bankes, 'there is plenty for everybody.'

ACTIVITY 3

1 Compare the physical effects of joy on the characters in the extracts. For instance, look at the three sentences beginning 'She was pale and expectant' from *Sons and Lovers* and the three lines beginning 'like a flag floated in an element of joy' from *To the Lighthouse*. What is similar in the effects of joy on the bodies of the two women? Which one seems to have more sexual connotations, and how?

2 Both writers suggest that the characters feel something beyond and above their own physical sensations. How does each writer try to convey this idea?

3 Look for descriptions of movement and stillness in each piece, and how they are conveyed. You should look particularly for repetitions of words and syntax, and sentence lengths. For instance, 'it was very still' is a short,

simple sentence. Where is there a similar sentence in *To the Lighthouse*, and how is the effect of a short sentence even stronger in this extract? 'In the face of the flowing, the fleeting, the spectral' from *To the Lighthouse* conveys movement – how, exactly? Look at sound and punctuation. Can you find a similar moment in the extract from *Sons and Lovers*?

4 Look for reference to:

- religion
- sexuality
- light and colour
- humour, or seriousness.

This might help you to sum up the differences between the two extracts. How are the tones of the extracts different? What do you conclude about the writers' intentions?

Language is a key feature in both of these texts. If you were comparing the two texts, you could look at:

- the way each writer conveys childhood
- sentence forms
- differences in structure
- invented language.

Meanings

The central meaning of texts could obviously form a basis for comparison, but if you are choosing texts for coursework it would be better to choose texts where the links and comparisons could be developed into other areas. A 'rites of passage' novel like *A Portrait of the Artist as a Young Man* could be compared with another novel, such as J. D. Salinger's *The Catcher in the Rye*. The phrase 'rites of passage' refers to key times in people's lives when common experiences such as birth, marriage and death have to be dealt with. In literature, 'rites of passage' often refers to experiences which highlight the joys and difficulties of adolescence, as teenagers move towards the adult world. These 'rites' might concern spiritual or political awareness, exploration, independence, or sexual drive.

Activity 4 takes another extract from *Sons and Lovers* by D. H. Lawrence, this time for comparison with an extract from *A Suitable Boy*, by Vikram Seth. Texts can be compared in a number of ways of course, with the same or other texts.

In this extract from *Sons and Lovers*, Miriam Leivers is attracted to Paul Morel. They are both in their teens:

Paul had been many times up to Willey Farm during the autumn. He was friends with the two youngest boys. Edgar, the eldest, would not condescend at first. And Miriam also refused to be approached. She was afraid of being set at nought, as by her own brothers. The girl was romantic in her soul. Everywhere was a Walter Scott heroine being loved by men with helmets or with plumes in their caps. She herself was something of a princess turned into a swine-girl in her own imagination. And she was afraid lest this boy, who, nevertheless, looked something like a Walter Scott hero, who could paint and speak French, and knew what algebra meant, and who went by train to Nottingham every day, might consider her simply as the swine-girl, unable to perceive the princess beneath; so she held aloof.

Her great companion was her mother. They were both brown-eyed, and inclined to be mystical, such women as treasure religion inside them, breathe it in their nostrils, and see the whole of life in a mist thereof. So to Miriam, Christ and God made one great figure, which she loved tremblingly and passionately when a tremendous sunset burned out the western sky, and Ediths, and Lucys, and Rowenas, Brian de Bois Guilberts, Rob Roys, and Guy Mannerings, rustled the sunny leaves in the morning, or sat in her bedroom aloft, alone, when it snowed. That was life to her. For the rest, she drudged in the house, which work she would not have minded had not her clean red floor been mucked up immediately by the trampling farm-boots of her brothers. She madly wanted her little brother of four to let her swathe him and stifle him in her love; she went to church reverently, with bowed head, and quivered in anguish from the vulgarity of the other choir-girls and from the common-sounding voice of the curate; she fought with her brothers, whom she considered brutal louts; and she held not her father in too high esteem because he did not carry any mystical ideals cherished in his heart but only wanted to have as easy a time as he could, and his meals when he was ready for them.

She hated her position as swine-girl. She wanted to be considered. She wanted to learn, thinking that if she could read, as Paul said he could read, 'Colomba', or the 'Voyage autour de ma Chambre' the world would have a different face for her and a deepened respect. She could not be princess by wealth or standing. So she was mad to have learning whereon to pride herself. For she was different from other folk, and must not be scooped up among the common fry. Learning was the only distinction to which she thought to aspire.

Her beauty – that of a shy, wild, quiveringly sensitive thing – seemed nothing to her. Even her soul, so strong for rhapsody, was not enough. She must have something to reinforce her pride, because she felt different from other people. Paul she eyed rather wistfully. On the whole, she scorned the male sex. But here was a new specimen, quick, light, graceful, who could be gentle and who could be sad, and who was clever, and who knew a lot, and who had a death in the family. The boy's poor morsel of learning exalted him almost sky-high in her esteem. Yet she tried hard to scorn him, because he would not see in her the princess but only the swine-girl. And he scarcely observed her.

Then he was so ill, and she felt he would be weak. Then she would be stronger than he. Then she could love him. If she could be mistress of him in his weakness, take care of him, if he could depend on her, if she could, as it were, have him in her arms, how she could love him!

This is the opening of Vikram Seth's novel *A Suitable Boy*, set in India. It was first published in 1993.

'You too will marry a boy I choose,' said Mrs Rupa Mehra firmly to her younger daughter.

Lata avoided the maternal imperative by looking around the great lamp-lit garden of Prem Nivas. The wedding-guests were gathered on the lawn. 'Hmm,' she said. This annoyed her mother further.

'I know what your hmms mean, young lady, and I can tell you I will not stand for hmms in this matter. I do know what is best. I am doing it all for you. Do you think it is easy for me, trying to arrange things for all four of my children without His help?' Her nose began to redden at the thought of her husband, who would, she felt certain, be partaking of their present joy from somewhere benevolently above. Mrs Rupa Mehra believed, of course, in reincarnation, but at moments of exceptional sentiment, she imagined that the late Rughubir Mehra still inhabited the form in which she had known him when he was alive: the robust, cheerful form of his early forties before overwork had brought about his heart attack at the height of the Second World War. Eight years ago, eight years, thought Mrs Rupa Mehra miserably.

'Now, now, Ma, you can't cry on Savita's wedding day,' said Lata, putting her arm gently but not very concernedly around her mother's shoulder.

'If He had been here, I could have worn the tissue-patola sari I wore for my own wedding,' sighed Mrs Rupa Mehra. 'But it is too rich for a widow to wear.'

'Ma!' said Lata, a little exasperated at the emotional capital her mother insisted on making out of every possible circumstance. 'People are looking at you. They want to congratulate you, and they'll think it very odd if they see you crying in this way.'

Several guests were indeed doing namasté to Mrs Rupa Mehra and smiling at her; the cream of Brahmpur society, she was pleased to note.

'Let them see me!' said Mrs Rupa Mehra defiantly, dabbing at her eyes hastily with a handkerchief perfumed with 4711 eau-de-Cologne. 'They will only think it is because of my happiness at Savita's wedding. Everything I do is for you, and no one appreciates me. I have chosen such a good boy for Savita, and all everyone does is complain.'

Lata reflected that of the four brothers and sisters, the only one who hadn't complained of the match had been the sweet-tempered, fair-complexioned, beautiful Savita herself.

'He is a little thin, Ma,' said Lata, a bit thoughtlessly. This was putting it mildly. Pran Kapoor, soon to be her brother-in-law, was lank, dark, gangly, and asthmatic.

'Thin? What is thin? Everyone is trying to become thin these days. Even I have had to fast the whole day and it is not good for my diabetes. And if Savita is not complaining, everyone should be happy with him. Arun and Varun are always complaining: why didn't they choose a boy for their sister then? Pran is a good, decent, cultured khatri boy.'

There was no denying that Pran, at thirty, was a good boy, a decent boy, and belonged to the right caste. And, indeed, Lata did like Pran. Oddly enough, she knew him better than her sister did – or, at least, had seen him for longer than her sister had. Lata was studying English at Brahmpur University, and Pran Kapoor was a popular lecturer there. Lata had attended his class on the Elizabethans, while Savita, the bride, had met him for only an hour, and that too in her mother's company.

'And Savita will fatten him up,' added Mrs Rupa Mehra. 'Why are you trying to annoy me when I am so happy? And Pran and Savita will be happy, you will see. They will be happy,' she continued emphatically. 'Thank you, thank you,' she now beamed at those who were coming up to greet her. 'It is so wonderful – the boy of my dreams, and such a good family. The Minister Sahib has been very kind to us. And Savita is so happy. Please eat something, please eat: they have made such delicious gulab-jamuns, but owing to my diabetes I cannot eat them even after the ceremonies. I am not even allowed gajak, which is so difficult to resist in winter. But please eat, please eat. I must go in to check what is happening: the time that the pandits have given is coming up, and there is no sign of either bride or groom!' She looked at Lata, frowning. Her younger daughter was going to prove more difficult than her elder, she decided.

ACTIVITY 4

1 The basis for comparison here is 'rites of passage'. Begin by comparing and contrasting the preoccupations of the characters in the two extracts. Think about the events that take place, the lives and states of mind of the characters, their expectations and the nature of the 'rites of passage' being referred to. Notice that several are evoked in the second passage.

2 Now compare the ways in which meanings are conveyed in the two extracts. Look at the diction of each extract, and the tone – which extract has humour, and how is it conveyed? Examine how Miriam's character is presented in the first extract, and the character of Mrs Rupa Mehra in the second. Look at narrative viewpoint, too. Compare the way in which the single viewpoint is given in the first extract with the presentation of the two viewpoints in the second.

3 The contexts of the writing are quite different. The first text was published in 1913, and the second in 1993. The first is set in England, and the second in India. Both have strong religious elements – how are they different? There are social and cultural contexts too. Look for the influence of these contexts in the details and language of the extracts, considering what are the most important contextual influences.

4 Now you could write a comparison of the two extracts.

Alternatively, you could compare a 'rites of passage' novel with a play – perhaps Neil Simon's *Brighton Beach Memoirs* or *Broadway Bound*. In this case, you could analyse differences of form in dealing with a similar subject as well, as you did in Activities 1 and 2 on *Birdsong* and the war poems of Wilfred Owen.

Assessment Objective 4

articulate independent opinions and judgements, informed by different interpretations of literary texts by other readers

Thinking about critical stances can be a good starting point for comparisons. One of the ways of interpreting texts such as *The Color Purple* by Alice Walker and *Oranges Are Not the Only Fruit* by Jeanette Winterson is to see them from a feminist perspective.

In this letter from *The Color Purple*, Celie is describing the preparations for Sofia's mother's funeral:

Harpo say, Whoever heard of women pallbearers. That all I'm trying to say.

Well, said Sofia, you said it. Now you can hush.

I know she your mother, say Harpo. But still.

You gon help us or not? say Sofia.

What it gon look like? say Harpo. Three big stout women pallbearers look like they ought to be home frying chicken.

Three of our brothers be with us, on the other side, say Sofia. I guess they look like field hands.

But peoples use to men doing this sort of thing. Women weaker, he say. People think they weaker, say they weaker, anyhow. Women spose to take it easy. Cry if you want to. Not try to take over.

Try to take over, say Sofia. The woman dead. I can cry and take it easy and lift the coffin too. And whether you help us or not with the food and the chairs and the get-together afterward, that's exactly what I plan to do.

In this extract from *Oranges Are Not the Only Fruit*, Jeanette, the central character, has started to preach in her church:

By Sunday the pastor had word back from the council. The real problem, it seemed, was going against the teachings of St Paul, and allowing women power in the church. Our branch of the church had never thought about it, we'd always had strong women, and the women organized everything. Some of us could preach, and quite plainly, in my case, the church was full because of it. There was uproar, then a curious thing happened. My mother stood up and said she believed this was right: that women had specific circumstances for their ministry, that the Sunday School was one of them, the Sisterhood another, but the message belonged to the men. Until this moment my life had still made some kind of sense. Now it was making no sense at all. My mother droned on about the importance of missionary work for a woman, that I was clearly such a woman, but had spurned my call in order to wield power on the home front, where it was inappropriate. She ended by saying that having taken on a man's world in other ways I had flouted God's law and tried to do it sexually. This was no spontaneous speech. She and the pastor had talked about it already. It was her weakness for the ministry that had done it. No doubt she'd told Pastor Spratt months ago. I looked around me. Good people, simple people, what would happen to them now? I knew my mother hoped I would blame myself, but I didn't. I knew now where the blame lay. If there's such a thing as spiritual adultery, my mother was a whore.

So there I was, my success in the pulpit being the reason for my downfall. The devil had attacked me at my weakest point: my inability to realize the limitations of my sex.

ACTIVITY 5

1 In the two extracts above, look for the similarities and differences in how the two women's lives are limited by the societies in which they live.

2 Are these limitations rules or customs? Look carefully for evidence from each extract.

3 What information is given in the extracts to help you to define the culture each woman lives in?

4 Compare the language used by Alice Walker and Jeanette Winterson.

A broader comparison of these two texts might include:

- the treatment of sexuality

- how feminist issues are reflected in secondary narrative in each text – the letters from Africa in *The Color Purple*, and the developing myth in *Oranges Are Not the Only Fruit*

- the power struggles between male and female in the texts, and their very different outcomes.

The position of women in society could be an important element in looking at less overtly feminist texts. *The Scarlet Letter* by Nathaniel Hawthorne could be compared from this point of view with either Charlotte Brontë's *Jane Eyre* or Margaret Atwood's *The Handmaid's Tale*.

The presentation of power and class in texts – a Marxist perspective, in other words – could be another point of comparison to focus on. *Hard Times* by Charles Dickens and J. B. Priestley's play *An Inspector Calls* offer similar perspectives here, but in different social and historical contexts and in different forms. Read the extracts from these two texts below, and then work through the questions in Activity 6.

In this extract from *Hard Times*, 'millers' in the third paragraph refers to the mill-owners – the employers in Coketown:

A sunny midsummer day. There was such a thing sometimes, even in Coketown.

Seen from a distance in such weather, Coketown lay shrouded in a haze of its own, which appeared impervious to the sun's rays. You only knew the town was there, because you knew there could have been no such sulky blotch upon the prospect without a town. A blur of soot and smoke, now confusedly tending this way, now that way, now aspiring to the vault of Heaven, now murkily creeping along the earth, as the wind rose and fell, or changed its quarter: a dense formless jumble, with sheets of cross light in it, that showed nothing but masses of darkness: – Coketown in the distance was suggestive of itself, though not a brick of it could be seen.

The wonder was, it was there at all. It had been ruined so often, that it was amazing how it had borne so many shocks. Surely there never was such fragile china-ware as that of which the millers of Coketown were made. Handle them never so lightly, and they fell to pieces with such ease that you might suspect them of having been flawed before. They were ruined, when they were required to send labouring children to school; they were ruined, when inspectors were appointed to look into their works; they were ruined, when such inspectors considered it doubtful whether they were quite justified in chopping people up with their machinery; they were utterly undone, when it was hinted that perhaps they need not always make quite so much smoke. Besides Mr Bounderby's gold spoon which was generally received in Coketown, another prevalent fiction was very popular there. It took the form of a threat. Whenever a Coketowner felt he was ill-used – that is to say, whenever he was not left entirely alone, and it was proposed to hold him accountable for the consequences of any of his acts – he was sure to come out with the awful menace, that he would 'sooner pitch his property into the Atlantic'. This had terrified the Home Secretary within an inch of his life, on several occasions.

However, the Coketowners were so patriotic after all, that they had never pitched their property into the Atlantic yet, but on the contrary, had been kind enough to take mighty good care of it. So there it was, in the haze yonder; and it increased and multiplied.

In *An Inspector Calls*, a police inspector is visiting the house of the Birling family after the death of a girl called Eva Smith. During the visit he shows how each member of the family was in some way responsible for the death. In Extract A, he is dealing with Mr Birling, the owner of the factory in which Eva was employed. In Extract B, he leaves the house after exposing the complicity of all the family.

Extract A

BIRLING [. . .] and she'd been working in one of our machine shops for over a year. A good worker too. In fact, the foreman there told me he was ready to promote her into what we call a leading operator – head of a small group of girls. But after they came back from their holidays that August, they were all rather restless, and they suddenly decided to ask for more money. They were averaging about twenty-two and six, which was neither more nor less than the average in our industry. They wanted the rates raised so they could average about twenty-five shillings a week. I refused, of course.

INSPECTOR Why?

BIRLING [*surprised*] Did you say 'Why?'?

INSPECTOR Yes. Why did you refuse?

BIRLING	Well, Inspector, I don't see that it's any concern of yours how I choose to run my business. Is it now?
INSPECTOR	It might be, you know.
BIRLING	I don't like that tone.
INSPECTOR	I'm sorry. But you asked me a question.
BIRLING	And you asked me a question before that, a quite unnecessary question too.
INSPECTOR	It's my duty to ask questions.
BIRLING	Well, it's my duty to keep labour costs down, and if I'd agreed to this demand for a new rate we'd have added about twelve per cent to our labour costs. Does that satisfy you? So I refused. Said I couldn't consider it. We were paying the usual rates and if they didn't like those rates, they could go and work somewhere else. It's a free country, I told them.
ERIC	It isn't if you can't go and work somewhere else.
INSPECTOR	Quite so.
BIRLING	[to Eric] Look – just you keep out of this. You hadn't even started in the works when this happened. So they went on strike. That didn't last long, of course.
GERALD	Not if it was just after the holidays. They'd all be broke – if I know them.
BIRLING	Right, Gerald. They mostly were. And so was the strike, after a week or two. Pitiful affair. Well, we let them all come back – at the old rates – except the four or five ring-leaders, who'd started the trouble. I went down myself and told them to clear out. And this girl, Eva Smith, was one of them. She'd had a lot to say – far too much – so she had to go.
GERALD	You couldn't have done anything else.
ERIC	He could. He could have kept her on instead of throwing her out. I call it tough luck.
BIRLING	Rubbish! If you don't come down sharply on some of these people, they'd soon be asking for the earth.
GERALD	I should say so!
INSPECTOR	They might. But after all it's better to ask for the earth than to take it.

Extract B

INSPECTOR   [. . .] [*Rather savagely, to Birling.*] You started it. She wanted twenty-five shillings a week instead of twenty-two and sixpence. You made her pay a heavy price for that. And now she'll make you pay a heavier price still.

BIRLING   [*unhappily*] Look, Inspector – I'd give thousands – yes, thousands –

INSPECTOR   You're offering the money at the wrong time, Mr Birling.

[*He makes a move as if concluding the session, possibly shutting up notebook, etc. Then surveys them sardonically.*]

No, I don't think any of you will forget. Nor that young man, Croft, though he at least had some affection for her and made her happy for a time. Well, Eva Smith's gone. And you can't do her any good now, either. You can't even say 'I'm sorry, Eva Smith.'

SHEILA   [*Who is crying quietly*] That's the worst of it.

INSPECTOR   But just remember this. One Eva Smith has gone – but there are millions and millions and millions of Eva Smiths and John Smiths still left with us, with their lives, their hopes and fears, their suffering and chance of happiness, all intertwined with our lives, and what we think and say and do. We don't live alone. We are members of one body. We are responsible for each other. And I tell you that the time will soon come when, if men will not learn that lesson, then they will be taught it in fire and blood and anguish. Good night.

He walks straight out, leaving them staring, subdued and wondering.

ACTIVITY 6

1   Compare how the working classes are shown being exploited by their employers in the two extracts. How do the employers justify or maintain their positions? The political message extends beyond the workers in the factories in both extracts. How do the writers do this?

2   How do the two writers convey their points of view? Think about the structure of the extract from *Hard Times*, in which the description of Coketown adds to the oppressive effect, and the use of syntax and irony convey the deadening effect of the town on its people. In considering the extract from *An Inspector Calls* you could think about how Priestley uses the exchanges between characters, the interventions of other characters, the language of the Inspector at the end, and his exit to achieve effects. After considering their points of view, compare how the writers use different forms to the same purpose.

3 *Hard Times* was written in 1854, and *An Inspector Calls* in 1945, though it was set in 1912. Which of these are significant contexts, in your view? Think about events going on and the state of society during these years.

4 Now write a comparison of the extracts.

A psychoanalytic reading of the nature of obsession in the novel *Enduring Love* by Ian McEwan and in either *Hamlet* or *Othello* by William Shakespeare would provide some illuminating connections and comparisons. *King Lear* is also open to a Marxist interpretation, but comparing it with Thomas Hardy's *Far From the Madding Crowd* would raise issues of family and power, gender and power, and nature and man as well.

Assessment Objective 5ii

evaluate the significance of cultural, historical and other contextual influences on literary texts and study

Your experience of AS English Literature will have taught you to look at all texts in terms of how they are written (AO3), different ways in which they might be interpreted (AO4), and the contexts involved in the writing of the text (AO5). AO5ii is not tested as such in this module, but AO2 'respond with knowledge and understanding to literary texts of different types and periods' is, and considering different contexts is a fruitful way of comparing texts (AO2ii). Examples are given below of a number of broad contextual areas for you to consider, with texts used to illustrate them.

Historical context

Many texts have a historical context which is significant for the reader. In pairing texts, the contexts themselves might be comparable, or the ways in which the writers use the contexts might be similar. For instance, J. G. Farrell's *The Siege of Krishnapur* and Peter Carey's *The True History of the Kelly Gang* are both modern novels set in the nineteenth century in British colonies of that time, India and Australia, but the writing reveals very different societies and social attitudes. Read the extracts from these novels below, and work through the questions that follow in Activity 7.

In this extract from *The Siege of Krishnapur* the Residency has been under siege for a considerable time, and supplies of food are running low.

On September 10th, which was Louise's birthday, Fleury bartered his gold cufflinks, a silver snuff-box and a pair of shoes with Rayne in exchange for two lumps of sugar. He ground the sugar into a powder, mixed it with water and with his daily handful of flour, adding a little curry powder to give it a spicy taste: then he grilled the result on a flat stone beside the fire. He also bought a teaspoonful of tea from one of the artillery women for ten pounds, to be paid after the siege was over or, in case of death, by his executors to certain of her relations; to lend substance to this rather nebulous arrangement which at first only seemed to excite the suspicion of the woman selling the tea, Fleury had drawn up an elaborate letter which began impressively: 'To Whomsoever May Find This Missive, I, George Fleury, Being Then Deceased,' and which seemed to Fleury to give a certain legal solemnity to the transaction. Thus provisioned, he invited Louise to come to the banqueting-hall to celebrate her birthday, though in a very quiet way, he assured her; he had not forgotten that she must still be suffering on account of her father, who had only recently taken his last dive down the well in the Residency yard in the wake of so many of his former patients.

Fleury's cakes had not turned out very well; in fact they had dried as hard as the stone they were baked on, and had to be chipped off with a bayonet. But even so, Louise was so hungry that she stared at them with a fearful concentration, ignoring Fleury's polite conversation as he made the tea. Unfortunately, when the time came to devour the cakes, she found she had difficulty in eating hers because of its hardness. She tried exchanging it for Fleury's but that was just as hard. The trouble was that Louise, like a number of other members of the garrison, was suffering from scurvy; there had been several cases of partial blindness and of swollen heads, but the most common symptom, and the one which was troubling Louise, was the loosening of teeth. She felt that her teeth would come out altogether if she tried to bite Fleury's cake. Fleury was not sure that his own teeth were very sound either so they decided that the best thing to do was to suck the cakes and perhaps dip them in the tea to soften them. Besides, in one way it was an advantage that they were so hard, because they would last longer. But in spite of their hardness they seemed to vanish in no time. Louise looked at Fleury and felt so vulnerable that presently she began to cry.

'Oh I say, what's the matter?'

But Louise could not tell him. Apart from the fact that she believed her teeth to be on the point of falling out, she had not had her period for several weeks and was afraid that she was barren. She wanted desperately to confide in someone about this, but once again found it impossible to find anyone suitable … her mother was too distraught, her father was dead and she could not bring herself to mention it to Miriam for fear of provoking some too blunt observations on the mysterious workings of a lady's insides. After a while, however, she forced herself to smile and dried her eyes on one of Fleury's shirt sleeves that looked fairly clean. She promised herself that she could continue sobbing later on, after she had gone to bed in the billiard room. Sobbing there was so commonplace that nobody noticed any more.

In this extract from *The True History of the Kelly Gang* Ned Kelly and his gang are on the run from the police when he receives a telegram telling him that his partner, who has fled to America, has had his child.

Read Ned read the thing.

DAM AND FILLY AT PASTURE IN SAN FRANCISCO FEED IS PENTIFUL.

It is her?

It is indeed.

My daughter it were you. You was born. You was in a foreign land but safe at your mother's breast I roared like a bull my breath burst forth & froze in that clean Australian air. Galloping in a circle round the paddock then a figure 8 I stood astride the mare one legged my pistols in my hands and all the boys stared they thought their moody Captain were finally insane.

He is a da called Kate.

Then what a show of riding they put on to welcome you and what a knees up promptly followed even if the porridge were still bubbling in the shanty pot.

The Kellys are here. Barefoot boys ran through the frost a girl on a Timor pony set off to bring the word these was our friends. Our hard won money flowed like wheat from a broken bag.

The police was in all in the hills & towns about but the country were not theirs they had not the least notion of the celebration which now spread like yellow gorse across the hills. Joe Byrne sang Rose O'Connell and his great baritone echoed out across the paddocks even the daggy sheep even the wall eyed donkey heard that you was born. Steve danced a jig in the middle of the track he were nimble & pretty as a pony. Dan were quickly drunk he wrote your name upon his hand then swore an oath to sail and bring you back to where you did belong.

These were your own people girl I mean the good people of Greta & Moyhu & Euroa & Benalla who come drifting down the track all through the morn & afternoon & night. How was they told of your birth did the bush telegraph alert them I do not know only that they come the men the women with babies at their breast shivering kiddies with cotton coats their eyes slitted against the wind. They arrived in broken cart & drays they was of that type THE BENALLA ENSIGN named the most frightful class of people they couldn't afford to leave their cows & pigs but they done so because we was them and they was us and we had showed the world what convict blood could do. We proved there were no taint we was of true bone blood and beauty born.

Through the dusk & icy starbright night them visitors continued to rise from the earth like winter oats their cold faces was soon pressed through doorway and window and even when the grog wore out they wd. not leave they come to touch my sleeve or clap my back they hitched great logs to their horses' tails to drag them out beside the track. 6 fires these was your birthday candles shining in 200 eyes.

ACTIVITY 7

1 Compare the celebrations in the two extracts. Think about:

- the elements of the celebrations
- the environments in which the celebrations take place
- the food
- the moods of the participants.

2 Overall, which seems more like a celebration, and why? How do the celebrations reflect the contexts of the action?

3 What are the attitudes to women in these extracts, and what do they reveal about the societies in which they are set?

4 Historical period and society are also reflected in the language. Compare and contrast the language of the extracts. How might the language reflect the societies in which the novels are set?

5 Compare how the language conveys mood in the two extracts.

If you were answering a question on these two texts as a pair, you would need to look at the wider picture of the period offered by each novel, and the way in which each text uses framing devices: the documents and accounts in *The True History of the Kelly Gang*, and the opening and ending of *The Siege of Krishnapur*. Social attitudes and language would also be focal points of comparison.

Social contexts

Many writers use their work to comment on the social context in which their text is set. Dickens is an obvious example, and his descriptions of Coketown in *Hard Times* or London in *Bleak House* could be compared and contrasted with William Blake's treatment of urban life in his poetry. This could be expanded, too, into an examination of form and language. Many writers also comment on their own society by setting their texts in other societies. Brian Friel's play *Translations*, for instance, is set in 1833, but at its first performance in Derry in 1980 the issues raised by the presence of English soldiers would have been very relevant to the lives of the audience.

Language, however, can also reflect the society being pictured. AO3 is tested in this Unit, and therefore the language of texts has to be considered; but language may also be a central feature of the text, as in *1984* by George Orwell, or in *Translations*, as the title suggests.

Two texts which combine both of these features are *A Clockwork Orange*, by Anthony Burgess, and *Riddley Walker*, by Russell Hoban. Both writers reflect concerns about their own society by creating a vision of a future society, but they are very different visions. *A Clockwork Orange* pictures a society with a dominant central government, rich in material possessions, but with a violent, disaffected teenage under-class who have developed a language of their own. In

Riddley Walker, Russell Hoban creates a society living in the wake of a nuclear holocaust. It has regressed to a Stone Age way of life, reflected in its unsophisticated language.

Read the passages from these two novels printed below, and answer the questions that follow in Activity 8. There is a glossary on page 160 to help you.

Below are two extracts from *A Clockwork Orange*. In the first, Alex, the narrator, has had a visit from P. R. Deltoid, his Post-Corrective Adviser, who suggests that he has been involved in violent incidents the previous night – which he has.

But when he'd ookadeeted and I was making this very strong pot of chai, I grinned to myself over this veshch that P. R. Deltoid and his droogs worried about. All right, I do bad, what with crasting and tolchocks and carves with the britva and the old in-out-in-out, and if I get loveted, well, too bad for me, O my little brothers, and you can't run a country with every chellovech comporting himself in my manner of the night. So if I get loveted and it's three months in this mesto and another six in that, and then, as P. R. Deltoid so kindly warns, next time, in spite of the great tenderness of my summers, brothers, it's the great unearthly zoo itself, well, I say: 'Fair, but a pity, my lords, because I just cannot bear to be shut in. My endeavour shall be, in such future as stretches out its snowy and lilywhite arms to me before the nozh overtakes or the blood spatters its final chorus in twisted metal and smashed glass on the highroad, to not get loveted again.' Which is fair speeching.

In the second extract, Alex is eating breakfast and reading an article in 'the gazetta' about 'Modern Youth'.

And there was a bolshy big article on Modern Youth (meaning me, so I gave the old bow, grinning like bezoomny) by some very clever bald chelloveck. I read this with care, my brothers, slurping away at the old chai, cup after tass after chasha, crunching my lomticks of black toast dipped in jammiwam and eggiweg. This learned veck said the usual veshches, about no parental discipline, as he called it, and the shortage of real horrorshow teachers who would lambast bloody beggary out of their innocent poops and make them go boohoohoo for mercy. All this was gloopy and made me smeck, but it was like nice to go on knowing one making the news all the time, O my brothers. Every day there was something about Modern Youth, but the best veshch they ever had in the old gazetta was by some starry pop in a doggy collar who said that in his considered opinion and he govoreeting as a man of Bog IT WAS THE DEVIL THAT WAS ABROAD and was like ferreting his way into like young innocent flesh, and it was the adult world that could take the responsibility for this with their wars and bombs and nonsense. So that was all right. So he knew what he talked of, being a Godman. So we young innocent malchicks could take no blame. Right right right.

Below are two extracts from *Riddley Walker*. In the first, Riddley, the narrator, is living a nomadic existence with Goodparley, and they have come to visit Goodparley's grandfather, who is a charcoal burner.

That morning it wer the 9th day from my naming day. That day when it come that las boars tern to dy on my spear in the grey morning girzel on them very same Bundel Downs. 9 days dont soun like a long time yet I stil cudnt take in all whatd happent. Seeing that boars face in my mynd that morning in the aulders and seeing it in my mynd now I have the same thot I had then: If you cud even jus see 1 thing clear the woal of whats in it you cud see every thing clear. But you never wil get to see the woal of any thing youre all ways in the middl of it living it or moving thru it. Never mynd.

We stoppit there then the Granser in the audlers it wer a good place to ly up. Granser he dint have no crowd there he wer oansome like the chard coal berners mosly wer. The forms all ways give them road crowd and hault ther fentsing 1 cutting to a nother then they fentst them in and lef them til they finisht ther berning and ready to move on. This year the chard coal berners ben doing the 6 year cutting in the aulder coppises all up and down the rivver. They had long flat boats for the fentsing and the chard coal there wer 1 tyd up by Gransers cutting with bags of chard coal covert with hard clof. All up and down the rivver you cud see the loppt off aulders when they wer fresh cut they wer red they ternt pink after. Red wood. Red wud. Seed of the red. All ways words in things. 6 year cuttings. Which this wer a Ardship year and a cutting year boath. Every 2nd cutting yearwd all ways be 1 of them 12th years when a Pry Mincer and a Ardship gone the Fools Circel 9wys. Them aulders wer trying to tel me some thing I knowit that much.

It wer on the forms to keap the chard coal berners in meat. Granser had a stoar of pittaters and sweads he had roady and sossage from Good Mercy plus some times they brung fresh meat. Goodparley and me we all ways kep low when any 1 ternt up. I gone foraging with the dogs every day we et good there.

In the second extract, Riddley is approaching Cambry, the ruins of Canterbury Cathedral, 'where the senter is'.

After a wyl I cud feal on my face a littl stilness where the wind wer cut off I cud hear the sylents of the stannings of the Power Ring. Feal the goast of old Power circeling hy over me. Only this time I felt a Power in me what circelt with it. Membering when that thot came to me: THE ONLYES POWER IS NO POWER. Wel now I sust that wernt qwite it. It aint that its *no* Power. Its the not sturgling for Power that's where the Power is. Its in jus letting your self be where it is. Its tuning in to the worl its leaving your self behynt and letting your self be where it says in *Eusa* 5:

> … in tu the hart uv the stoan hart uv the dans. Evere thing blippin & bleapin & movin in the shiftin uv thay Nos. Sum tyms bytin sum tyms bit.

Looking up in to the black where the goast of Power circelt blyn and oansome like a Drop John roun the los hump of Cambry I larft I yelt, 'SPIRIT OF GOD ROAD WITH ME!'

ACTIVITY 8

1 *Social context*

The two narrators, both young men, lead very different lives. Compare these elements in the extracts:
- food
- activities
- government.

2 *Language context*

The texts are written in different languages from our own and from each other. Compare the language of the extracts, keeping in mind the differences from contemporary English. There is a glossary on page 160 to help you.

Compare:
- the vocabulary and spelling
- the punctuation
- the syntax.

3 *Philosophical context*

Attitudes and ideas about life in the societies created in these texts can also be compared.

Identify and compare:
- the attitudes towards the self in the extracts
- the attitudes towards God (referred to as 'Bog' by Alex) in the extracts.

There are many socio-cultural areas which might also allow for interesting and illuminating comparisons. *Trainspotting* by Irving Welsh and the play *Shopping and Fucking* by Mark Ravenshill, for instance, both deal with drug culture, and you could make comparisons of language and structure. The novel *The French Lieutenant's Woman* by John Fowles and the play *Mrs Warren's Profession* by George Bernard Shaw both revolve around issues of love, marriage and prostitution, but make very different cultural assumptions. As well as the difference in form, one is a chronological narrative and one non-chronological, offering further scope for contrast. A comparison of *Oranges Are Not the Only Fruit* by Jeanette Winterson with *Wild Swans* by Jung Chang would offer, in two very different narratives, perspectives on growing up in restrictive cultures.

A particular socio-economic concept, which forms a context for many American texts, is the 'American Dream' – the idea that working to acquire money and material goods will bring success, and with it every kind of happiness. Two texts which both reflect on this are *The Great Gatsby* by Scott Fitzgerald and the play *Death of a Salesman* by Arthur Miller: extracts from both are given below.

In this extract from *The Great Gatsby*, the narrator, Nick, is describing the parties at the house of his new neighbour, Jay Gatsby:

At least once a fortnight a corps of caterers came down with several hundred feet of canvas and enough coloured lights to make a Christmas tree of Gatsby's enormous garden. On buffet tables, garnished with glistening hors-d'œuvre, spiced baked hams crowded against salads of harlequin designs and pastry pigs and turkeys bewitched to a dark gold. In the main hall a bar with a real brass rail was set up, and stocked with gins and liquors and with cordials so long forgotten that most of his female guests were too young to know one from another.

By seven o'clock the orchestra has arrived, no thin five-piece affair, but a whole pitful of oboes and trombones and saxophones and viols and cornets and piccolos, and low and high drums. The last swimmers have come in from the beach now and are dressing upstairs; the cars from New York are parked five deep in the drive, and already the halls and salons and verandas are gaudy with primary colours, and hair bobbed in strange new ways, and shawls beyond the dreams of Castile. The bar is in full swing, and floating rounds of cocktails permeate the garden outside, until the air is alive with chatter and laughter, and casual innuendo and introductions forgotten on the spot, and enthusiastic meetings between women who never knew each other's names.

The lights grow brighter as the earth lurches away from the sun, and now the orchestra is playing yellow cocktail music, and the opera of voices pitches a key higher. Laughter is easier minute by minute, spilled with prodigality, tipped out at a cheerful word. The groups change more swiftly, swell with new arrivals, dissolve and form in the same breath; already there are wanderers, confident girls who weave here and there among the stouter and more stable, become for a sharp, joyous moment the centre of a group, and then, excited with triumph, glide on through the sea-change of faces and voices and colour under the constantly changing light.

Suddenly one of these gypsies, in trembling opal, seizes a cocktail out of the air, dumps it down for courage and, moving her hands like Frisco, dances out alone on the canvas platform. A momentary hush; the orchestra leader varies his rhythm obligingly for her, and there is a burst of chatter as the erroneous news goes around that she is Gilda Gray's understudy from the *Follies*. The party has begun.

This scene from Miller's *Death of a Salesman* shows Willy Loman contemplating killing himself so that his family can get the insurance money. Willy, a salesman, is ill, and has been fired from his job. He feels guilty about his lack of success, the trouble his wife has had to endure, and the contempt that his son Biff feels for him. Here, he is 'talking' to his Uncle Ben, who was a successful entrepreneur; the conversation takes place in Willy's imagination:

WILLY   [. . .] What a proposition, ts, ts. Terrific, terrific. 'Cause she's suffered, Ben, the woman has suffered. You understand me? A man can't go out the way he came in, Ben, a man has got to add up to something. You can't, you can't – [*Ben moves towards him as though to interrupt.*] You gotta consider, now. Don't answer so quick. Remember, it's a guaranteed twenty-thousand-dollar proposition. Now look, Ben, I want you to go through the ins and outs of this thing with me. I've got nobody to talk to, Ben, and the woman has suffered, you hear me?

BEN   [*standing still, considering*] What's the proposition?

WILLY   It's twenty thousand dollars on the barrelhead. Guaranteed, gilt-edged, you understand?

BEN   You don't want to make a fool of yourself. They might not honour the policy.

WILLY   How can they dare refuse? Didn't I work like a coolie to meet every premium on the nose? And now they don't pay off! Impossible!

BEN   It's called a cowardly thing, William.

WILLY   Why? Does it take more guts to stand here the rest of my life ringing up a zero?

BEN   [*yielding*] That's a point, William. [*He moves, thinking, turns.*] And twenty thousand – that *is* something one can feel with the hand, it is there.

WILLY   [*now assured, with rising power*] Oh, Ben, that's the whole beauty of it! I see it like a diamond, shining in the dark, hard and rough, that I can pick up and touch in my hand. Not like – like an appointment! This would not be another damned-fool appointment, Ben, and it changes all the aspects. Because he thinks I'm nothing, see, and so he spites me. But the funeral – [*straightening up*] Ben, that funeral will be massive! They'll come from Maine, Massachusetts, Vermont, New Hampshire! All the old-timers with the strange licence plates – that boy will be thunderstruck, Ben, because he never realized – I am known! Rhode Island, New York, New Jersey – I am known, Ben, and he'll see it with his eyes once and for all. He'll see what I am, Ben! He's in for a shock, that boy!

BEN   [*coming down to the edge of the garden*] He'll call you a coward.

WILLY   [*suddenly fearful*] No, that would be terrible.

BEN   Yes. And a damned fool.

WILLY   No, no, he mustn't, I won't have that! [*He is broken and desperate.*]

BEN   He'll hate you, William.

ACTIVITY 9

1   In the extract from *The Great Gatsby*, look for the words and phrases which suggest:

  • abundance, and excess

  • a dream-like, or unreal quality

  • a transitory feeling

  • that things are false – although an effect has been aimed for, it hasn't quite succeeded.

2   In the extract from *Death of a Salesman*, look for evidence in Willy's language of his desire to succeed. What else seems to drive him?

3   Willy is planning to kill himself, but he describes it like a business deal. Look for evidence of this in the extract.

4   Find examples of Willy's sense of his own failure.

5   Willy has always deluded himself about his own achievements. Can you find allusions to this in the passage?

6   The extract from *The Great Gatsby* comes early on in the novel (Chapter 2) but both texts end in the failure and death of the central figures. Using all the evidence you've accumulated, show how both extracts present the American Dream as a false, dangerous concept.

Language context

All literary texts have a language context. In some, however, language is a pronounced feature. Brian Friel's play *Translations* and George Orwell's novel *1984* both deal with the power of language to affect society and the individual. Read these two extracts and work through Activity 10, which follows.

In this extract from *1984* the central character, Winston Smith, is listening to a colleague in the Ministry of Truth telling him about the advantages of Newspeak. Newspeak is the language of Big Brother, who is the figurehead of the totalitarian state in which the novel is set.

'[. . .] Do you know that Newspeak is the only language in the world whose vocabulary gets smaller every year?'

Winston did know that, of course. He smiled, sympathetically he hoped, not trusting himself to speak. Syme bit off another fragment of the dark-coloured bread, chewed it briefly, and went on:

'Don't you see that the whole aim of Newspeak is to narrow the range of thought? In the end we shall make thoughtcrime literally impossible, because there will be no words in which to express it. Every concept that can ever be needed will be expressed by exactly *one* word, with its meaning rigidly defined and all its subsidiary meanings rubbed out and forgotten. Already, in the Eleventh Edition, we're not far from that point. But the process will still be continuing long after you and I are dead. Every year fewer and fewer words, and the range of consciousness always a little smaller. Even now, of course, there's no reason or excuse for committing thoughtcrime. It's merely a question of self-discipline, reality-control. But in the end there won't be any need even for that. The Revolution will be complete when the language is perfect. Newspeak is Ingsoc and Ingsoc is Newspeak,' he added with a sort of mystical satisfaction. 'Has it ever occurred to you, Winston, that by the year 2050, at the very latest, not a single human being will be alive who could understand such a conversation as we are having now?'

'Except – ' began Winston doubtfully, and then stopped.

It had been on the tip of his tongue to say 'Except the proles,' but he checked himself, not feeling fully certain that this remark was not in some way unorthodox.

In this extract from Brian Friel's play *Translations*, Lancey, an English soldier, is warning the villagers of Ballybeg what will happen if his fellow officer, who has gone missing, is not found. In the play, set in the west of Ireland in 1833, Owen has been translating the officers' words into Irish, and has been helping to give English names to Irish places. Sarah, who was mute at the beginning of the play, has learned to speak during the course of it.

LANCEY   If that doesn't bear results, commencing forty-eight hours from now we will embark on a series of evictions and levelling of every abode in the following selected areas –

OWEN   You're not – !

LANCEY   Do your job. Translate.

OWEN   If they still haven't found him in two days' time they'll begin evicting and levelling every house starting with these townlands.

[*Lancey reads from his list.*]

LANCEY   Swinefort.

OWEN   Lis na Muc.

LANCEY   Burnfoot.

OWEN   Bun na hAbhann.

LANCEY   Dromduff.

OWEN   Druim Dubh.

LANCEY   Whiteplains.

OWEN   Machaire Ban.

LANCEY   Kings Head.

OWEN   Cnoc na Ri.

LANCEY   If by then the lieutenant hasn't been found, we will proceed until a complete clearance is made of this entire section.

OWEN   If Yolland hasn't been got by then, they will ravish the whole parish.

LANCEY   I trust they know exactly what they've got to do.

[*Pointing to Bridget*] I know you. I know where you live.

[*Pointing to Sarah*] Who are you? Name!

[*Sarah's mouth opens and shuts, opens and shuts. Her face becomes contorted.*]

What's your name?

[*Again Sarah tries frantically.*]

OWEN   Go on, Sarah. You can tell him.

[*But Sarah cannot. And she knows she cannot. She closes her mouth. Her head goes down.*]

OWEN   Her name is Sarah Johnny Sally.

LANCEY   Where does she live?

OWEN   Bun na hAbhann.

LANCEY   Where?

OWEN   Burnfoot.

ACTIVITY 10

1 Describe how language, and rules about language, are used to oppress people in the societies of each extract. Be as detailed and exact as you can.

2 *1984* is set in a society in the future, and *Translations* is set in a society in the past. What does each writer seem to be suggesting about the society they present?

3 In each extract one character does not speak, although Winston starts to and stops in *1984*. What might their silence suggest to the reader of *1984* and the audience of *Translations*? Look at the stage directions and work out how the play operates in a different way from the novel.

If you were comparing these two texts, you could go on to look at the importance of language in the whole texts. These two extracts would be good starting points.

Invented language is a feature of some texts, and could be an important element in comparing, say, *1984* with *A Clockwork Orange* by Anthony Burgess.

Literary and generic context

Comparing two texts by the same writer involves a literary context, that of the writer's work. Other contexts, such as period, will be involved too, and style and subject matter can also be compared. There are likely to be similarities, of course, but there may also be significant differences. The writer's intentions in the texts may be quite different, a range of conventions could be used, and the works may represent different stages in the writer's development.

Below are the openings to two novels by Jane Austen: *Pride and Prejudice* and *Mansfield Park*. Read these extracts, and work through Activity 11, which follows.

It is a truth universally acknowledged, that a single man in possession of a good fortune must be in want of a wife.

However little known the feelings or views of such a man may be on his first entering a neighbourhood, this truth is so well fixed in the minds of the surrounding families, that he is considered as the rightful property of someone or other of their daughters.

'My dear Mr Bennet,' said his lady to him one day, 'have you heard that Netherfield Park is let at last?'

Mr Bennet replied that he had not.

'But it is,' returned she; 'for Mrs Long has just been here, and she told me all about it.'

Mr Bennet made no answer.

'Do not you want to know who has taken it?' cried his wife impatiently.

'*You* want to tell me, and I have no objection to hearing it.'

This was invitation enough.

'Why, my dear, you must know, Mrs Long says that Netherfield is taken by a young man of large fortune from the north of England; that he came down on Monday in a chaise and four to see the place, and was so much delighted with it, that he agreed with Mr Morris immediately; that he is to take possession before Michaelmas, and some of his servants are to be in the house by the end of next week.'

'What is his name?'

'Bingley.'

'Is he married or single?'

'Oh! single, my dear, to be sure! A single man of large fortune; four or five thousand a year. What a fine thing for our girls!'

'How so? How can it affect them?'

'My dear Mr Bennet,' replied his wife, 'how can you be so tiresome! You must know that I am thinking of his marrying one of them.'

'Is that his design in settling here?'

'Design! Nonsense, how can you talk so! But it is very likely that he *may* fall in love with one of them, and therefore you must visit him as soon as he comes.'

'I see no occasion for that. You and the girls may go, or you may send them by themselves, which perhaps will be still better, for as you are as handsome as any of them, Mr Bingley might like you the best of the party.'

(J. Austen, *Pride and Prejudice*)

About thirty years ago, Miss Maria Ward, of Huntingdon, with only seven thousand pounds, had the good luck to captivate Sir Thomas Bertram, of Mansfield Park, in the county of Northampton, and to be thereby raised to the rank of a baronet's lady, with all the comforts and consequences of an handsome house and large income. All Huntingdon exclaimed on the greatness of the match, and her uncle, the lawyer, himself allowed her to be at least three thousand pounds short of any equitable claim to it. She had two sisters to be benefited by her elevation; and such of their acquaintances as thought Miss Ward and Miss Frances quite as handsome as Miss Maria, did not scruple to predict their marrying with almost equal advantage. But there certainly are not so many men of large fortune in the world as there are pretty women to deserve them. Miss Ward, at the end of half-a-dozen years, found herself obliged to be attached to the Rev. Mr Norris, a friend of her brother-in-law, with scarcely any private fortune, and Miss Frances fared yet worse. Miss Ward's match, indeed, when it came to the point, was not contemptible; Sir Thomas being happily able to give his friend an income in the living of Mansfield; and Mr and Mrs Norris began their career of conjugal felicity with very little less than a thousand a year. But Miss Frances married, in the common phrase, to disoblige her family, and by fixing on a lieutenant of marines, without education, fortune, or connections, did it very thoroughly. She could hardly have made a more untoward choice. Sir Thomas Bertram had interest which, from principle as well as pride – from a general wish of doing right, and a desire of seeing all that were connected with him in situations of respectability, he would have been glad to exert for the advantage of Lady Bertram's sister; but her husband's profession was such as no interest could reach; and before he had time to devise any other method of assisting them, an absolute breach between the sisters had taken place. It was the natural result of the conduct of each party, and such as a very imprudent marriage almost always produces.

(J. Austen, *Mansfield Park*)

ACTIVITY 11

1 Referring to both extracts, what does Jane Austen suggest is the most important element in making a marriage? What is unimportant? How are these things conveyed? Look for all the references to money, and notice which extract has the most references.

2 Find examples of humour in the extracts. Which extract has more humour? Notice whether the humour relies on language or character.

3 Look for the abstract nouns in each extract. Which extract has more? Do you see any condemnation in either extract?

4 Although the language in both extracts is naturally fairly similar, the form is used differently. Look at the way the two extracts are set out on the page and note the main differences. How is character conveyed in each extract?

5 Having worked through the questions above, try to sum up the differences in tone and intention of the two extracts.

If you were answering a question on these two texts, you could look at how marriage is viewed in each novel as a whole, and at the differences in tone.

Another type of literary context occurs when one text refers to another. This is the case with *Jane Eyre*, by Charlotte Brontë, and *Wide Sargasso Sea* by Jean Rhys, in which the author explores a character from Brontë's (earlier) novel; or *Precious Bane*, by Mary Webb, and *Cold Comfort Farm* by Stella Gibbons. Gibbons's novel is a parody of the rural genre to which *Precious Bane* belongs.

Developments in literary forms and conventions can also form a context, and comparisons between texts can illuminate the issues. In first-person narratives, for instance, the narrator might be 'reliable' or 'unreliable'. The effect on the reader of the 'unreliable' narrator in *The Remains of the Day* by Kazuo Ishiguro, for example, could be examined by comparing it with the effect of the narrative in *David Copperfield*, by Charles Dickens. On the other hand, comparing it with a similar narrative of self-delusion in Dickens's *Great Expectations* would also be interesting.

Texts within particular literary genres could be compared, too. In detective fiction, *The Lady in the Lake* by Raymond Chandler could be compared with any of the 'Aurelio Zen' novels by Michael Dibdin, or either of these could be compared with Ian McEwan's *Enduring Love*, which has strong elements of thriller writing, though used here for different purposes. Gothic or horror novels from different periods could also be compared.

Coursework

If you choose to enter for the coursework unit, you will have to study and compare at least two texts, one of which must be a prose text, and produce an essay of about 2,500 words in length. You can write the essays in school or at college or at home, and then they will be marked by your teacher. Finally, the moderator from the Examination Board will look at your work and all the work from your school or centre, and decide on a final mark. In order to do well in your coursework, you need to think about these points:

- choosing a task
- reading the text
- planning
- research
- writing
- drafting and redrafting
- sticking to word and time limits.

Choosing a task

It is vital to choose a task which is appropriate – a task that addresses the Assessment Objectives. This module represents 15% of the whole A Level examination, and 30% of A2. It assesses equally Assessment Objectives 1, 3 and 4, with special emphasis on AO2ii (this accounts for nearly half of the marks available). This means that you must choose a task which is not simply about two texts, but which offers good opportunities for a thorough comparison. You must choose a task which enables you to address writers' choices of form, language and structure, too, and one which leads you to an independent judgement. It is easy to get very involved in comparing subject matter and to forget that you have to do more than this. Your task needs to be achievable, as well: if you're setting out to write a 2,500-word piece, there's no point in setting yourself a task which can't be done in less than 10,000 words. Word limits are very important. As a general rule, the more sharply defined the task is, the better.

Reading the text

You'll probably read the texts in class, at least partially, where you'll have the chance to discuss them with your teacher and other students. But just like your exam texts for Module 4, you'll need to read them again yourself too. You need to show 'knowledge and understanding' of the texts (AO2ii) in your writing, and the more you read them the better your chances of finding and exploring connections and comparisons between them. This will enable you to draw on a wide range of evidence when you write your final essay.

Planning

Now you need to plan your essay. Here are three general points to bear in mind.

1   Your plan needs to be helpful to you in writing your essay, so that in working through it, you produce a logical sequence of ideas, which develop an argument and lead to a clear conclusion.

2   You need to check your plan against the Assessment Objectives. Is it clear how and at what point you're going to meet them?

3   You don't want to have to change your plan much once you've started writing, so think about length again at this stage. By the time your plan is fleshed out with argument and evidence, will the word count be about right? Too many words? Too few to create a solid argument? If it doesn't look right, change your plan now.

Research

Research may well involve reading articles or essays about your texts, from books or the internet, but the most important source of information is still the primary source – the texts themselves. For instance, if you decided to write about how the American Dream is presented in *The Great Gatsby* and *Death of a Salesman*, you'd begin with a selective re-reading of the texts, looking for ideas and passages which might be useful to you. You could then research the writers, or the concept of the American Dream, to see if you could add to the ideas you already have, or to find some new angles to develop, or to provide additional evidence. If you have read secondary sources as part of your research, you must mention them in the bibliography at the end of your essay.

Writing

A significant proportion of the marks available for this module are for writing, and in coursework you have the chance to score well – perhaps more easily than you can in timed examinations. Five of the thirty marks are for the ability to 'communicate clearly the knowledge, understanding and insight appropriate to literary study, using appropriate terminology and accurate and coherent written expression' (AO1). As long as you give yourself plenty of time to write, you can take more care over the accuracy and clarity of your coursework essay than you can in an examination – and you can take the time to check it, revise it and improve it when you've finished the first draft. There are specific marks for this, so do take the trouble to collect them.

Assessment Objective 2ii is the dominant Objective here. After all, this module is about 'literary connections', and the second part of this Objective asks you to explore and comment on 'relationships and comparisons between literary texts'. You still have to meet the first part of the Objective, though, and show your ability to 'respond with knowledge and understanding to a literary text'. Your understanding will be demonstrated in the quality of your argument; but knowledge has to underpin everything you write, in an examination or in coursework. In coursework you have the leisure to practise what you have to do under time pressure in the examinations – to provide evidence for what you say from the text. There are appropriate ways of showing knowledge, too. You can show it by referring to details or echoes of the text, or by quotation. Short quotations (usually the most effective) can be included in the body of your writing, while longer quotations can be written on separate lines, so that they are easier to read. If you're quoting lines of verse in the body of your writing, you should show the line divisions.

If you are quoting from a secondary source, such as a critic, this should be footnoted, by numbering the quotations and providing a guide to the numbers, either at the foot of the page or at the end of the essay. Here is an example:

'Blake's engravings also form a context, in that he seemed to want to make the experiences conveyed by the poems as concrete as possible. Perhaps he was suggesting that experience should be considered in physical as well as abstract terms.[1]

The note at the bottom of the page or the end of the essay would be:

[1] Childs, T., Moore, J.: p.74, *A2 English Literature for AQA A* (2001)

If you do use the words of other writers, such as critics, in your own writing, you must acknowledge them. You have to sign a declaration that the coursework is your own work. 'Lifting' from other writing without acknowledging it is regarded as malpractice, and it could lose you all your marks for the module.

Drafting and redrafting

When you have completed a first draft of your coursework essay, your teacher may allow you to redraft it, as long as there is enough time left to do so. Your teacher is only allowed to give general advice and guidelines as to how you might improve the work, *not* to correct it and rewrite it – the coursework essay must be your work, after all. Of course, you should heed any advice, but you should try and make your first draft as good as you can. It's a lot easier to make minor changes than major ones at this stage.

Sticking to word and time limits

The word limit for A2 coursework is 2,500 words. If you exceed it, you will run the risk of being penalised. If your first draft comes to 3,000 words, you can probably trim it fairly easily, and you can ask for your teacher's guidance as to which parts to prune. If it is 5,000 words, though, you may have problems. Cutting sentences here and there, and tightening expression, won't cut it by half. If this situation arises, you probably made a mistake early on – either in selecting the task, at the planning stage, or when you were partway through. If it looks as if you will run over the word limit, you should stop and review your work as soon as possible. Your teacher will give you the coursework deadlines, and it is important to stick to them – not just to please your teacher, but to improve your chances of success. You will only be able to cut/redraft/rethink if you've got the time to do it.

Planning coursework: some strategies

The first part of Module 5, Literary Connections, was designed to offer you a range of methods for comparing texts, and at the same time a choice of possible combinations of texts. Once you've chosen and read texts, and decided on and discussed a task with your teacher (who has to get the agreement of the coursework moderator), then it's time to start planning. Below are some strategies you could adopt. The principles outlined will apply to any choice of texts. The plans are based on the study of *Birdsong* by Sebastian Faulks and the war poetry of Wilfred Owen, both of which we looked at earlier in this module (pages 108–12). The task is: 'An exploration of the ways in which war is presented in *Birdsong* and Wilfred Owen's poetry'.

Methods 1 and 2 involve looking first at one text, then the other. Methods 3 and 4 involve looking at the two texts *alongside* each other. If you organise your work by looking at the two texts like this, 'systematic comparisons', and 'developing ideas by comparison and contrast' should both be possible. There are a number of ways of doing this; Methods 3 and 4 are just two examples.

Method 1

The simplest way to start is to deal with one text, then the other, then draw together comparisons and contrasts. However, this is unlikely to be the most effective method. The teachers and moderators who assess your work do not favour one method over another, but they do mark against the Assessment Criteria. The criteria for the top two bands for AO2ii for this module are:

- systematic comparisons of form, structure and language as well as subject and theme (Band 3 11–15)
- skilfully selects for analysis specific aspects of texts, clarifying and developing ideas by comparison and contrast (Band 4 16–20).

As you can see, 'systematic comparisons' and 'developing ideas by comparison and contrast' will be difficult to achieve with this method, especially within 2,500 words. A method which produces sharper focus will be more likely to score really well.

Method 2

A similar method would be to write about one text, and then to compare and contrast elements as you write about the second. Looking at the criteria quoted above, this would allow you to make 'systematic comparisons', but 'developing ideas by comparison and contrast' might be a little more difficult. Your thinking and writing about the texts will still have to be very organised, or you will find yourself including material on one of the texts – probably the first – for which there is no relationship in the other text. This material would then be irrelevant to your argument.

Method 3

You could organise your comparison by subject matter. In the case of the task on *Birdsong* and the poetry of Owen, there are elements of war which both writers deal with, so you could make a plan charting a logical sequence of elements, and then write about how the writers present these elements. It might look something like this:

1 Introduction

2 Trench conditions – mud, cold, disease, effects of noise, madness

3 Wounds – including self-inflicted

4 Death – types of death inc. gas, mines, tunnelling, death of the young

5 Attitudes to officers and generals

6 Attitudes to the enemy

7 Conclusion, linking writers' tones and intentions

This would work well enough, and should allow you to develop and explore ideas about relationships and comparisons which remain relevant. A danger here would be over-enthusiasm for the subject matter, to the exclusion of style. Remember, you have to address AO3, and the question asked 'how the writers present' – an invitation to write about 'how writers' choices of form, structure and language shape meanings'.

Method 4

You could organise your comparison by style instead of subject matter, by working through a comparison of the ways in which the writers choose form, structure and language to shape meanings. You can't overlook AO3 if you do this, and the subject matter should be easier to deal with. A plan might look like this:

1   *Introduction* You could begin by comparing the two extracts about shellholes from the two texts given on pages 108–9 of this book. This would both illustrate some commonality of subject, and lead you into a discussion of form.

2   *Form* You could pick up from the extracts Faulks's use of dialogue, although Owen uses dialogue too ('The Chances', for instance, is entirely in dialogue, and several other poems make use of speech). *Birdsong* makes use of letters, a form which is not really available to Owen, though 'S.I.W.' contains a fragment of a letter. Owen's distinctive poetic style and use of half-rhyme, however, highlight a genre difference.

3   *Structure* The structures used by the writers are mostly very different, which is a reflection of genre as much as anything. The complex narrative structure of *Birdsong*, with its time shifts and perspectives, opens up angles not available to Owen, especially as Faulks has the advantage of writing from a later period. On the other hand, Owen also uses shifts in time to make his statements. 'Disabled', 'S.I.W.', and 'The Send-Off' could all be looked at here. Owen uses some dramatic beginnings and endings in ways that would be very unusual in prose, which tends to be less concentrated and intense. Prose tends to explain, where poetry suggests.

4   *Language* Despite the differences in genre – you might expect to find more striking use of language in the intense nature of poetry – both texts shape meanings with choices of language which are often similar. If you look at Pair 1 on page 110 you will find some evidence for this. Of course, there is also a range of poetic language devices employed by Owen which Faulks does not use.

5   *Conclusion* – attitudes/intentions. Despite the differences which will have emerged during the essay, it is clear that Faulks and Owen, in their individual ways and from their different perspectives, share some attitudes about the war. There is much evidence of this, some of which will already have been used, but in Pair 2 on pages 111–12 the final word about war seems to be common to both. Nevertheless, Owen's intention was more immediate than Faulks's in one sense, as he intended his poetry to speak to people at the time, an option not open to Faulks.

Methods 3 and 4 may still have their pitfalls. For example, Method 4 runs the risk of being too technical, and failing to link subject matter. The best thing to do is to plan according to your texts and task. With any method, it is essential to remember that you must offer your own views about the effectiveness of the texts, or about how they can be read.

How to secure good marks

When you've followed all the advice above about selecting texts and task, and planning and writing your essay, you need to have an idea of how well you're going to score. Your teacher will help you here, but it is worth knowing exactly how teachers and moderators judge your essay.

The dominant Assessment Objective in this module is AO2ii, which states that:

> Candidates should be able to respond with knowledge and understanding to literary texts of different types and periods, exploring and commenting on relationships between literary texts.

There are four mark bands. Here are the criteria in the top band, which offers 16–20 marks:

- sound knowledge and understanding of text
- mature skills of analysis and synthesis
- range of ideas supported by detailed reading
- crucial aspects of a question clearly identified
- developed, sustained discussion
- secure conceptual grasp
- skilfully selects for analysis specific aspects of texts, clarifying and developing ideas by comparison and contrast.

That's what you have to aim for. By contrast, here are the criteria for the bottom band (which offers 0–6 marks), which will tell you what to avoid if you want to move up the bands:

- simple narration, description of plot
- simple assertion
- unsupported unconnected comments
- frequent irrelevance
- unassimilated notes
- comparisons between texts are mainly on their superficial features.

Assessment Objective 2ii counts for nearly half the marks, but that means that the other three Objectives tested here are also very important, taken together:

> AO1   Candidates should be able to communicate clearly the knowledge, understanding and insight appropriate to literary study, using appropriate terminology and accurate written expression.

Top band:

- technically accurate, sophisticated style
- a cogent, well-structured argument
- accurate use of an appropriate, extensive critical vocabulary
- a vocabulary that can cope with the needs of analysis and criticism.

Bottom band:

- frequent lapses in spelling, punctuation, grammar, sentence construction
- limited vocabulary hinders expression
- technical terms often misunderstood
- unclear lines of argument and/or poor deployment of knowledge/evidence.

AO3	Candidates should be able to show detailed understanding of the ways in which choices of form, structure and language shape meanings.

Top band:

- Mature and sophisticated analysis of the ways in which different kinds of form, structure and language shape meaning.

Bottom band:

- few (if any) form, structural or language features identified
- very limited (if any) discussion of how language shapes meaning.

AO4	Candidates should be able to articulate informed independent opinions and judgements, showing understanding of different interpretations of literary texts by different readers.

Top band:

- mature understanding of the significance of differing critical positions
- sophisticated judgement of text based upon an informed consideration of various possibilities.

Bottom band:

- little (if any) understanding of different interpretive approaches
- little personal response based upon slender or misinterpreted evidence or insensitive reading of other opinions or text
- narrow range of meaning asserted.

Examination

If you select the examination unit, you will have to study and compare at least one of the named pairs of texts in the specification. In the examination, you will have to answer one question on one pair of texts in 1 hour 30 minutes. You can take your texts into the examination, and should do so, as the questions are tailored to an open-book examination.

Preparing for the examination

In class, you will no doubt look at various angles of the texts which you are going to write about in the examination, and think about how you might tackle questions. Immediately before the examination, however, you will probably have some time to do the final preparation yourself. What should you do in this time?

The first thing to say is that you should not rely on having your texts with you in the examination to provide information to answer the questions. The texts are simply there for you to use in response to questions which focus on particular passages in the texts. You won't have time to look up other parts of the texts for quotations or information; you need to know all that before you go in.

'Revision' does not just mean looking again at what you've already done. It may be useful to do this when you start to revise, but then you need to re-read as much of your two texts as you can, as close to the examination as you reasonably can, and within a relatively short period of time. The re-reading will refresh information for you, so you have more chance of drawing on it quickly in the exam. You are bound to find new things each time you read a text, and in this case you'll be reading the texts with relationships and comparisons in mind. A plan of action might be:

1 Read over what you've already done – notes, essays, etc.

2 Remind yourself of the sorts of comparisons you might find – reading through the opening pages of the section about Module 5 might be a help.

3 Read the texts, recognising features which fit with the connections you've already recognised, and looking for more.

In the examination – deconstructing the question

When you look at the two questions you have to choose from, and particularly when you have chosen your question, you need to look carefully at the wording to ensure that you know exactly what you have to do – what you have to write about, and how. 'How', of course, will be in line with the Assessment Objectives which you know are being tested. Because they're being tested, they have to be incorporated into the question.

Here are two questions on *The Bell Jar* by Sylvia Plath and *One Flew Over the Cuckoo's Nest* by Ken Kesey. The passages to which they refer are reproduced on pages 151–3.

> **1** Remind yourself of the episode in *The Bell Jar* from the beginning of Chapter 14 to 'You'll marry a nice blind man some day', before the break in the text. (*Passage A*)
>
> Also remind yourself of the episode in Part 1 of *One Flew Over the Cuckoo's Nest* from 'The Big Nurse is able to set the wall clock' to 'till green sparks flash and buzz across my forehead'. (*Passage B*)
>
> Compare and contrast the subject matter and style of these two extracts and consider their importance in the novels.
>
> **2** Compare the presentation of heroic figures in *The Bell Jar* and *One Flew Over the Cuckoo's Nest*.

If you choose the first question, the key words to focus on are:

- 'compare and contrast' – which is the dominant Assessment Objective, AO2ii
- 'subject matter' – the first part of AO2ii
- 'style' – AO3
- 'consider' – AO4; you're being asked for your view on their importance
- 'importance' – a reminder that in these extract-based questions you also have to relate these passages to the rest of the text, which is showing both your knowledge and your ability to find relationships within texts.

If you choose the second question, the key words to focus on are:

- 'compare' – again, this refers to the dominant AO2ii
- 'presentation' – AO3. This is the invitation to show your knowledge of this aspect of the texts. What 'choices of form, structure and language' have the two writers used in creating heroic figures?
- 'heroic figures' – invites you to think about subject matter, the characters in the novels who might be considered heroic in some way. This therefore refers to the first part of AO2. It also refers to AO4, as it is connected to the reader's response – who might you consider heroic in each novel, and why?

Planning your response

Sample plans of responses to these two tasks are given below. There are a few important things to remember. First, you must take the time to plan properly. You need to think about the things you want to say, the material to use, and the order to work in. If you are attempting an extract-based question, you may well need to look for the material to use in the extracts as a first step, and this should then be inserted in the right place in your plan. Planning is vital: you need to do it when you're balancing two texts; you've got the time to do it, as you've only got to answer one question in an hour and a half; and planned answers are much more likely to produce high-scoring responses.

Sample questions and plans

The same two questions on the texts *The Bell Jar* and *One Flew Over the Cuckoo's Nest* are repeated below, followed by indications of the elements in the novels that you could use in your answers, in a planned sequence. This will give you an idea of the sort of approach you could take with other pairs of texts or similar questions.

1 Remind yourself of the episode in *The Bell Jar* from the beginning of Chapter 14 to 'You'll marry a nice blind man some day,' before the break in the text. (*Passage A*)

Also remind yourself of the episode in Part 1 of *One Flew Over the Cuckoo's Nest* from 'The Big Nurse is able to set the wall clock' to 'till green sparks flash and buzz across my forehead.' (*Passage B*)

Compare and contrast the subject matter and style of these two extracts and consider their importance in the novels.

In the examination itself the passages you are asked to look at are a little longer than these examples, which are printed below. The principles of looking at the passages, selecting material, linking to the rest of the novels, and planning are the same.

Passage A

Esther starts to come round after attempting suicide by taking an overdose.

It was completely dark.

I felt the darkness, but nothing else, and my head rose, feeling it, like the head of a worm. Someone was moaning. Then a great, hard weight smashed against my cheek like a stone wall and the moaning stopped.

The silence surged back, smoothing itself as black water smooths to its old surface calm over a dropped stone.

A cool wind rushed by. I was being transported at enormous speed down a tunnel into the earth. Then the wind stopped. There was a rumbling, as of many voices, protesting and disagreeing in the distance. Then the voices stopped.

A chisel cracked down on my eye, and a slit of light opened, like a mouth or a wound, till the darkness clamped shut on it again. I tried to roll away from the direction of the light, but hands wrapped round my limbs like mummy bands, and I couldn't move.

I began to think I must be in an underground chamber, lit by blinding lights, and that the chamber was full of people who for some reason were holding me down.

Then the chisel struck again, and the light leapt into my head, and through the thick, warm, fuzzy dark, a voice cried, 'Mother!'

Air breathed and played over my face.

I felt the shape of a room around me, a big room with open windows. A pillow moulded itself under my head, and my body floated, without pressure, between thin sheets.

Then I felt warmth, like a hand on my face. I must be lying in the sun. If I opened my eyes, I would see colours and shapes bending in upon me like nurses.

I opened my eyes.

It was completely dark.

Somebody was breathing beside me.

'I can't see,' I said.

A cheery voice spoke out of the dark. 'There are lots of blind people in the world. You'll marry a nice blind man some day.'

Passage B

Chief Bromden imagines that the Big Nurse can alter the speed of time.

The Big Nurse is able to set the wall clock at whatever speed she wants by just turning one of those dials in the steel door; she takes a notion to hurry things up, she turns the speed up, and those hands whip around that disc like spokes in a wheel. The scene in the picture-screen windows goes through rapid changes of light to show morning, noon, and night – throb off and on furiously with day and dark, and everybody is driven like mad to keep up with that passing of fake time; awful scramble of shaves and breakfasts and appointments and lunches and medications and ten minutes of night so you barely get your eyes closed before the dorm light's screaming at you to get up and start the scramble again, go like a sonofabitch this way, going through the full schedule of a day maybe twenty times an hour, till the Big Nurse sees everybody is right up to the breaking point, and she slacks off on the throttle, eases off the pace on that clock-dial, like some kid been fooling with the moving-picture projection machine and finally got tired watching the film run at ten times its natural speed, got bored with all that silly scampering and insect squeak of talk and turned it back to normal.

She's given to turning up the speed this way on days like, say, when you got somebody to visit you or when the VFW brings down a smoker show from Portland – times like that, you'd like to hold and have stretch out. That's when she speeds things up.

But generally it's the other way, the slow way. She'll turn that dial to a dead stop and freeze the sun there on the screen so it don't move a scant hair for weeks, so not a leaf on a tree or a blade of grass in the pasture shimmers. The clock hands hang at two minutes to three and she's liable to let them hang there till we rust. You sit solid and you can't budge, you can't walk or move to relieve the strain of sitting, you can't swallow and you can't breathe. The only thing you can move is your eyes and there's nothing to see but petrified Acutes across the room waiting on one another to decide whose play it is. The old Chronic next to me has been dead six days, and he's rotting to the chair. And instead of fog sometimes she'll let a clear chemical gas in through the vents, and the whole ward is set solid when the gas changes into plastic.

Lord knows how long we hang this way.

Then, gradually, she'll ease the dial up a degree, and that's worse yet. I can take hanging dead still better'n I can take that syrup-slow hand of Scanlon across the room, taking three days to lay down a card. My lungs pull for the thick plastic air like getting in through a pinhole. I try to go to the latrine and I feel buried under a ton of sand, squeezing my bladder till green sparks flash and buzz across my forehead.

Plan

The plan and notes below outline a possible response to this question. There are several ways of approaching the question, of course. Here comparison (AO2ii) is kept at the forefront of the writing all the time, as well as finding opportunities to show the skills appropriate to Assessment Objectives 3 and 4.

Similarities and differences

- Both passages clearly reflect the perceptions of disturbed minds, affecting senses and thoughts. Both paranoid – Esther imagines 'people . . . holding me down' (BJ), Chief sees Big Nurse as a malignant controller, and 'you can't swallow and you can't breathe' (CN).

- Both narrators very aware of light: 'It was completely dark' (BJ) – phrase repeated suggests reflection of obsessional mind. Light seems to have life – 'darkness clamped shut' (BJ), 'the dorm light's screaming at you' (CN) Light here aggressive, as are the 'blinding lights' (BJ).

- Vision affected in other ways – Chief thinks the ward is filled wth 'fog' or 'a clear chemical gas' so that it sets solid as plastic (CN). Esther imagines 'colours and shapes' then 'can't see', and is enclosed in 'thick, warm, fuzzy dark' (BJ).

- Both feel disembodied, in a way – Esther 'my body floated' plus disembodied sounds, Chief hanging in time.

- Both under pressure or restraint. Chief feels 'buried under a ton of sand', Esther 'a great, hard weight'. She escapes from pressure, though –'I felt warmth, like a hand on my face' – Chief does not, as the weight squeezes his bladder.

- Both delusional: 'A chisel cracked down on my eye' (BJ), Chief seeing 'petrified Acutes' (CN).

- Some similarities/differences in AO3: Kesey captures Chief's perceived pace of time/desperation with vocabulary, 'furiously', 'like mad', 'scramble', plus a 14-line sentence, full of long phrases and commas. Plath uses short sentences and paragraphs to capture stasis, though the pace of perceived time alters in both.

- Both employ disturbing imagery: light personified as 'like a mouth or a wound' (BJ), Chief sees a Chronic 'rotting to the chair' (CN), though Plath employs figurative language much more extensively.

- Esther's experience is entirely personal, reflected in 'I' throughout, Chief feels part of the general experience of the inmates, in a way, reflected in predominance of 'you'.

- Shift of feeling in BJ, unlike CN. Esther's body 'floated, without pressure' unlike continuing pressure on Chief; passage from BJ relieved by black humour of the 'cheery voice' at the end, unlike CN. Idea of nurses appear welcome to Esther, unlike persecution by Big Nurse in CN.

Importance of passage and evaluation

- Both are strong examples of the effects of delusion and paranoia in the novels, as detailed above. The close personal focus is typical of BJ, and the longer passages detailing delusions typical of CN.

- Both of these passages occur at low points in the narratives for the central figures. BJ – final suicide attempt before committal to psychiatric hospital. Here still 'completely dark', but warmth, even humour, perhaps presages ending. CN – 'Fog' which envelopes Chief's mind still around, but 'today something's happened: there hasn't been any of these things worked on us all day' (CN, page after passage). Like Esther, much suffering to come before end, but beginning of effect of McMurphy on Chief, which results in his recovery.

- The personal/general difference, detailed above, perhaps indicates an element in the scheme of both novels. Both are set in the same socio-historical context, and detail similar treatments for madness, including electric shock therapy, but CN was widely seen at the time as condemning treatment regimes, whereas BJ was simply taken to be about the experience of the writer. The feelings towards authority are quite different, as shown in these passages, and at the end of BJ Esther is released as the result of successful treatment; the Chief breaks out, leaving behind the body of McMurphy, destroyed by the system.

> **2** Compare the presentation of heroic figures in *The Bell Jar* and *One Flew Over the Cuckoo's Nest*.

Plan

The plan and notes below outline a possible response to this question. As with question 1, there are several ways of approaching the task, keeping comparison (AO2ii) at the forefront of the writing all the time, as well as finding opportunities to show the skills appropriate to Assessment Objectives 3 and 4.

- Both novels offer characters who could be considered heroic, including the narrators, though not centrally concerned with heroism. In CN there is one central heroic figure, whereas in BJ there is a succession of temporary hero figures for Esther. Difference symbolises the different problems and needs of the narrators.

- In CN a heroic figure is central to the plot. McMurphy begins change in ward and Chief. Dominates text – appears 7 pages in, present till 2 pages from end. Whole swathes lose sight of Chief, even though told in his voice, when describing McMurphy's actions. Heroic figure in Chief's mental and emotional journey – makes him 'big' again, produces his impulses to speak and act, breaking him out of semi-catatonic state. A therapeutic figure in an institution where conventional therapy fails and destroys, poignantly summed up in his own destruction. Action driven by McMurphy – Chief does not act. The dramatic episodes are all initiated by McMurphy – the card game, the fishing trip, the night before the 'escape' – but final action belongs to Chief, who kills McMurphy and breaks out – hero at the last.

- BJ offers a number of possible heroic figures, all of whom fail, unlike McMurphy in both senses. Esther's lack of a sense of her own individuality leads her to adopt other personalities, but each is found wanting, increasing her sense of alienation and isolation. She idolises Jay Cee's accomplishments, as the Chief does McMurphy's. She admires the worldly, experienced Doreen, as the Chief does McMurphy – 'being with Doreen made me forget my worries'. The pure, simple Betsy also falls from Esther's grace to become 'Pollyanna Cowgirl'. Esther sees the faults in each of these 'heroes' – apart from one episode, the Chief does not see McMurphy's flaws – this is left to the reader. Dr Nolan is heroic in a different sense – an authority figure who removes the 'bell jar'. It's McMurphy who removes the Chief's bell jar, not the Big Nurse, who holds it down.

- Esther herself an unlikely hero. Personally weak – repeatedly attempts suicide, runs away, hides – but struggles against controlling figures such as her mother throughout, eventually becomes 'perfectly free'. Symbolised by last sentence 'I stepped into the room'. Also a sympathetic figure for feminist readers – hates roles women have been designated to follow in her society, the superiority of men over women, women's expected maternal role.

- Chief also an apparently unlikely hero, paralysed in speech and action by his condition. Exhibits personal heroism in small ways, as Esther does – the lifting of his hand to vote, breaking his silence. At end becomes heroic in action, ironically by killing McMurphy to save him, and by breaking free, literally. Similar presentation to Esther at end – he steps out rather than in, taking 'huge strides . . . I felt like I was flying. Free.'

Overview/evaluation

One novel, CN, seems much more concerned with heroism. All heroic figures are flawed, including McMurphy. Heroic tone at end of both, however – maybe both celebrate the heroism of the human spirit in the end.

Sample questions

Two more sample questions are given below, with some reminders of the sort of approach you should take in answering them.

> 1 Remind yourself of the end of Chapter 17 of *The Bell Jar*, from 'I think we can take you right away, Esther', and the beginning of Chapter 18, up to 'I was open to the circulating air.' (*Passage A*)
>
> Also remind yourself of two descriptions in Part 4 of *One Flew Over the Cuckoo's Nest*: (a) from from 'Twist some dials' to 'The machine hunches on me'; and (b) from 'There had been times when I'd wandered around' to 'It was the last treatment they gave me.' (*Passage B*)
>
> Compare and contrast the subject matter and style of these two extracts and consider their importance in the novels.

Passage A

These extracts describe Esther undergoing electric shock therapy, and her awakening afterwards.

Extract 1

> 'I think we can take you right away, Esther,' Miss Huey said. 'Mr Anderson won't mind waiting, will you, Mr Anderson?'
>
> Mr Anderson didn't say a word, so with Miss Huey's arm around my shoulder, and Doctor Nolan following, I moved into the next room.
>
> Through the slits in my eyes, which I didn't dare open too far, lest the full view strike me dead, I saw the high bed with its white, drumtight sheet, and the machine behind the bed and the masked person – I couldn't tell whether it was a man or a woman – behind the machine, and the other masked people flanking the bed on both sides.

Miss Huey helped me climb up and lie down on my back.

'Talk to me,' I said.

Miss Huey began to talk in a low, soothing voice, smoothing the salve on my temples and fitting the small electric buttons on either side of my head. 'You'll be perfectly all right, you won't feel a thing, just bite down …' And she set something on my tongue and in panic I bit down, and darkness wiped me out like chalk on a blackboard.

Extract 2

'Esther.'

I woke out of a deep, drenched sleep, and the first thing I saw was Doctor Nolan's face swimming in front of me and saying, 'Esther, Esther.'

I rubbed my eyes with an awkward hand.

Behind Doctor Nolan I could see the body of a woman wearing a rumpled black-and-white checked robe and flung out on a cot as if dropped from a great height. But before I could take in any more, Doctor Nolan led me through a door into fresh, blue-skied air.

All the heat and fear had purged itself. I felt surprisingly at peace. The bell jar hung, suspended, a few feet above my head. I was open to the circulating air.

Passage B

These extracts describe Chief Bromden about to undergo electric shock therapy, and his recovery afterwards.

Extract 1

Twist some dials, and the machine trembles, two robot arms pick up soldering irons and hunch down on him. He gives me the wink and speaks to me, muffled, tells me something, says something to me around the rubber hose just as those irons get close enough to the silver on his temples – light arcs across, stiffens him, bridges him up off the table till nothing is down but his wrists and ankles and out around that crimped black rubber hose a sound like *hoveel* and he's frosted over completely with sparks.

And out the window the sparrows drop smoking off the wire.

They roll him out on a Gurney, still jerking, face frosted white. Corrosion. Battery acid. The technician turns to me.

Watch that other moose. I know him. Hold him!

It's not a will-power thing any more.

Hold him! Damn. No more of these boys with Seconal.

The clamps bite my wrists and ankles.

The graphite salve has iron fillings in it, temples scratching.

He said something when he winked. Told me something.

Man bends over, brings two irons towards the ring on my head.

The machine hunches on me.

Extract 2

There had been times when I'd wandered around in a daze for as long as two weeks after a shock treatment, living in that foggy, jumbled blur which is a whole lot like the ragged edge of sleep, that grey zone between light and dark, or between sleeping and waking or living and dying, where you know you're not unconscious any more but don't know yet what day it is or who you are or what's the use of coming back at all – for two weeks. If you don't have a reason to wake up you can loaf around in that grey zone for a long, fuzzy time, or if you want to bad enough I found you can come fighting right out of it. This time I came fighting out of it in less than a day, less time than ever.

And when the fog was finally swept from my head it seemed like I'd just come up after a long, deep dive, breaking the surface after being under water a hundred years. It was the last treatment they gave me.

Think about the following comparative elements before you write your answer.

1 Both passages show aggressive therapy being applied. Both have some impersonality, but BJ more sympathetically presented. Is this true of other incidents of aggressive therapy in each novel – i.e. CN violent, BJ not?

2 Compare the attitudes, words, descriptions of the attendants in each of the passages describing the application of therapy. How are they personalised, or not?

3 How does the extract from CN present the machinery as being vicious? How is the machine in BJ presented?

4 Compare the descriptions of awakening in the two novel extracts. Why does Kesey spend more time on this, do you think? Think about where each of the characters is in the course of their illness.

5 Compare the attitudes of each of the narrators to the figures who were in charge of the therapy. Is the difference representative of differences in the novels as a whole?

6 Compare carefully the last four lines of each of the Passage B extracts, paying attention to diction and imagery.

7 Place each of these moments of release in the contexts of the structure of the novels. Are they of equal significance?

2 Compare the presentation of madness in *The Bell Jar* and *One Flew Over the Cuckoo's Nest*.

This question clearly addresses AO2ii, and AO3 – 'presentation' instructs you to find ways to show your understanding of 'the ways writers' choices of form, structure and language shape meanings'. You need to show your own response to the relevant issues in the texts (AO4), and structure your response carefully (AO1).

Here is a sample plan for your answer:

1 Compare the ways in which the first-person narratives portray madness – range of mental states/delusions through voice/senses – see notes on first sample question (pages 158–9 above).

2 Examine differences in structure. BJ goes from apparently normal life, descends into madness gradually via suicide attempts, gradual distortion of reality, near-death experience, EST, release. CN begins in the middle of this curve – Chief catatonic, gradual movement towards recovery via McMurphy, breaks out to freedom.

3 Compare range of madness presented, and nature of therapy regimes. CN regime clearly disapproved of; BJ two models shown, one more liberal, progressive, resulting in recuperation.

4 Overview/evaluation. A view, developed from the writing you've done, of the nature of the presentation of madness in the texts, and a view of the effects of each of these on the reader.

Whether you choose to do a passage-based question or not, the mark schemes are the same. You need to know what you have to do in order to do well, and what you have to avoid. Here are some key descriptors which might help:

Assessment Objective 2ii is the dominant objective here. The descriptors for 14–15 marks out of 20, the top of Band 3, are:

• clearly able to evaluate and analyse issues in extracts and whole texts; exploratory; analyses links between and differences of form, structure and language; detailed analysis of writers' techniques; systematic textual detail.

The descriptors for 0–6 marks, Band 1, are:

- simple narrative; usually irrelevant/assertive; factual errors; reliant on re-worked notes; no real grasp of how language shapes writers' meanings.

Assessment Objectives 1, 3 and 4 are less important here, but taken together still carry a lot of weight.

The descriptors for 14–15 marks (top of Band 3) are:

- coherent and well-developed lines of argument; pertinent, well-chosen vocabulary showing a command of the technical rules of English; coherent informed, personal response to extracts and whole texts.

The descriptors for 0–6 marks, Band 1, are:

- frequent technical lapses; no obvious line of argument or meaningful discussion of interpretative approaches; narrow range of meanings; confused responses to texts; limited vocabulary; poor deployment of knowledge.

Working on this module will have enabled you to compare and contrast texts, and to analyse how writers work in ways which are often similar, but very different too, even when their subjects might appear to be the same. This will have helped you as you approach Module 6, when all the skills you have learned over two years are tested, particularly as there is a comparative element in the examination.

Glossary for Activity 8 (pages ooo)

The four extracts on pages 130–132 include words which have been invented by the authors, although they are mostly derived from known words. The meanings of the words become apparent when reading the whole texts, but it may be helpful to include some meanings here, to assist reading.

A Clockwork Orange

ookadeeted	left	oddy knockies	own (as in 'on our own')
vesch	thing		
crasting	robbery	malenky	little, tiny
tolchock	a blow, beating	moloko	milk
britva	razor	sladky	sweet
in-out-in-out	copulation	smeck	laugh
loveted	caught	horrorshow	good
nozh	knife	govoreeting	speaking
malchick	boy		
lewdies	people		

Riddley Walker

girzel	drizzle	Pry Mincer	a key figure in the area's skeletal 'authority'
oansome	alone		
forms	farms	Fools Circel	a ritual journey in attempting to discover the ancient truths, based on a children's game
fentsing	fencing, fence posts		
Ardship	Archbishop originally, as in the Ardship of Cambry		

Module 6 Reading for Meaning

This module carries 40% of the final A2 mark, 20% of the final A level mark. The marks are divided amongst the Assessment Objectives like this:

ASSESSMENT OBJECTIVES

AO1 communicate clearly the knowledge, understanding and insight appropriate to literary study, using appropriate terminology and accurate and coherent written expression
(9% of the final A2 mark; 4.5% of the final A Level mark)

AO2ii respond with knowledge and understanding to literary texts of different types and periods, exploring and commenting on relationships and comparisons between literary texts
(7% of the final A2 mark; 3.5% of the final A Level mark)

AO3 show detailed understanding of the ways in which writers' choices of form, structure and language shape meanings
(8% of the final A2 mark; 4% of the final A Level mark)

AO4 articulate independent opinions and judgements, informed by different interpretations of literary texts by other readers
(7% of the final A2 mark; 3.5% of the final A Level mark)

AO5ii evaluate the significance of cultural, historical and other contextual influences on literary texts and study
(9% of the final A2 mark; 4.5% of the final A Level mark)

The purpose of this module

The aim of this module is to test the skills, knowledge and understanding of English Literature you have gained throughout the course, by looking at some unprepared material. In other words, to see how well you can apply the five Assessment Objectives to unfamiliar material. For that reason, all the Assessment Objectives are tested here.

The key preparation for this module is to complete the rest of the course – if you've followed it sensibly, you'll already have a good working knowledge of the requirements of this module, because they're the requirements of the whole course. Here you will be required to look at prose, poetry, drama and non-fiction, and pre-twentieth century as well as twentieth-century literature. This module will test your ability to:

• trace connections between texts

• show knowledge and understanding of form, structure and language

• present your own and others' interpretations of text

• evaluate the significance of contextual influences.

These should come as no surprise to you: you've tackled them all during the course, and they are set out in the Assessment Objective list above.

There are two specific elements to think about in approaching this module. Although the material in the examination is unseen, it is taken from an identified area of English Literature, and you will be expected to have undertaken a course of wide reading in this area, which you will then be able to draw on in the examination. In the first three years of the specification this will be 'War in Literature', with specific emphasis on literature written about and during the First World War. You need to plan your reading and, more importantly, how to read for maximum effect. Secondly, you will need to look closely at the requirements of the exam itself, which are quite different from those of the other modules, in the sense that there are *no set texts*.

Preparing for the module: wide reading

There are many texts you could read which deal with the First World War, some of which you may have studied for GCSE. There are also many texts which deal with other wars, and with war generally. A list of suitable texts is supplied in the specification, and more texts are suggested in the material provided in this section. Before you start reading, though, you need to think very carefully about the purpose of your reading. You're not going to be tested on any of these 'background' texts, after all, – what you are doing is providing yourself with a bank of material which you might refer to in the exam, when you are writing about the extracts provided. It will be useful to measure the extracts against your own reading, in a number of ways. Below (pages 162–185) is a list of features it would be useful to bear in mind as you choose material to read, and then as you read, so that you can provide yourself with a variety of useful information and ideas.

Range of genres

The questions in the exam cover the full range of genres, so you should aim to do the same in your background reading. Here are some of the obvious choices for reading material:

Prose (fiction):

- *Birdsong* (Sebastian Faulks). There are some excerpts from this text in this book, in Module 5.
- *The Regeneration Trilogy* (Pat Barker).
- *Strange Meeting* (Susan Hill).
- *The Ice Cream War* (William Boyd).

Prose (non-fiction):

- *Somme* (Lyn MacDonald). A synopsis of first-hand accounts of the Battle of the Somme.

- *Letters from a Lost Generation* (eds. A. Bishop and M. Bostridge). Correspondence between Vera Brittain and three young soldiers, which formed the basis of: *Testament of Youth, Chronicles of Youth, Diaries* (Vera Brittain).

- *Goodbye To All That* (Robert Graves). Autobiography, including his experience as a young officer in the war.

Poetry

- Wilfred Owen, who died in the last days of the war, was arguably the finest war poet, and his work certainly cannot be ignored. Some of his poems are in this book, in Module 5.

- Poems by Siegfried Sassoon should also be read, along with Rupert Brooke, whose patriotic poems are very much at odds with the work of Owen and Sassoon.

- There are many other poets to read whose work is widely anthologised, for example Isaac Rosenberg and Ivor Gurney. There are a number of good anthologies of First World War poetry.

- The publication of the anthology of women's First World War poetry, *Scars Upon My Heart* (ed. Catherine W. Reilly) in 1981 was a breakthrough in the study of literature of the period. Hardly any of the earlier anthologies covering this period had featured women's writing.

- *The Penguin Book of First World War Poetry* (ed. J. Silkin).

Drama

- *Journey's End* (R. C. Sherriff).
- *Not About Heroes* (Stephen MacDonald).
- *Oh What A Lovely War!* (Theatre Workshop).
- *The Accrington Pals* (Peter Whelan).
- *Observe the Sons of Ulster Marching Towards the Somme* (Frank McGuinness).

Collections and commentaries

- *Virago Book of Women and the Great War* (ed. Joyce Marlowe).
- *The Great War and Modern Memory* (ed. Paul Fussell).
- *Women's Writing on the First World War* (ed. Agnes Cardinal).
- *The Great War in British Literature* (Adrian Barlow).

Features of war

When you start reading texts about the war, the first points of comparison you are likely to notice are the features of the war that the writers deal with. A phrase you might come across in the exam is 'Examine how typical in both style and treatment of subject matter these writings are . . .'. The question is asking you to compare the way texts are written, and how they deal with their subjects, with other texts about the First World War – which is why you need a good background of purposeful reading. Identifying features of the war doesn't enable you to write about style and treatment by itself, but nevertheless it is an important first step in making connections in subject matter.

Here are some of the features you might expect to come across, and bear in mind for comparison with other texts:

- trench conditions, including mud, cold, etc.
- fighting and killing – including gas, mines, bayonets, barbed wire as well as shooting
- death in various ways – exposure and drowning as well as combat deaths
- other outcomes – injury and sickness, madness, desertion
- life behind the lines
- life at home – on leave, attitudes of people at home, relationships between home and front via letters, etc.
- political concerns – the conduct and outcome of battles and the war, political objectives, etc.
- love – love expressed in letters to and from home, and the love in comradeship in war.

Feelings and attitudes

Recognising and comparing the feelings and attitudes expressed towards these features in the texts you read takes you one step closer to dealing with 'treatment' of subject matter. An important distinction to make here is between the feelings and attitudes expressed by characters in the text, whether 'real' or otherwise, and the feelings and attitudes of the writers. It is the latter which is more likely to feed into discussion of 'treatment of subject matter', and to lead on to style. This can be seen in Siegfried Sassoon's poem 'Lamentations':

LAMENTATIONS

I found him in the guard-room at the Base.
From the blind darkness I had heard his crying
And blundered in. With puzzled, patient face
A sergeant watched him; it was no good trying
To stop it; for he howled and beat his chest.
And, all because his brother had gone west,

Raved at the bleeding war; his rampant grief
Moaned, shouted, sobbed, and choked, while he was kneeling
Half-naked on the floor. In my belief
Such men have lost all patriotic feeling.

An attitude is expressed in the last line – but whose view is it, and what is it directed towards? It is difficult to believe that the attitude is really that of the poet. A reading of other poems by Sassoon will reveal that this could hardly be the case, and the whole poem implies that the reader cannot take it literally. The soldier is rendered pathetic by the 'blind' darkness in which he is crying, and the poet says that he 'blundered' in, suggesting an awkwardness at intruding on the man's grief. The sergeant is 'puzzled', presumably at the extent of the emotion, and 'patient', presumably he recognises the man's sincerity. The diction of the next few lines emphasises the extremity of the soldier's despair: 'howled', 'raved', 'rampant', 'moaned, shouted, sobbed, and choked'. The 'bleeding war' is ambiguous, both a curse and a literal fact, and the soldier's state and position of 'kneeling/ Half-naked on the floor' emphasises his vulnerability and loss of dignity. In the middle of this, 'all because his brother had gone west' may well be viewed by the reader as sarcasm – 'all because', allied to the casual diction of 'had gone west' obviously belies the depth of the man's feelings. In the face of this, 'In my belief/ Such men have lost all patriotic feeling' becomes deeply sarcastic; the poet is attacking the attitude that could express such a sentiment. This in itself leads to a wider questioning, about the nature and effects of 'patriotic feeling' in the war.

Below is a poem by Wilfred Owen in which similar features can be identified and explored. First read the poem, looking for the feelings and attitudes expressed, and then work through the questions in Activity 1.

THE DEAD-BEAT

He dropped, – more sullenly than wearily,
Lay stupid like a cod, heavy like meat,
And none of us could kick him to his feet;
Just blinked at my revolver, blearily;
– Didn't appear to know a war was on,   5
Or see the blasted trench at which he stared.
'I'll do 'em in,' he whined. 'If this hand's spared,
I'll murder them, I will.'
                                        A low voice said,
'It's Blighty, p'raps, he sees; his pluck's all gone,
Dreaming of all the valiant, that aren't dead: 10
Bold uncles, smiling ministerially;
Maybe his brave young wife, getting her fun
In some new home, improved materially.
It's not these stiffs have crazed him; nor the Hun.'

We sent him down at last, out of the way.   15
Unwounded; – stout lad, too, before that strafe.
Malingering? Stretcher-bearers winked, 'Not half!'

Next day I heard the Doc's well-whiskied laugh:
'That scum you sent last night soon died. Hooray!'

ACTIVITY 1

1 There are a number of features of the war mentioned here. Make a list of them and think about:

- the man's condition

- the trench

- the causes of madness

- the officer's behaviour (first stanza)

- life at home

- the doctor, and what his attitude and 'well-whiskied laugh' tell you.

2 Identify the various attitudes expressed in this poem. Think about the attitudes of:

- the officer (first stanza)

- various people at home

- the stretcher-bearers

- the doctor.

3 The 'I' in the last stanza of the poem is clearly an officer's voice – Wilfred Owen was an officer in the trenches himself. If you believe that, like Sassoon's poem 'Lamentations', the view expressed in the last line is the opposite of the poet's view, what evidence can you find in the rest of the poem to back this up?

Look at line 16: who is it who is thinking 'stout lad'?

Look also at line 18: what is the effect of 'well-whiskied'?

Think about the title of the poem as well. Whose voice do you think the phrase 'The Dead-Beat' belongs to, and what does it reveal about the attitude of the speaker?

4 Whose is the 'low voice' (line 8) do you think? If your answer is 'just another soldier', does the expression fit? Is this a problem with the poem? Can you think of any other interpretation?

You will obviously come across many attitudes in your reading, both of characters and writers, and trying to categorise them would be futile. But registering different attitudes to the various features of the war that you read about is certainly worthwhile.

In the activity on 'The Dead-Beat' you identified features of the war, moving towards 'knowledge and understanding' (AO2) and knowledge of context (AO5), and started to 'explore and comment on relationships between literary texts' (AO2). Exploring interpretations of the poem (Question 4) and comparing with another poem (Question 3) leads you towards AO4. The last two suggestions in Question 3 also address 'an understanding of the ways writers' choices of form, structure and language shape meanings' (AO3).

The elements of AO3 need thinking about separately and in detail, though, as they are the key elements of 'style' which you will be tested on in the exam. Of course, there are too many possible variations here to think about them all, but there are some elements which appear regularly in First World War literature, and which may therefore feature either in the examination extracts, or can be used in comparison or contrast to them.

Form

Form goes beyond simply the broad forms of the three genres of prose, drama and poetry. Non-fiction *prose* forms you may come across regularly are letters, diaries, journals, and other forms of first-hand accounts, as in *Somme* and *Letters from a Lost Generation*. Because of the nature of the First World War and the writing associated with it, these forms are used by fiction writers too.

The nature of the war also influences the forms taken by *drama*, as rendering the realities of trench warfare on stage in a naturalistic way is clearly a difficult task, the only enduring example being *Journey's End*. The war of 1914–18 became modern, in the sense that it became increasingly mechanised and fought at a distance; this, and the sheer scale of the battlefield, made it much more difficult to represent than smaller-scale conflicts in predominantly hand-to-hand battle. Of course, Shakespeare could not depict the whole of the battle of Agincourt, for instance; but by showing snapshots of situations in various parts of the field the whole picture could be suggested with reasonable accuracy. This could not be done with the subsequent involvement of tanks and aircraft, and long-distance shelling. Later wars than the First World War have hardly been the subject of stage drama at all, except in miniature in such plays as *The Long, the Short and the Tall* by Willis Hall, which concerns a platoon of British soldiers in the Malayan jungle during the Second World War. The resources of film have proved more suitable to showing modern warfare. It would be easy to list dozens of films about the Second World War and the Vietnam War, for instance, but few plays come to mind.

Dramatists have therefore used various techniques to cope with the problems of portraying the First World War on stage: the use of voices, stage positions and sound in *Not About Heroes*, the surreal elements of *The Accrington Pals*, and the range of strategies developed by Joan Littlewood with the Theatre Workshop group for *Oh What A Lovely War!*. Forms here include song, dance and slides, as well as the device of seeing the war through a particular dramatic setting which is itself a dramatic form.

The following extract from Peter Whelan's *The Accrington Pals* illustrates some of the problems and solutions. *The Accrington Pals* was one of the volunteer regiments raised in the early years of the First World War. The Pals went into action on the first day of the Battle of the Somme, 1 July 1916. Between 7.20 a.m. and 8.30 a.m., 584 of the 720 men were killed, wounded or missing, and there was a total of 60,000 British casualties on that day. The play shows the recruiting in the town, and intercuts action in battle with life 'at home', as the women and children of the town hear initial optimistic reports, before the awful truth is known.

RALPH	I'm not going to drown. Shot or blown to bits but not drowned. Loose your straps. I reckon if you're out of your pack quick enough and get it under your feet you might keep up. But tie your water bottle separate. Fuck all use not drowning if you die of thirst! Oh these straps. I'll never get out fast enough.
TOM	You could cut them.
RALPH	I've tried. Bayonet's too blunt!
TOM	Borrow this.
RALPH	That's your leather knife . . . What will you do?
TOM	Oh aye . . .
RALPH	What you made of Tom? You going over there to talk philosophy with them?
TOM	There's a lot of good German philosophers.
RALPH	Well, there's fuck-all of them over there! Wake up Arthur, get up.
VOICE	[*off*] Move up nine platoon. Move!
ARTHUR	[*to his pet pigeon England's Glory*] Now sweet . . . now my beauty . . . the sun is shining and the air is clear . . .
RALPH	Hold on to me Tom. Oh mother, I've got the movies. Push me if you see me falling back . . . don't let them see me go back. Christ I'm clasped so tight I'll bust!
	[*CSM Rivers dashes in to join them.*]
RIVERS	Heads down! Get your heads down! Seven-thirty ack-emma . . . mines detonating.
VOICES	Stand by! Stand by! Take cover!
RIVERS	Brace yourselves!
	A vast deep roaring sound as the Hawthornden Ridge mine goes off. They cower and sway as the shock waves go through the trench.

Well the Pals! Next stop, Serre for Beaumont Hamel, Bapaume and Berlin!

[*Shouts off*] Mr Williams, sir! Move your platoon up! [*Quietly, to Tom*] Think of her, shall we, Hackford . . . think of her? If you lose your officers don't make for the gaps in the wire . . . Jerry's got his Spandaus trained on the gaps and he'll rip you to pieces . . . cut your own; understood? Got your wire cutters?

TOM   Yes sir.

RIVERS Let glory shine from your arseholes today boys. Rise on the whistle . . . dress from the right . . . rifles at the port . . . go steady and we'll be drinking schnappes and eating sausages by sundown. Boggis . . . let's have a prayer.

ARTHUR Oh God . . . do you smile still? Do you smile to see your handiwork?

Whistles begin to blow around the theatre, merging into one another.

RIVERS Over we go . . . stay in line . . . right marker!

VOICES Come on the Pals. Up the Accringtons! Nine platoon! Ten platoon! With me, with me, with me! Dress from the right. Leave that man! Leave him!

They go over the top. Mingling with the machine guns stuttering we hear an awkward, heavy piano introduction to Edward German's 'Oh Peaceful England' being played. Eva appears in her Britannia costume. She is singing at the fund raising concert. She looks tense and nervous . . . almost angry. She begins to sing.

EVA   [*sings*]

Oh peaceful England, while I my watch am keeping,
Thou like Minerva weary of war art sleeping.
Sleep on a little while and in thy slumber smile.
While thou art sleeping I my watch am keeping.
Sword and buckler by thy side, rest on the shore of battle-tide,
Which like the ever hungry sea, howls round this Isle.
Sleep till I awaken thee, and in thy slumber smile.
England, fair England, well hast thou earned thy slumber,
Yet though thy bosom no breast-plate now encumber . . .

Suddenly she breaks off. She's lost the next line. The accompanyist falters. Eva begins to shake with fury at the situation she's put herself in. She exclaims something and runs off.

The playwright can show some of the conditions and feelings of the war through the small group of soldiers, but the size of the field can only be suggested by Rivers shouting offstage to the next platoon in the line. The nature of the battle has to be suggested by sound effects, and when the men go over the top realistic portrayal is impossible. Later in the play a dream-like, surreal sequence of action is used; Whelan ends the scene by cutting to a 'home' scene which suggests loss and a horrible mistake, while remaining in the context of war and patriotism – German's famous patriotic song becomes ironic here. There are a number of other features of the war in the extract which you should recognise by now: the trench conditions, the expectation of death, thoughts of home, attitude to the enemy, and despair of religion.

Poetry of the time used the full range of poetic forms available, and in addition much poetry has been written later, using more modern techniques. There was one significant development in poetic form which you should look at. This was the development by Wilfred Owen of half-rhyme, sometimes called pararhyme or consonantal rhyme, in which the vowel sounds are not the same, but the consonants are. For example, 'moan' and 'blown' rhyme, because the vowel sounds are the same; 'moan' and 'mourn' don't rhyme – the vowel sounds are different – but there is clearly a strong link between the sounds of the two words, as the consonants are the same. Owen found that this rhyme form was more 'in tune' with the destruction and despair that he wanted to write about than the more harmonious effect of full rhyme. With 'moan' and 'mourn', for example, the sound actually deepens. Owen made use of this pair of words several times, along with others which deepened the tone. His technique has affected the writing of poetry profoundly since the time in which he was writing, but during the war most writers were oblivious to it, as Owen's poetry was not published until very late in or after the war.

Here is an example of this technique at work, from 'Strange Meeting':

> With a thousand pains that vision's face was grained;
> Yet no blood reached there from the upper ground,
> And no guns thumped, or down the flues made moan.
> 'Strange friend,' I said, 'here is no cause to mourn.'

The 'moan/mourn' pair is used here, and the effect is increased by the pairing of 'grained/ground', another step down in sound. (The next pair in the poem is 'years/yours'.) Owen uses other resources of form here to deepen the effect. The long 'a' sound of 'grained' is the third in the same line; the assonance of 'pains', 'face', and 'grained' makes the reader feel the pain. The sound of the next line immediately deepens even before 'ground', with 'no', 'blood' and 'upper', the latter being the first of four 'u' sounds in these lines.

Here is another example of a complex pattern of sounds and half-rhymes, in the last verse of Owen's poem 'Insensibility'. Read the lines and work through Activity 2.

But cursed are dullards whom no cannon stuns,
That they should be as stones;
Wretched are they, and mean
With paucity that never was simplicity.
By choice they made themselves immune
To pity and whatever moans in man
Before the last sea and the hapless stars;
Whatever mourns when many leave these shores;
Whatever shares
The eternal reciprocity of tears.

ACTIVITY 2

1 Pick out the first half-rhyme in these lines.

2 Where is the half-rhyme for 'mean'? (Read the lines very carefully.)

3 'Simplicity' doesn't seem to have an obvious rhyme – but check all the lines here. There are in fact two echoes of it – can you find them?

4 Where are the half-rhymes for 'stars' and 'shores'?

5 Whereabouts in the lines does the 'moans/mourns' half-rhyme appear? What else echoes this pairing?

6 The poem is about 'insensibility' – the various ways in which soldiers in the war became insensible to suffering, through fatigue, madness, loss of senses, or just simple-mindedness. This last verse attacks those who choose not to feel. Given this, why does Owen choose 'tears' as the last word of the poem? ('Reciprocity' means 'sharing' or 'common feeling'.)

The choice of this word – 'insensibility' – reflects how Owen has used all three elements of 'form, language and structure to shape meaning'.

Structure

You will probably come across various distinctive uses of *structure* in your reading, without any of them being characteristic of either war literature or specifically First World War literature. This war was such a significant event in the history of the twentieth century, however, its effects were so far-reaching, and its nature so distressing, that writers have continued to write about it ever since. A desire to 'place' the war experience, both historically and in human terms, produces structures like that of the novel *Birdsong*, which focuses on times before, during and after the war years, which are the defining experiences for all the characters, even those born after the war itself had ended.

One of the aims of *war poets* such as Owen and Sassoon was to 'tell the truth' about their experiences, as they felt the truth was not known, or being told, at home. This aim is often achieved through very direct or abrupt endings, in other words, the meaning is shaped by the structure. Here are some examples:

O Jesus, make it stop!

(S. Sassoon, 'Attack')

Sneak home and pray you'll never know
The hell where youth and laughter go.

(S. Sassoon, 'Suicide in the Trenches')

Oh what made fatuous sunbeams toil
To break earth's sleep at all?

(W. Owen, 'Futility')

Snatching after us who smote them, brother,
Pawing us who dealt them war and madness.

(W. Owen, 'Mental Cases')

'E's wounded, killed, and pris'ner, all the lot,
The bloody lot all rolled in one. Jim's mad.

(W. Owen, 'The Chances')

Structures in many *drama texts* work in the same way, seeking to remind audiences of the desperation of the war through dramatic means at key points. Below are two short extracts from R. C. Sherriff's *Journey's End*. The first is the opening to Act 3, Scene 1, and the second is the end of the play, when Raleigh is lying fatally wounded in the dug-out as the men prepare to go over the top.

Extract 1

The following day, towards sunset. The earth wall of the trench outside glows with a light that slowly fades with the sinking sun.

Stanhope is alone, wandering to and fro across the dug-out. He looks at the steps for a moment, crosses to the table, and glances down at the map. He looks anxiously at his watch, and, going to the servant's dug-out, calls:

STANHOPE   Mason!

Extract 2

RALEIGH Could we have a light? It's – it's so frightfully dark and cold.

STANHOPE [*rising*] Sure! I'll bring a candle and get another blanket.

[*Stanhope goes to the left-hand dug-out, and Raleigh is alone, very still and quiet, on Osborne's bed. The faint rosy glow of the dawn is deepening to an angry red. The grey night sky is dissolving, and the stars begin to go. A tiny sound comes from where Raleigh is lying – something between a sob and a moan. Stanhope comes back with a blanket. He takes a candle from the table and carries it to Raleigh's bed. He puts it on the box beside Raleigh and speaks cheerfully.*]

Is that better, Jimmy? [*Raleigh makes no sign.*] Jimmy . . .

[*Still Raleigh is quiet. Stanhope gently takes his hand. There is a long silence. Stanhope lowers Raleigh's hand to the bed, rises, and takes the candle back to the table. He sits on the bench behind the table with his back to the wall, and stares listlessly across at the boy on Osborne's bed. The solitary candle-flame throws up the lines on his pale, drawn face, and the dark shadows under his tired eyes. The thudding of the shells rises and falls like an angry sea.*

A Private Soldier comes scrambling down the steps, his round, red face wet with perspiration, his chest heaving for breath.]

SOLDIER Message from Mr Trotter, sir – will you come at once.

[*Stanhope gazes round at the soldier – and makes no other sign.*]

Mr Trotter, sir – says will you come at once!

[*Stanhope rises stiffly and takes his helmet from the table.*]

STANHOPE All right, Broughton, I'm coming.

[*The soldier turns and goes away.*

Stanhope pauses for a moment by Osborne's bed and lightly runs his fingers over Raleigh's tousled hair. He goes stiffly up the steps, his tall figure black against the dawn sky.

The shelling has risen to a great fury. The solitary candle burns with a steady flame, and Raleigh lies in the shadows. The whine of a shell rises to a shriek and bursts on the dug-out roof. The shock stabs out the candle-flame; the timber props of the door cave slowly in, sandbags fall and block the passage to the open air.

There is darkness in the dug-out. Here and there the red dawn glows through the jagged holes of the broken doorway.

Very faintly there comes the dull rattle of machine-guns and the fevered spatter of rifle fire.]

ENDS

ACTIVITY 3

Many of the choices the playwright makes here are structural. Look at the following features, and their effects on the audience.

1 Look at the lighting in the first extract. What does this time of day, and the 'sinking sun' suggest? What is Stanhope preoccupied with, and how does that connect with the context and the battle to come?

2 Look at the lighting at the beginning of the second extract. What does the 'angry red' of the dawn suggest? What does the disappearance of the stars suggest?

3 Look at the effect of the candle in the second extract. It is one light in the darkness. What does its extinction symbolise?

4 Sherriff chooses the end of the play to show Raleigh's death. What reasons could he have for doing this? Think about the structure of the play.

5 Look at all the stage directions for sound, and decide why each sound has to come at that exact moment. Why does Sherriff want the shells to sound 'like an angry sea'?

6 In the last minute of the play, Sherriff introduces a 'private soldier' who has not appeared before. Why does he do this? Why does he want Stanhope silhouetted against the dawn sky?

7 What does the final scene in the play, including sound, suggest to the audience? Remember that the performance might well end with lights fading to black.

Prose often spells out meanings rather than suggesting them, as the ending of Sherriff's play does. Even in the usually prosaic form of the *letter*, though, writers wanted to draw the lessons from what they were experiencing and shaped their material accordingly.

Here is the end of a letter written by Vera Brittain to her brother, Edward Brittain, in February 1916:

I would like to think of you as never forgetting that one day the War will end and the things that used to matter will matter again; even if you are not to see them I still think it is better to remember, for otherwise your work & life is lived only for the moment and not for all time. And as the effects of this War will be for all time the people who are playing their part in it will play that part for all time too, and to remember this seems to make one's lot – whether it be life or work or horror or death – so much more worthwhile.

Language

From your work on language during the course, you'll be well aware of the many resources writers use to shape meanings, for example diction, syntax, imagery, sounds. Some of these resources are more widely used in First World War literature than others because of the nature of the conflict and the attitudes towards it. Some of them are discussed below.

Use of dialogue in poetry

Many poets wanted to show convincingly the voices of 'common soldiers'. Owen's poem 'The Chances', quoted on page 177, is one example. Other voices were represented too, such as those of officers and women.

Questions

The nature and the length of the war led people to question many things – the conduct of the war, the motives of generals and politicians, religion, and the purpose of life itself – and this was inevitably reflected in literature.

Here are the opening and closing lines of 'Afterwards' by Margaret Postgate Cole:

> Oh, my beloved, shall you and I
> Ever be young again, be young again?

and

> What use is it to you? What use
> To have your body lying here
> In Sheer, underneath the larches?

The last two lines of Owen's 'Futility' are:

> Oh what made fatuous sunbeams toil
> To break earth's sleep at all?

Questions about the purpose of life also appear in the letters of the time, and the questions were often much more immediate here, as in this letter from Lieutenant Cyril Drummond, written on 30 June 1916:

Lying beside a pile of boxes was the body of a soldier who had been killed earlier in the day. He was covered by a blanket, but one corner was awry, exposing an arm, torn, shattered, and dusty. Suddenly, for the first time, the thought crossed my mind, 'Shall I be looking like that this time tomorrow?'

Exclamations

For much the same reasons as questions, exclamations are often found in contemporary texts, echoing strength of feeling. The lines from 'Futility' above, though technically a rhetorical question, are really more of an exclamation. 'Oh Jesus, make it stop!' (in Sassoon's 'Attack', quoted on page 172) is certainly an exclamation. The same feeling often appeared in letters, as in this ending to a letter from Vera to Edward Brittain on 8 March 1916:

But if I escape Zeppelins at home, and torpedoes, enteric or dysentery abroad, I promise you to go to Uppingham on behalf of us all . . . And as I told you before you went out, if the War spares me, it will be my one aim to immortalise in a book the story of us four, with the friendship of the Three Musketeers playing so large a part . . . Just as you, if you come through, will immortalise it all in music. Oh! If only it could *end*! We are all so weary.

Religious diction and imagery

Because of the strength of feeling and despair occasioned by the war, religion was frequently either appealed to or questioned. In 'Sacrament' by Margaret Sackville, for instance, she questions the actions of God in sacrificing lives, through the imagery of the sacrament, in the third verse:

This wine of awful sacrifice outpoured;
  This bread of life – of human lives. The Press
Is overflowing, the Wine-Press of the Lord! . . .
  Yet doth he tread the foaming grapes no less.

In the sacrament, wine and bread represent the blood and body of Christ. Sackville is explicit in saying that the 'bread of life' here means 'human lives', and that the wine is not just the wine of sacrifice, but 'awful'. The emotive effect is enhanced by the word 'outpoured', suggesting volume, placed at the end of the line. The idea of excess blood is picked up by the metaphor of 'the Wine-Press of the Lord' overflowing, and given further impact by the final image of Christ wantonly continuing to tread the grapes. The grapes are human beings, of course, and 'foaming' in this context gives an awful vision of foaming blood.

Owen's 'At a Calvary near the Ancre' and Sassoon's 'The Redeemer' are both powerful accounts of Christ on the battlefield, although the former also echoes the contempt that many soldiers had for the actions of churchmen in the war, as does another poem by Sassoon, 'They'.

Romantic v. realistic

There is a sharp distinction, particularly in poetry, between those writers who perceived the actions of the war as romantic, and therefore used language to portray it in this way, and those whose writing reflects a desire to paint the details of war as graphically and realistically as possible, to suggest the degradation and futility of war. The terms 'romantic' and 'realistic' are in common usage here, but are different to the literary concept of Romanticism.

One of the most famous patriotic war poems, which depends heavily on its romantic diction and imagery, is 'The Soldier', by Rupert Brooke. In this poem, the English soldier's body is 'a richer dust' in 'some corner of a foreign field'.

Here is the opening to Brooke's 'The Dead':

Blow out, you bugles, over the rich Dead!
   There's none of these so lonely and poor of old,
   But, dying, has made us rarer gifts than gold.

By contrast, here is the description of a gas victim in 'Dulce Et Decorum Est', a direct attack by Owen on patriotism:

And watch the white eyes writhing in his face,
His hanging face, like a devil's sick of sin;
If you could hear, at every jolt, the blood
Come gargling from the froth-corrupted lungs . . .

Here is an extract from *Goodbye To All That* by Robert Graves:

Going and coming, by the only possible route, I passed by the bloated and stinking corpse of a German with his back propped against a tree. He had a green face, spectacles, close-shaven hair; black blood was dripping from the nose and beard. I came across two other unforgettable corpses: a man of the South Wales Borderers and one of the Lehr regiment had succeeded in bayoneting each other simultaneously. A survivor of the fighting told me later that he had seen a young soldier of the Fourteenth Royal Welch bayoneting a German in parade-ground style, automatically exclaiming: 'In, out, on guard!'

In Brooke's poem, an emblem of military and patriotic feeling – the bugle – is invoked in an exclamation, over the 'rich Dead!' The upper case 'D' in itself glorifies the dead soldiers, who are 'rich'. This is not just heightened language –

picked up again in 'rarer' and 'gold' — it also suggests that soldiers who were 'lonely' and 'poor' are somehow enriched and enriching others by their deaths. This is further emphasised by the weight of the rhyming couplet falling on 'gold'.

The other two extracts are quite different in attitude. Owen's poem is a direct attack on the attitude of Brooke, and here he spells out exactly the details of death in the effect of the gas on the eyes, the face, the blood and the lungs of the soldier. The words 'writhing', 'hanging', 'gargling' and 'froth-corrupted' are deliberately emotive, heightened by the repetition of 'his face', as though the viewer could not take his eyes from the awful sight, and the repulsive idea of 'like a devil's sick of sin'.

Graves, though not using the poetic resources of Owen, nevertheless signals the same attitude in similar ways. The corpse is 'bloated' and 'stinking', with a 'green face' and 'black blood [. . .] dripping from the nose' — a reminder of Owen's description, and far removed from the 'rich' language and attitude of Brooke. The mutually bayoneted figures are grotesque, and in both these recollections the German corpses are equivalent to the British; there is no sense of 'rarer gifts than gold' being given to the countrymen of one side.

The poem below shows how language can be used to *suggest* things, as well as stating them directly. Ivor Gurney was both a poet and a composer, who served as a private soldier in France with his local regiment, the Gloucesters. Read the poem, and attempt the questions which follow in Activity 4.

THE SILENT ONE

Who died on the wires, and hung there, one of two –
Who for his hours of life had chattered through
Infinite lovely chatter of Bucks accent;
Yet faced unbroken wires; stepped over, and went,
A noble fool, faithful to his stripes – and ended.
But I weak, hungry, and willing only for the chance
Of line – to fight in the line, lay down under unbroken
Wires, and saw the flashes, and kept unshaken.
Till the politest voice – a finicking accent, said:
'Do you think you might crawl through, there; there's a hole.' In the
     afraid
Darkness, shot at; I smiled, as politely replied –
'I'm afraid not, Sir.' There was no hole, no way to be seen.
Nothing but chance of death, after tearing of clothes.
Kept flat, and watched the darkness, hearing bullets whizzing –
And thought of music – and swore deep heart's deep oaths
(Polite to God –) and retreated and came on again,
Again retreated – and a second time faced the screen.

ACTIVITY 4

1 Who is 'The Silent One' of the title, do you think? There are at least two interpretations. Find evidence to support each one, and then see if you can think of any more.

2 How does Gurney present the soldier who has died on the wire? Think about what his attitude on the wire might suggest, and what the five adjectives used about him convey about the surviving soldier's attitude to him.

3 What features of trench warfare are referred to in this poem?

4 What does the dialogue tell you about the soldier and the officer? What does each of the three forms of the word 'polite' suggest?

5 Look for all the repetitions of words, language forms or actions used in the last six lines. Taken together, what do they say to you about the nature of the conflict?

Contexts

Assessment Objective 5ii on contexts requires you to 'evaluate the significance of cultural, historical and other contextual influences on literary texts and study'. The over-arching context here is the First World War, of course, but within that there are a number of other contexts which specifically influence individual writers and their texts. Below are some of the contexts which you should recognise in your reading, and which you can then refer to in the exam.

Social

The central social context in most of the writing during and about this war relates to class, and reflects the stratified class system of the time. It emerges chiefly in the attitudes of ordinary soldiers, officers and generals to each other. In Gurney's poem 'The Silent One', consider what the 'polite' exchange of words masks – what the soldiers are being asked to do, and the attitudes towards class differences that lie behind it.

The differences between ranks also included differences between field officers such as Owen and Sassoon and those behind the lines, as reflected in this poem by Sassoon:

BASE DETAILS

If I were fierce, and bald, and short of breath,
    I'd live with scarlet Majors at the Base,
And speed glum heroes up the line to death.
    You'd see me with my puffy petulant face,
Guzzling and gulping in the best hotel,
    Reading the Roll of Honour. 'Poor young chap,'

I'd say – 'I used to know his father well;
　　Yes, we've lost heavily in this last scrap.'
And when the war is done and youth stone dead,
I'd toddle safely home and die – in bed.

Class is a significant context for the writing here, not only because of what it says, but because Sassoon himself belonged to the same class as many of the 'scarlet Majors'. Similarly, the outburst of the writer of the following diary entry (from *Tommy Goes to War* by Malcolm Brown), Sapper Garfield Powell of the Royal Engineers, is strengthened by his own background. Powell had a B.Sc. in Chemistry and Mathematics but as a miner's son was not officer material.

As an army we are darned badly treated. Officers claim to get leave every three months and get it. Battalion and Company Sergeant-Majors claim leave every four months and again get it (being called 'Sir' by their inferiors in rank not being sufficient sop to their self-love). In what army (barring the national armies of Germany or Russia) would such a system be in vogue? The officers in most regiments take very little more risk than their privates. Their bodies are not fatigued by constant and hard work and they are no more useful to the Army than privates. Why should the fools in higher command allow it? Why should 'gentlemen' take it as nothing less than their due? Ay, what fools we all are!

The significance of the context of class, and not just officer/ordinary soldier, becomes much clearer towards the end of this piece.

Historical

Although the war itself lasted only four years, which is a short period in history, much changed during this time, even though the lines of battle hardly moved. Early optimism, which produced more optimistic, romantic literary responses, was replaced by the hard slog of the trenches, and after 1916 by a slaughter which became increasingly mechanistic as the new instruments of destruction appeared on the battlefields. The period being written about, therefore, is a significant contextual influence on the writing. Similarly, those writing after the war began to view the war differently, as the surviving combatants struggled to come to terms with 'ordinary' life. This is shown in this extract from Sassoon's 'A Footnote to the War':

But how can I co-ordinate this room –
Music on piano, pictures, shelves of books,
And Sunday morning peace – with him for whom
Nine years ago the world wore such wild looks?
How can my brain join up with the plutonian
Cartoon? . . . The trench; and a fair-haired Cameronian

> Propped in his pool of blood while we were throwing
> Bombs at invisible Saxons . . . War's a mystery
> Beyond my retrospection.

The significance of the context here could hardly be greater; the writer's problem is that in 'ordinary' life the war is inescapable for him, and continues to shape his thoughts and his writing.

Writer's biography and gender

Given the significance of class, rank and period, the *biography* of any writer of the time is bound to be a significant contextual influence. *Gender* is also a very significant contextual influence. Some of the women's poetry of the time shows women in war-time occupations such as nursing, as in Mary Henderson's 'An Incident' (see page 201), and munitions work, as in Mary Gabrielle Collins's poem 'Women at Munitions Making'. The use of women for this sort of work was highly significant in a political and historical context, as many commentators saw it as an important step on the road to women's suffrage. Suffragettes such as Mrs Pankhurst also played a key role as pacifists, and this is reflected in literature too. Much of the poetry, though, simply reflects the feelings of women 'left behind', as in this poem by Gabrielle Elliott. Read the poem below, and work through Activity 5 that follows.

PIERROT GOES TO WAR

In the sheltered garden, pale beneath the moon,
(Drenched with swaying fragrance, redolent with June!)
There, among the shadows, some one lingers yet –
Pierrot, the lover, parts from Pierrette.

Bugles, bugles, bugles, blaring down the wind,
Sound the flaming challenge – *Leave your dreams behind!*
Come away from shadows, turn your back on June –
Pierrot, go forward to face the golden noon!

In the muddy trenches, black and torn and still,
(How the charge swept over, to break against the hill!)
Huddled in the shadows, boyish figures lie –
They whom Death, saluting, called upon to die.

Bugles, ghostly bugles, whispering down the wind –
Dreams too soon are over, gardens left behind.
Only shadows linger, for love does not forget –
Pierrot goes forward – but what of Pierrette?

ACTIVITY 5

Only the last line is a clear plea from the woman's point of view, although the writer has structured the poem so that this plea remains in the reader's mind. The contrasts in the woman's and the man's situation are implied in other ways, as well. Look for the contrasts between:

- the first verse and the third verse

- the lines in brackets

- the different times of year mentioned or hinted at

- the different implications of 'shadows'

- the two mentions of bugles, and the sounds they make

- the poet's references to nature.

Is war, or love, or gender the most significant context here, do you think?

Literary

There are a number of literary contexts for the work of this period. Just as the war proved a watershed in society and history, it affected the development of literature, as writers strove to find new ways of expressing what they saw and felt. The old ways would not do. The difference between the writing of the pre-war years and post-war writing is huge, and is a study in itself. The shift in the poetry of Thomas Hardy, who spans this time period, and the style and attitude of the early war 'patriotic' poems such as those of Rupert Brooke, as shown on page 177, against the later poets, are interesting literary contexts. The development can be seen most clearly, perhaps, in Owen's poetry. At the beginning of the war his poems were still very clearly imitations of Keats, but by the end of the war he was writing in the preface for his planned collection of poems, 'Above all I am not concerned with poetry'. In other words, he had found his own voice. He had become determined to write poetry that 'the dullest Tommy' could understand. His specific literary legacy, apart from the poems themselves, was the use of half-rhyme, as discussed on pages 170–1.

Pre-twentieth-century war literature

The specification requires that this module should also include pre-twentieth-century literature. As the area of literature for the first three years of the specification is First World War literature, it follows that you will be asked to compare a pre-twentieth-century extract with one or more of the First World War extracts, to think about the different ways the writers present war, and to offer a view about them. This offers you a very wide choice – for example, you could look at Shakespeare's treatment of war in many of his plays, or at texts about the American Civil War or the Boer War.

The poem below, 'The Due of the Dead' by W. M. Thackeray, was set in the Crimean War, as was 'The Charge of the Light Brigade' by Tennyson. You could look at similarities and differences between the two poems. The most important thing to bear in mind, however, is that when you are reading pre-twentieth-century literature you should choose and explore texts which can be compared to a work of literature from the later period.

Read the poem below, by W. M. Thackeray (1811–63), and work through Activity 6.

THE DUE OF THE DEAD

I sit beside my peaceful hearth,
    With curtains drawn and lamp trimmed bright
I watch my children's noisy mirth;
    I drink in home, and its delight.

I sip my tea, and criticise
    The war, from flying rumours caught;
Trace on the map, to curious eyes,
    How here they marched, and there they fought.

In intervals of household chat,
    I lay down strategic laws;
Why this manoeuvre, and why that;
    Shape the event, or show the cause.

Or, in smooth dinner-table phrase,
    'Twixt soup and fish, discuss the fight;
Give to each chief his blame or praise;
    Say who was wrong and who was right.

Meanwhile o'er Alma's bloody plain
    The scathe of battle has rolled by –
The wounded writhe and groan – the slain
    Lie naked staring to the sky.

The out-worn surgeon plies his knife,
    Nor pauses with the closing day;
While those who have escaped with life
    Find food and fuel as they may.

And when their eyes in sleep they close,
    After scant rations duly shared,
Plague picks his victims out, from those
    Whom chance of battle may have spared.

Still when the bugle sounds the march,
    He tracks his prey through steppe and dell;
Hangs fruit to tempt the throats that parch,
    And poisons every stream and well.

All this with gallant hearts is done;
    All this with patient hearts is borne:
And they by whom the laurel's won
    Are seldom they by whom 'tis worn.

No deed, no suffering of the war,
    But wins us fame, or spares us ill:
Those noble swords, though drawn afar,
    Are guarding English homesteads still.

Owe we a debt to these brave men,
    Unpaid by aught that's said or sung;
By leaders from a ready pen,
    Or phrases from a flippant tongue.

The living, England's hand may crown
    With recognition, frank and free;
With titles, medals and renown;
    The wounded shall our pensioners be.

But they, who meet a soldier's doom –
    Think you, it is enough, good friend,
To plant the laurel at their tomb,
    And carve their names – and there an end?

No. They are gone: but there are left
    Those they loved best while they were here –
Parents made childless, babes bereft,
    Desolate widows, sisters dear.

All these let grateful England take;
    And, with a large and liberal heart,
Cherish, for her plain soldiers' sake,
    And of her fullness give them part.

Fold them within her sheltering breast;
    Their parent, husband, brother prove.
That so the dead may be at rest,
    Knowing those cared for whom they love.

ACTIVITY 6

1 The setting of the first five verses is at home in England, discussing the progress of war. How does Thackeray emphasise how far the narrator is removed from the war itself? Can you think of any First World War texts which deal with this setting in a similar way?

2 The next four verses deal with the horrors of war. Compare Thackeray's treatment of the subject with that in any First World War text(s) that you have read.

3 Plague is personified over six lines in these verses. Can you think of any similar use of personification in the First World War literature you have read? If you can't, read 'The Next War', by Wilfred Owen. Which of the personifications seems more effective, and why?

4 The next six verses deal with military honours and decorations. What attitudes does Thackeray express here? What attitudes, either similar or different, have you come across in your reading of First World War literature?

5 The feelings and attitudes of those left behind also feature strongly in these verses. Compare any of these with similar thoughts expressed in the First World War texts you have read, being careful to think about *how* the thoughts are expressed as well as the actual ideas.

6 How do you respond to the patriotism of the last two verses? Compare the attitude and expression here to Rupert Brooke's 'The Soldier'.

- Do you consider this poem to be romantic in nature?
- Is it far removed from First World War poetry in attitudes and style?
- Is the form successful, in your view?
- Think of any other comparisons you might make with the First World War texts you have looked at.

Further sample extracts and activities

Over the next few pages you will find more poems and extracts from First World War literature. They provide additional reading in prose, drama and poetry, but also give you the opportunity to compare and contrast them with other texts you have read. Texts 5, 6 and 7 are by women who were writing at the time of the First World War.

With each extract, try to answer the following questions once you have read and re-read each piece. You could also use these questions as a useful checklist for any other relevant reading you have done.

1 What features of the war can you identify in the text?

2 Identify the feelings and attitudes in the text, being careful to differentiate between the writer's attitude and the attitude of characters, whether real or imagined, in the text.

3 How has the writer used form, structure and language to shape his or her meanings?

4 What contexts can you see, and how significant are they to your reading and understanding of the text?

5 Having worked through the questions above, compare and contrast your findings about the text with other First World War texts, or pre-twentieth-century texts about war. Make some judgements about the comparative strengths and weaknesses of the style and treatment of subject matter in the texts, and consider any other interpretations of the texts you are looking at.

Text 1

Isaac Rosenberg was a front-line soldier. This poem was written in 1916, two years before his death in action in the last year of the war.

BREAK OF DAY IN THE TRENCHES

The darkness crumbles away –
It is the same old druid Time as ever.
Only a live thing leaps my hand –
A queer sardonic rat –
As I pull the parapet's poppy
To stick behind my ear.
Droll rat, they would shoot you if they knew
Your cosmopolitan sympathies.
(And God knows what antipathies).
Now you have touched this English hand
You will do the same to a German –
Soon, no doubt, if it be your pleasure
To cross the sleeping green between.
It seems you inwardly grin as you pass
Strong eyes, fine limbs, haughty athletes
Less chanced than you for life,
Bonds to the whims of murder,
Sprawled in the bowels of the earth,
The torn fields of France.
What do you see in our eyes
At the shrieking iron and flame
Hurled through still heavens?
What quaver – what heart aghast?
Poppies whose roots are in man's veins
Drop, and are ever dropping;
But mine in my ear is safe,
Just a little white with the dust.

Text 2

This is an excerpt from *The Ghost Road*, the final part of *The Regeneration Trilogy* by Pat Barker. W. H. R. Rivers was an army psychologist who met Siegfried Sassoon at Craiglockhart hospital in 1917.

After Wansbeck had gone, Rivers sat quietly for a few minutes before adding a note to the file. Sassoon had been much in his mind while he was speaking to Wansbeck, Sassoon and the apparitions that gathered round his bed and demanded to know why he was not in France. Also, another of his patients at Craiglockhart, Harrington, who'd had dreadful nightmares, even by Craiglockhart standards, and the nightmares had continued into the semi-waking state, so that they acquired the character of hypnagogic hallucinations. He saw the severed head, torso and limbs of a dismembered body hurtling towards him out of the darkness. A variant of this was a face bending over him, the lips, nose and eyelids eaten away as if by leprosy. The face, in so far as it was identifiable at all, was the face of a close friend whom Harrington had seen blown to pieces. From these dreams he woke either vomiting or with a wet bed, or both.

At the time he witnessed his friend's death Harrington had already been suffering from headaches, split vision, nausea, vomiting, disorder of micturition, spells of forgetfulness and a persistent gross tremor of the hands, dating from an explosion two months before in which he'd been buried alive. Despite these symptoms he had remained on duty (shoot the MO, thought Rivers) until his friend's death precipitated a total collapse.

What was interesting about Harrington was that instead of treatment bringing about an elaboration of the nightmares, so that the horrors began to assume a more symbolic, less directly representational form – the normal path to recovery – something rather more remarkable had happened. His friend's body had begun to reassemble itself. Night after night the eaten-away features had fleshed out again. And Harrington talked to him. Long conversations, apparently, or they seemed long to him on waking, telling his friend about Rivers, about life at Craiglockhart, about the treatment he was receiving . . .

After several weeks of this, he awoke one day with his memory of the first hour after the explosion restored. He had, even in his traumatized state and under heavy fire, crawled round the pieces of his friend's body collecting items of equipment – belt, revolver, cap and lapel badges – to send to the mother. The knowledge that, far from having fled from the scene, he had behaved with exemplary courage and loyalty, did a great deal to restore Harrington's self-esteem, for, like most of the patients at Craiglockhart, he suffered from a deep sense of shame and failure. From then on the improvement was dramatic, though still the conversations with the dead friend continued, until one morning he awoke crying, and realized he was crying, not only for his own loss but also for his friend's, for the unlived years.

Text 3

Edgell Rickword fought on the Western Front and published many poems in periodicals. Most of them were written in the 1920s.

WINTER WARFARE

Colonel Cold strode up the Line
  (Tabs of rime and spurs of ice).
Stiffened all where he did glare,
  Horses, men, and lice.

Visited a forward post,
    Left them burning, ear to foot;
Fingers stuck to biting steel,
    Toes to frozen boot.

Stalked on into No Man's Land,
    Turned the wire to fleecy wool,
Iron stakes to sugar sticks
    Snapping at a pull.

Those who watched with hoary eyes
    Saw two figures gleaming there;
Hauptman Kälte, Colonel Cold,
    Gaunt, in the grey air.

Stiffly, tinkling spurs they moved
    Glassy eyed, with glinting heel
Stabbing those who lingered there
    Torn by screaming steel.

Text 4

This is an extract from *Oh What A Lovely War!*, which was devised by Joan Littlewood's Theatre Workshop Group, and first performed in 1953. The play tells the story of the First World War by setting the action in an Edwardian pierrot show, using slides of war action and songs of its time. At the beginning of this extract, the Nurse and the Medical Officer are discussing the problem of disposing of the huge number of unburied bodies.

MEDICAL OFFICER	We'll have to start burning them soon, nurse.
NURSE	Yes, it's such an unpleasant duty, doctor. The men always try to get out of it.
MEDICAL OFFICER	Oh, well, it'll be good farming country after.
NURSE	If there are any of us left to see it.
FIRST SOLDIER	Still got my water on the knee, doc.
MEDICAL OFFICER	I'll fix you up with a number nine later.
FIRST SOLDIER	On my knee! – I said, sir!
SERGEANT	All right, you men. I want this trench clear in half an hour; get stuck in. Come on, jump to it!
	[*The men form up, as in a slit trench, digging.*]
BAND	'Oh It's A Lovely War' [*Very slow*]
HAIG	[*reading a letter*] From Snowball to Douglas. Water and mud are increasing and becoming horrible. The longer days when they come will be most welcome, especially to

the officers, who say the conditions are impairing their efficiency. The other ranks don't seem to mind so much.

FIRST SOLDIER	Look out – we're awash! Hey, give us a hand; he's going under.
SECOND SOLDIER	Cor – he's worse than old Fred.
THIRD SOLDIER	Here, whatever happened to old Fred?
SECOND SOLDIER	I dunno. Haven't seen him since his last cry for help.
FOURTH SOLDIER	That's right; he got sucked under.
THIRD SOLDIER	Oh no, he went sick.
FIFTH SOLDIER	No, he went under.
THIRD SOLDIER	He went sick.
SECOND SOLDIER	He got sucked under, mate.
THIRD SOLDIER	Well, I bet you a fag he went sick.
SECOND SOLDIER	Don't be daft. You can't go sick here. You've got to lose your lungs, your liver, your lights . . .
SERGEANT	Watch it!
	[*The Nurse crossing in front stumbles.*]
FIRST SOLDIER	I think she's lost hers.
NURSE	Thank you.
MEDICAL OFFICER	Put that man on a charge, sergeant.
FIRST SOLDIER	On a raft.
HAIG	Everything points to a complete breakdown in enemy morale. Now is the time to hit him resolutely and firmly. I understand the Prime Minister has been asking questions about my strategy. I cannot believe a British Minister could be so ungentlemanly.
	[*The soldiers go off.*]
NURSE	[*writing*] Thank you for the copy of *The Times*. I am glad that in spite of all it is still a victory; it does not seem so here. It is beyond belief, the butchery; the men look so appalling when they are brought in and so many die.
HAIG	September 17th. Glass still falling. A light breeze blows from the south. Weather unsettled.
NEWSPANEL:	*Average life of a machine gunner under attack . . . four minutes*

Text 5

REPORTED MISSING

My thought shall never be that you are dead:
Who laughed so lately in this quiet place.
The dear and deep-eyed humour of that face
Held something ever living, in Death's stead.
Scornful I hear the flat things they have said
And all their piteous platitudes of pain.
I laugh! I laugh! – For you will come again –
This heart would never beat if you were dead.
The world's adrowse in twilight hushfulness,
There's purple lilac in your little room,
And somewhere out beyond the evening gloom
Small boys are culling summer watercress.
Of these familiar things I have no dread
Being so very sure you are not dead.

Anna Gordon Keown

Text 6

DRAFTS

Waking to darkness; early silence broken
By seagulls' cries, and something undefined
And far away. Through senses half-awoken,
A vague enquiry drifts into one's mind.
What's happening? Down the hill a movement quickens
And leaps to recognition round the turning –
Then one's heart wakes, and grasps the fact, and sickens –
'Are we down-hearted' . . . 'Keep the homefires burning'.
They go to God-knows-where, with songs of Blighty,
While I'm in bed, and ribbons in my nightie.

Sex, nothing more, constituent no greater
Than those which make an eyebrow's slant or fall,
In origin, sheer accident, which, later,
Decides the biggest differences of all.
And, through a war, involves the chance of death
Against a life of physical normality –
So dreadfully safe! O, damn the shibboleth
Of sex! God knows we've equal personality.
Why should men face the dark while women stay
To live and laugh and meet the sun each day.

They've gone. The drumming escort throbs the distance,
And down the hill the seagulls' cries are rife
And clamorous. But in their shrill persistence
I think they're telling me – 'We're all one Life'.
As much one life as when we flamed together,
As linked, as indivisible, as then;
When nothing's separate, does it matter whether
We live as women or we die as men?
Or swoop as seagulls! Everything is part
Of one supreme intent, the deathless heart.

Nora Bomford

Text 7

THE CENOTAPH

September 1919
Not yet will those measureless fields be green again
Where only yesterday the wild sweet blood of wonderful youth was shed;
There is a grave whose earth must hold too long, too deep a stain,
Though for ever over it we may speak as proudly as we may tread.
But here, where the watchers by lonely hearths from the thrust of an
   inward sword have more slowly bled,
We shall build the Cenotaph: Victory, winged, with Peace, winged too, at
   the column's head.
And over the stairway, at the foot – oh! here, leave desolate, passionate
   hands to spread
Violets, roses, and laurel, with the small, sweet, twinkling country things
Speaking so wistfully of other Springs,
From the little gardens of little places where son or sweetheart was born
   and bred.
In splendid sleep, with a thousand brothers
            To lovers – to mothers
            Here, too, lies he:
Under the purple, the green, the red,
It is all young life: it must break some women's hearts to see
Such a brave, gay coverlet to such a bed!
Only, when all is done and said,
God is not mocked and neither are the dead.
For this will stand in our Market-place –
            Who'll sell, who'll buy
            (Will you or I
Lie each to each with the better grace)?
While looking into every busy whore's and huckster's face
As they drive their bargains, is the Face
Of God: and some young, piteous, murdered face.

Charlotte Mew

Preparing for the examination

In a sense, the whole course is a preparation for this examination, as you have worked on all the Assessment Objectives which are tested here. Hopefully you will have read a range of First World War texts, and some pre-twentieth-century texts, and thought about them in the ways suggested in this book. Some practice in the type of questions you will have to answer is a good idea, and you will find two sets of materials and questions below. The first set of materials and questions has some suggested responses to give you an idea of what the examiners will be looking for.

In the examination room

The Module 6 examination is different from any other that you sit for this A Level course, as you are presented with *unseen* material. Although you know what the prescribed area of study is, it is unlikely that you will have read the texts which you have to write about in the exam – they will be new to you on the day.

There are some important things to remember as you start the examination.

- You will have *two* questions to answer in three hours. The paper will advise you how to divide your time between the two questions, and will also tell you that the time includes 'reading time'. It must also include *thinking time* if you are to do well. You haven't seen these texts before; remember how much time you've spent reading and re-reading texts for your other exams before you felt prepared.

- After the first reading of the first extract, one element of all your subsequent reading should be comparative – looking for links between this extract and the others, and between this extract and texts you have read in the course of your background reading. At the same time, your planning should not consist of trying to signal every bit of reading you've done. You should be selecting appropriately, and not dragging as much wide reading in as you can at the expense of writing about the extracts.

- As you read, make some notes and underline key words and phrases in the extracts. Then take some more time to draw a plan together, in the light of the question. Although you will be anxious to get on with writing, there are so many things to think about here that planning is necessary for you to create a clear and coherent response. This will not only ensure that you are able to address all the Assessment Objectives 2, 3, 4 and 5, and be rewarded for addressing them, but it will also enhance your performance in Assessment Objective 1, the ability to 'communicate clearly the knowledge, understanding and insight appropriate to literary study, using appropriate terminology and accurate and coherent written expression'. This Assessment Objective is tested on both questions.

- When you've formed a plan, start to write, making sure you choose the right words for the task. Don't be afraid of changing your mind about the extracts as you work; after all, you've never seen them before, so as you revisit them during the course of writing you may well find new things to comment on. Incorporate these new thoughts into your writing, rather than starting again.

- As you write, keep your mind on two key elements – the question and the Assessment Objectives. You should be sure that what you are writing is a direct response to the question you've been asked, and that you don't lose your focus on it. It might be very tempting to insert as much as you can about the texts you've read about the First World War – but you could easily drift away from the question and the extracts on the paper if you follow that course. You should only refer to elements of your wide reading which are relevant to the question and comparable to the extracts. There are no prizes for particularly long answers, either – it's quality that counts, not quantity.

The question paper will remind you about the Assessment Objectives targeted by each question, but you should be able to identify them yourself by reading the questions carefully, and recognising what you are being asked to do.

On the following pages are two sample question papers. Outline responses are given for the first paper. You could attempt the question first, and then compare your responses with the outlines, or do this first if you need to. The second sample question paper is for you to attempt on your own.

Sample Paper 1

1 Reading

- Here is the selection of material taken from the <u>prescribed area for study</u>. You will be using this material to answer the questions in this examination.

- Alongside the three pieces (B, C and D) about the First World War (the prescribed area for study) you will find a piece of pre-twentieth-century writing (A). This also has <u>war</u> as its theme.

- Read all four pieces and their introductions very carefully and closely. Then read them again several times in the light of the specific questions set.

2 The questions, what they test, and how to manage your time

All questions test your ability to:

- *communicate clearly*

- *explore and comment on the relationships between texts*

- *show detailed understanding of the ways in which writers' choices of form, structure and language shape meanings.*

Question 1a

- You should plan to spend about 1 hour and 15 minutes on question 1a; this will include reading time.

  This question especially tests your ability to:

  explore and comment on relationships and comparisons between literary texts

  and

  articulate independent judgements, informed by different interpretations of literary texts by other readers.

Question 1b

- You should spend about 1 hour and 45 minutes on question 1b; this will include reading time.

  This question especially tests your ability to:

  explore and comment on relationships and comparisons between literary texts

  and

  evaluate the significance of cultural, historical and other contextual influences on literary texts and study.

3 Wider reading

The paper tests your wider reading on the subject of *War in Literature* with specific reference to literature of and about the *First World War*.

In your answers, you should take every opportunity to refer to this wider reading and to your knowledge of this specific area of study.

Extract A

Walt Whitman (1819–92) was an American writer who published a collection of poems about the American Civil War.

FROM THE WOUND-DRESSER

2

[. . .] Bearing the bandages, water and sponge,
Straight and swift to my wounded I go,
Where they lie on the ground after the battle brought in,
Where their priceless blood reddens the grass the ground,
Or to the rows of the hospital tent, or under the roof'd hospital,
To the long rows of cots up and down each side I return,
To each and all one after another I draw near, not one do I miss,
An attendant follows holding a tray, he carries a refuse pail,
Soon to be fill'd with clotted rags and blood, emptied, and fill'd again.

I onward go, I stop,
With hinged knees and steady hand to dress wounds,
I am firm with each, the pangs are sharp yet unavoidable,
One turns to me his appealing eyes – poor boy! I never knew you,
Yet I think I could not refuse this moment to die for you, if that would
    save you.

3

On, on I go, (open doors of time! open hospital doors!)
The crush'd head I dress, (poor crazed hand tear not the bandage away,)
The neck of the cavalry-man with the bullet through and through I
    examine,
Hard the breathing rattles, quite glazed already the eye, yet life struggles
    hard,
(Come sweet death! be persuaded O beautiful death!
In mercy come quickly.)

From the stump of the arm, the amputated hand,
I undo the clotted lint, remove the slough, wash off the matter and blood,
Back on his pillow the soldier bends with curv'd neck and side falling head,
His eyes are closed, his face is pale, he dares not look on the bloody stump,
And has not yet look'd on it.

I dress a wound in the side, deep, deep,
But a day or two more, for see the frame all wasted and sinking,
And the yellow-blue countenance see.

I dress the perforated shoulder, the foot with the bullet-wound,
Cleanse the one with a gnawing and putrid gangrene, so sickening, so
    offensive,
While the attendant stands behind aside me holding the tray and pail.

I am faithful, I do not give out,
The fractur'd thigh, the knee, the wound in the abdomen,
These and more I dress with impassive hand, (yet deep in my breast a fire,
   a burning flame.)

4

Thus in silence in dreams' projections,
Returning, resuming, I thread my way through the hospitals,
The hurt and wounded I pacify with soothing hand,
I sit by the restless all the dark night, some are so young,
Some suffer so much, I recall the experience sweet and sad,
(Many a soldier's loving arms about this neck have cross'd and rested,
Many a soldier's kiss dwells on these bearded lips.)

Extract B

This is an extract from *Oh What A Lovely War!*, which was devised by Joan
Littlewood's Theatre Workshop Group, and first performed in 1953. The play tells
the story of the First World War by setting the action in an Edwardian pierrot
show, using slides of war action and songs of its time.

*Voices offstage sing 'Gassed Last Night' as a sequence of slides appear on the
screen.*

*Slide 22: Infantry advancing along the crest of a hill, silhouetted against a large
white cloud.*

*Slide 23: Two German infantrymen running to escape an advancing cloud of
poison gas.*

*Slide 24: A group of 'walking wounded' Tommies, some with bandaged eyes
owing to being gassed.*

*Slide 25: Group of four German soldiers, carrying one of their gassed in a
blanket.*

*Slide 26: Line-up, Indian file, of gassed Tommies, all with bandaged eyes, and
one hand on the shoulder of the person immediately in front of them.*

*Slide 27: Another picture of 'walking wounded': two French Poilus, eyes
bandaged, walking hand in hand, escorted by another Frenchman and
a Tommy.*

*Slide 28: Photograph of a German infantryman diving for cover, beside a field
gun, as a shell explodes nearby.*

*Slide 29: Three British infantrymen, full pack, standing in mud and slush,
firing over the parapet of a trench.*

*Slide 30: Three Germans in a dugout, silhouetted against clouds of smoke
caused by a plane bombing overhead.*

Slide 31: Four Tommies sitting in dugouts, which are merely holes, waist deep in mud.

Slide 32: A dead German soldier, lying in a slit trench.

SONG: '*Gassed Last Night*'.

[22] Gassed last night and gassed the night before, [23]
Going to get gassed tonight if we never get gassed any more. [24]
When we're gassed we're sick as we can be,
'Cos phosgene [25] and mustard gas is much too much for me.
They're warning [26] us, they're warning us,
One [27] respirator for the four of us.
Thank your lucky stars that three of us can run,
So one of us can use it all alone. [29]
Bombed last night and bombed the night before,
Going to get bombed tonight if we never get bombed any more.
When we're bombed we're [29] scared as we can be.
God strafe the bombing planes from High Germany.

They're [30] over us, they're over us,
One shell hole for just the [31] four of us,
Thank your lucky stars there are no more of us,
'Cos [32] one of us could fill it all alone.

A group of five British soldiers enter and build a barricade.

SERGEANT	Get this barricade up, quickly. Keep your heads down.
LIEUTENANT	Have you got the trench consolidated, sergeant?
SERGEANT	All present and correct, sir.
LIEUTENANT	The C.O. is going to have a word with the men.
SERGEANT	Right, lads – attention!
	[*The Commanding Officer enters.*]
COMMANDING OFFICER	You can stand the men at ease, sergeant.
	[*Sound of machine-gun fire. They throw themselves down.*]
LIEUTENANT	On your feet, lads.
SERGEANT	Come on – jump to it!
COMMANDING OFFICER	You can let them smoke if they want to.
SERGEANT	The C.O. says you can smoke. But don't let me catch you.
COMMANDING OFFICER	Now, you men, I've just come from having a powwow with the colonel; we think you've done some damn fine work – we congratulate you.

SOLDIERS	Thank you, sir.
COMMANDING OFFICER	I know you've had it pretty hard the last few days, bombs, shells, and snipers; we haven't escaped scot-free back at staff either, I can tell you. Anyway, we're all here – well, not all of us, of course; and that gas of ours was pretty nasty – damned wind changing.
LIEUTENANT	Indeed, sir.
COMMANDING OFFICER	But these mishaps do happen in war, and gas can be a war-winning weapon. Anyway, so long as we can all keep smiling; you're white men all. [*To the Lieutenant*] Sector all tidy now, Lieutenant?
LIEUTENANT	Well, we've buried most of the second Yorks and Lancs, sir; there's a few D.L.I.s and the men from our own company left.
COMMANDING OFFICER	I see. Well, look, let the lads drum up some char . . . [*Sound of exploding shell.*]
LIEUTENANT	Get down, sir.
COMMANDING OFFICER	Good God!
VOICE	[*offstage*] Stretcher bearers! . . . Stretcher bearers! . . .
COMMANDING OFFICER	You have no stretcher bearers over there?
LIEUTENANT	No, I'm afraid they went in the last attack, sir. I'm waiting for reliefs from H.Q.
COMMANDING OFFICER	Oh well, they're stout chaps! [*Explosion.*]
COMMANDING OFFICER	Yes, you'd better let the men keep under cover.
LIEUTENANT	Thank you, sir.
COMMANDING OFFICER	Damn place still reeks of decomposing bodies.
LIEUTENANT	I'm afraid it's unavoidable, sir; the trench was mainly full of Jerries.
COMMANDING OFFICER	Yes, of course, you were more or less sharing the same front line for a couple of days, weren't you?
LIEUTENANT	Yes, sir.
COMMANDING OFFICER	Oh well, carry on.
LIEUTENANT	Thank you, sir.
COMMANDING OFFICER	Ye Gods! What's that?
LIEUTENANT	Oh, it's a Jerry, sir.

COMMANDING OFFICER	What?
LIEUTENANT	It's a leg, sir.
COMMANDING OFFICER	Well, get rid of it, man. You can't have an obstruction sticking out of the parapet like that. [*He goes off.*]
LIEUTENANT	Hardcastle. Remove the offending limb.
SERGEANT	Well, we can't do that, sir; it's holding up the parapet. We've just consolidated the position.
LIEUTENANT	Well, get a shovel and hack it off; and then dismiss the men. [*He goes off.*]
SERGEANT	Right, sir. What the bloody hell am I going to hang my equipment on now. All right, lads, get back, get yourselves some char. Heads, trunks, blood all over the place, and all he's worried about is a damned leg. [*The soldiers go off.*]

Extract C

Below are extracts from two letters Robert Graves sent home in 1915. They feature in his autobiography, *Goodbye To All That*.

May 28th. [. . .] Last night a lot of German stuff was flying about, including shrapnel. I heard one shell whish-whishing towards me and dropped flat. It burst just over the trench where 'Petticoat Lane' runs into 'Lowndes Square'. My ears sang as though there were gnats in them, and a bright scarlet light shone over everything. My shoulder got twisted in falling and I thought I had been hit, but I hadn't been. The vibration made my chest sing, too, in a curious way, and I lost my sense of equilibrium. I was ashamed when the sergeant-major came along the trench and found me on all fours, still unable to stand up straight.

A corpse is lying on the fire-step waiting to be taken down to the grave-yard tonight: a sanitary-man, killed last night in the open while burying lavatory stuff between our front and support lines. His arm was stretched out stiff when they carried him in and laid him on the fire-step; it stretched right across the trench. His comrades joke as they push it out of the way to get by. 'Out of the light, you old bastard! Do you own this bloody trench?' Or else they shake hands with him familiarly. 'Put it there, Billy Boy.' Of course, they're miners, and accustomed to death. They have a very limited morality, but they keep to it. It's moral, for instance, to rob anyone of anything, except a man in their own platoon. They treat every stranger as an enemy until he proves himself their friend, and then there's nothing they won't do for him. They are lecherous, the young ones at least, but without the false shame of the English lecher. I had a letter to censor the other day, written by a lance-corporal to his wife. He said that the French girls were nice to sleep with, so she mustn't worry on his account, but that he far preferred sleeping with her and missed her a great deal.

June 9th. I am beginning to realize how lucky I was in my gentle introduction to the Cambrin trenches. We are now in a nasty salient, a little to the south of the brick-stacks, where casualties are always heavy. The company had seventeen casualties yesterday from bombs and grenades. The front trench averages thirty yards from the Germans. Today, at one part, which is only twenty yards away from an occupied German sap, I went along whistling 'The Farmer's Boy' to keep up my spirits, when suddenly I saw a group bending over a man lying at the bottom of the trench. He was making a snoring noise mixed with animal groans. At my feet lay the cap he had worn, splashed with his brains. I had never seen human brains before; I somehow regarded them as a poetical figment. One can joke with a badly-wounded man and congratulate him on being out of it. One can disregard a dead man. But even a miner can't make a joke that sounds like a joke over a man who takes three hours to die, after the top part of his head has been taken off by a bullet fired at twenty yards' range.

Beaumont, of whom I told you in my last letter, also got killed – the last unwounded survivor of the original battalion, except for the transport men. He had his legs blown against his back. Everyone was swearing angrily, but an R.E. officer came up and told me that he had a tunnel driven under the German front line, and that if my chaps wanted to do a bit of bombing, now was the time. So he sent the mine up – it was not a big one, he said, but it made a tremendous noise and covered us with dirt – and we waited for a few seconds for the other Germans to rush up to help the wounded away, and then chucked all the bombs we had.

Beaumont had been telling how he had won about five pounds' worth of francs in the sweepstake after the Rue du Bois show: a sweepstake of the sort that leaves no bitterness behind it. Before a show, the platoon pools all its available cash and the survivors divide it up afterwards. Those who are killed can't complain, the wounded would have given far more than that to escape as they have, and the unwounded regard the money as a consolation prize for still being here.

Extract D

An Incident

He was just a boy, as I could see,
For he sat in the tent there close by me.
I held the lamp with its flickering light,
And felt the hot tears blur my sight
As the doctor took the blood-stained bands
From both his brave, shell-shattered hands –
His boy hands, wounded more pitifully
Than Thine, O Christ, on Calvary.

I was making tea in the tent where they,
The wounded, came in their agony;
And the boy turned when his wounds were dressed,
Held up his face like a child at the breast,
Turned and held his tired face up,
For he could not hold the spoon or cup,
And I fed him. . . . Mary, Mother of God,
All women tread where thy feet have trod.

And still on the battlefield of pain
Christ is stretched on His Cross again;
And the Son of God in agony hangs,
Womanhood striving to ease His pangs.
For each son of man is a son divine,
Not just to the mother who calls him 'mine',
As he stretches out his stricken hand,
Wounded to death for the Mother Land.

Mary H. J. Henderson

Answer **all** questions.

1a Basing your answer on **Extract A** and <u>one</u> of the other three extracts, write a comparison of the ways the writers present attitudes to injury and death in war.

How far do you agree with the view that Whitman presents his subject in a far more sentimental and unrealistic way than the writer of the extract of your choice?

1b By comparing **Extracts B, C and D**, and by referring to your own wider reading, examine how typical in both style and treatment of subject matter these writings are of literature from or about the First World War.

You should consider:

• language, form and structure

- the ways the writers use the genre of their choice to express their thoughts and feelings
- the writers' attitudes to war and contemporary society
- the influence of the time of composition
- the gender of the writers.

Deconstructing the questions

Question 1a

- 'Write a comparison' invites you to '*explore and comment on the relationships and comparisons between literary texts*' (AO2ii).

- 'the ways the writers present' invites you to '*show detailed understanding of the ways in which writers' choices of form, structure and language shape meanings*' (AO3), as does 'presents his subject' in the second part of the question.

- 'How far do you agree with' invites you to '*articulate independent opinions and judgements, informed by different interpretations of literary texts by other readers*' (AO4).

- Another key element here is choice. You have to choose which extract to compare with **A**, bearing the question in mind, which here concerns 'attitudes to injury and death in war'. So, which extract seems most easily comparable with **A**? Which extract can you most easily analyse in terms of presentation? Which extract offers you the chance to refer to some of your wider reading? Don't try and do a lot of analysis on each extract to make this choice, though – make a choice and then start to work.

Question 1b

- 'By comparing' asks you again to '*explore and comment on the relationships and comparisons between literary texts*' (AO2ii).

- 'referring to your own wider reading' is a specific invitation to refer to other texts, so this is a more important element here than it is in **1a**, perhaps, addressing 'how typical'.

- 'style and treatment of subject matter' asks you to '*show detailed understanding of the ways in which writers' choices of form, structure and language shape meanings*' (AO3). The first two elements 'language, form and structure' and 'the ways the writers use the genre of their choice to express their thoughts and feelings' also address AO3.

- 'how typical' and the list of elements test your ability to '*evaluate the significance of cultural, historical and other contextual influences on literary texts and study*' (AO5ii).

Example of response to 1a

Here are some notes which could be shaped into a response to **1a**, assuming that **Extract B** was chosen as the extract for comparison. At the end of this there are some notes on aspects of the other two extracts which might be used in a comparison with **A**.

Extract B

First part of question.

- Suffering of soldiers (injury or death) are presented differently – **A** in first person verse, **B** in song, slides, dialogue, giving multiple viewpoints.

- Slides in **B** show British, German, French – emphasise suffering of all sides – only one side in **A**. Implies universal attitude of writer. Perhaps refer to Owen 'Strange Meeting', end of *Birdsong* extract in Module 5 material, others showing both sides.

- Focus of **A** always on emotions of narrator, through to end. **B** more diverse, though slides/song in combination give an unrelenting focus on suffering and death, either potentially or actually.

- Both writers use repetition to shape and convey their attitudes. Sense of rush and purpose in **A** given by repetition of 'on, on', working throughout with unconventional use of commas where full stops should be – a sense of a continuous, never-ending task. 'Deep, deep' for emotive effect. In **B**, song form naturally uses repetitions, here picking out key words – 'gassed' 5 times in first verse, 'Bombed' in second. 'Last night/the night before', 'much too much for me', and 'they're warning us, they're warning us' all repetitions implying attitude. Refer to other songs if known.

- Both extracts use graphic words and images – 'matter and blood', 'the bloody stump', 'gnawing and putrid gangrene' (**A**), 'damn place still reeks of decomposing bodies' (**B**). Refer quickly to a similar example in wider reading. Presentation of attitudes different, though – direct giving of feelings in **A** 'so sickening, so offensive', which combines with direct appeal to an imagined onlooker: 'For see the frame all wasted . . . the yellow-blue countenance see'.

- Attitude of writer indirectly given in **B**, reflecting genre. Difference between officers and men in **B** – form of **A** doesn't allow this. Understatement of officer in 'pretty nasty', unrealistic encouragement of 'so long as we can all keep smiling'. Callousness of officers implied in 'all tidy', meaning how many bodies buried, and in refs. to leg – 'an obstruction', 'get a shovel and hack it off'. None of this in **A**.

- Humour in **B** too, unlike seriousness of **A**. Black humour – 'well, not all of us, of course', 'What the bloody hell am I going to hang my equipment on now?' (could refer to Grave's remark about brains on cap in **Extract C** – 'even a miner can't make a joke . . .').

Second part of question – **A** more sentimental and unrealistic?

- Yes, with this pairing. (*Remember this is only an example – you have to say and support what you think, taking other interpretations into account.*)

- **A** uses sentiment directly 'priceless blood', 'appealing eyes', 'poor boy', 'poor crazed hand', and so on. Sentimental about death, too; 'sweet death', 'O beautiful death!' Injured soldier's attitude described 'with curv'd neck and side falling head', like a Rossetti portrait. The experience is 'sweet and sad'. Most sentiment reserved for narrator himself – seems to be the hero of his own story: 'I am faithful, I do not give out', 'not one do I miss', 'I am firm', and the romantic idea of the soldier's 'appealing eyes' causing the doctor to offer his own life to save him. Easy reference to Brooke's 'The Soldier' here. Does not ignore some of the 'realistic' graphic detail, however.

- **B** not sentimental, despite use of popular song. Uses understatement rather than exaggeration of **A** – 'tidy' could be seen as this instead of callous. Lieutenant makes bald statements without adjectives, saying 'we've buried most of the second Yorks and Lancs'. The Sergeant's reply is practical and realistic, but also chilling. Could refer to Owen's 'Insensibility'. Could lead to a view of **A** as being more acceptable to modern reader as there is sentiment expressed. We *should* feel something about this awful suffering.

Extract C

If you had chosen to compare **A** with **C**, here are some of the things you might have thought about:

- The direct attitude of the narrator/writer to the fear of injury and death is similar to the narrator of **A**, at least in the direct 'telling' of feeling; the narrator in **C** is self-critical, though, unlike **A**: 'I was ashamed . . .'. The writer of **C** feels he 'can joke with a badly-wounded man'; **A** has no room for this, who doesn't 'struggle' to 'disregard a dead man', though he does note with approval his own 'impassive hand'.

- There is clearly humour in the attitude of the soldiers to the dead man's arm, 'Put it there, Billy Boy', but the writer forgives the men for any apparent callousness – 'they're miners, and accustomed to death'. In this way the writer uses their attitude to stress the horror of what he sees – more subtle than approach of the narrator in **A**, despite this being autobiographical.

- Both writers use graphic details for effect, the 'blood and matter' of **A**, and the cap 'splashed with his brains' in **C**. Compare other similar texts, e.g. Owen's 'Dulce Et Decorum Est'.

- Clearly the attitudes of the soldiers to death are very unsentimental – the sweepstake story in the last para. of the June 9th letter. Nothing of the sort of adjectives that are used in **A**.

- Realism partly result of genre – this is autobiographical non-fiction, and told without much direct authorial comment, even in a letter, where more personal comment might be expected. Compare with other letters in wider reading.

Extract D

If you had chosen to compare **A** with **D**, here are some of the things you might have thought about:

- As in **A**, first-person poem centring on care of wounded. However, no sense of this narrator's views about her own actions, unlike **A**. **A** very personal – many instances of 'I' – **D** much less so, and depersonalises and deglorifies her own actions by universalising them, through reference to Mother of God: 'All women tread where thy feet have trod'. This could be aggrandisement, comparing herself to Mary, but not with *all* women.

- **D** also refers to 'just a boy', and shows a strong emotional effect – 'felt the hot tears blur my sight'. **A** mentions 'a fire, a burning flame' but 'deep in my breast' rather than openly manifested. This may reflect character, or gender. **D** refers to the boy as 'like a child at the breast' – again perhaps reflecting the gender of the writer, though the pose seems more natural and less artistic than the attitude of the soldier described in **A**. This again reflects the attitude of the speaker.

- **D** seems more deliberately wrought than **A** – uses structure and language to emphasise the religious nature of the feelings. **A** is an unbroken narrative stream, but **D** becomes completely universal in stanza 3 to express the writer's attitude to injury and death, 'each son of man is a son divine', likening each soldier's death to Christ on the cross, and the mother becoming 'the Mother Land', a patriotic concept not touched on in **A**.

For the second part of the question:

- **D** seems comparatively more sentimental than either **B** or **C** when compared with **A**. 'The lamp with its flickering light', the tears, the 'blood-stained' bands, the 'brave' hands, conjure a scene and an attitude more directly comparable in sentiment with **A**, and lacking even that poem's graphic detail. A final view, though, might depend on your response to the strong religious agenda here, as to whether you consider the poem 'sentimental' or 'unrealistic'. With reference 'unrealistic', **A** does stay with the incident described, whereas **D** moves beyond it into more abstract realms – more 'unrealistic', then?

Example of response to 1b

There are a number of ways of organising your response, once you've read through the extracts carefully, noting elements of the individual pieces and how they might relate to each other and to texts you have covered in your wider reading. You could follow the list of prompts in the question, choose one extract as key and compare the other two to it, or find another method. Below are some of the relevant things you might have found in each of the extracts, with comparative links to other extracts and wider reading. The organisation is up to you.

Extract B

- Form of songs, slides in drama unusual – no equivalent in lit. about period.

- Structure episodic – free-wheeling style typical of later period – time of writing significant influence.

- Song typical of songs of time, though – compare to any known. Heavy rhythm picks out 'gassed', 'bombed', etc.

- Expression of thoughts/feelings/attitudes to audience indirect – they have to infer them from slides/songs, dialogue. No authorial voice, unlike other two extracts.

- Words of song insist on camaraderie ('we', 'us', not 'I') – as in much lit., such as **C**, and other texts known (refer). 1 in 4 significant – it was the basic unit of men in the front line, referred to in accounts. Fallen soldiers had to be replaced in the 4.

- Bad conditions in trenches stressed here, as in much other war lit. – gas, waist-deep mud, shellholes, numbers of dead in trench, military blunders – compare last line of Sassoon 'The General' – 'but he did for them both by his plan of attack' and many other refs. to all elements. Gas refs. here almost light-hearted – contrast with Owen's 'Dulce Et Decorum Est'.

- Leg in trench episode also referred to in **C**, and famous war photo. Attitudes here and in Graves comparable.

- Ref. to 'sharing the same trench' indication of static nature of war and close proximity. Also suggests that experiences of Allies and Germans were similar – compare Owen's 'Strange Meeting', Faulks's *Birdsong*, Graves's poem 'A Dead Boche', Sassoon's 'Reconciliation'.

- Stratified military system here reflects class system of the time. Ordinary soldiers not involved in this discussion. CO not used to front line – surprised by shell, explosion – compare Sassoon 'Base Details'. Understatement in language – compare **C** 'a lot of German stuff flying about'.

Extract C

- This extract is non-fiction – autobiography and letters within it. Compare similar forms in accounts, *Letters from a Lost Generation*, *Testament of Youth*, etc.

- Onomatopoeia of 'whish-whishing' compares with Owen's 'Anthem for Doomed Youth' and 'The Last Laugh'. Sensations of the individual in battle personal/direct, unlike **B**, **D** – sound, sight, and shame.

- Narrower canvas than **D** – reflects genre, and letter form. Letter is immediate – no wider perspective, or hindsight, possible.

- Trench conditions, as in **B**, at centre of extract. Corpse and arm a direct reminder of **B** and photo of arm in trench wall. Grim humour here, but in next letter humour is impossible, indicating depth of effect of brains on cap. Even miners 'accustomed to death' moved – further indication. Insensibility to death – compare Owen's 'Insensibility' – also shown in account of sweepstake. Morality of troops also here, not in other extracts.

- Brothels behind lines – ref. to other lit. Mining in front line in Owen's 'Strange Meeting', Faulks's *Birdsong*.

- Camaraderie and fierce loyalty to members of same platoon also in **B**. Letter June 1915 mentions 'last survivor of original battalion' – death rate in trenches – historical stats.

- Voice of officer in letters – shows in language, maybe attitude, but less sharply distinguished than in **B** – maybe reflecting less exaggeration in factual text, maybe viewpoint or character of narrator.

Extract D

- Content and diction more emotional than **B**, **C** – mentions of bravery and pain. 'agony', 'tears' might be expected in situation, but only mentioned here in three of the extracts.

- Focus here not trench conditions, but result – 'shell-shattered hands', though wounded and bandaged soldiers feature in slides in **B**. Religious attitudes and questioning of religion widespread in lit. – ref. to some. Owen 'At a Calvary near the Ancre': 'One ever hangs where shelled roads part' – though 'love of God seems dying' ('Exposure').

- No elements of humour here – passionate. Patriotism of 'Mother Land' might remind of Brooke's 'The Soldier', but no sense of glory/richness here.

- Gender central to this text – ref. to contemporary society in issue of women's occupations and position in society, and coming change.

- Focus on woman, child – language refers to 'like a child at the breast'. Speaker identifies with 'Mary, Mother of God'.

- Stanza 3 conceptualises, universalises war experience, unlike **B** or **C**. Prepared for by move at end of stanza 2. Soldier likened to Christ 'each son of man is a son divine', and each soldier's mother to Mary, and to the 'Mother Land'.

Sample Paper 2

1 Reading

- Here is the selection of material taken from the <u>prescribed area for study</u>. You will be using this material to answer the questions in this examination.

- Alongside the three pieces (B, C and D) about the First World War (the prescribed area for study) you will find a piece of pre-twentieth-century writing (A). This also has <u>war</u> as its theme.

- Read all four pieces and their introductions very carefully and closely. Then read them again several times in the light of the specific questions set.

2 The questions, what they test, and how to manage your time

All questions test your ability to:

- *communicate clearly*

- *explore and comment on the relationships between texts*

- *show detailed understanding of the ways in which writers' choices of form, structure and language shape meanings.*

Question 1a

- You should plan to spend about 1 hour and 15 minutes on question 1a; this will include reading time.

This question especially tests your ability to:

explore and comment on relationships and comparisons between literary texts

and

articulate independent judgements, informed by different interpretations of literary texts by other readers.

Question 1b

- You should spend about 1 hour and 45 minutes on question 1b; this will include reading time.

This question especially tests your ability to:

explore and comment on relationships and comparisons between literary texts

and

evaluate the significance of cultural, historical and other contextual influences on literary texts and study.

3 Wider reading

The paper tests your wider reading on the subject of *War in Literature* with specific reference to literature of and about the *First World War.*

In your answers, you should take every opportunity to refer to this wider reading and to your knowledge of this specific area of study.

Extract A

FROM THE FRUITS OF WAR

I set aside to tell the restless toil,
The mangled corpse, the maimed limbs at last,
The shortened years by fret of fever's foil,
The smoothest skin with scabs and scars disgraced,
The frolic favour frounced and foul defaced,
The broken sleeps, the dreadful dreams, the woe,
Which wone with war and cannot from him go.
I list not write, for it becomes me not,
The secret wrath which God doth kindle oft,
To see the sucklings put into the pot,
To hear their guiltless blood send cries aloft,
And call for vengeance unto him, but soft!
The soldiers they commit those heinous acts,
Yet kings and captains answer for such facts.

What need we now at large for to rehearse
The force of Fortune, when she list to frown?
Why should I here display in barren verse
How realms are turned topsy-turvy down,
How kings and Caesars lost both claim and crown,
Whose haughty hearts to hent all honour haunt,
Till high mishaps their doughtiest deed do daunt?

All these, with more, my pen shall overpass,
Since Haughty Heart has fixed his fancy thus.
'Let chance,' saith he, 'be fickle as it was,
Sit bonus, in re mala, animus.
Nam omne solum viro forti ius.
And fie,' saith he, 'for goods or filthy gain!
I gape for glory; all the rest is vain.'

Vain is the rest, and that most vain of all:
A smouldering smoke which flieth with every wind,
A tickle treasure, like a trendling ball,
A passing pleasure mocking but the mind,
A fickle fee as fancy well can find,
A summer's fruit which long can never last,
But ripeneth soon and rots again as fast.

And tell me, Haughty Heart, confess a truth,
What man was aye so safe in glory's port
But trains of treason (oh, the more the ruth!)
Could undermine the bulwarks of this fort
And raze his ramparts down in sundry sort?
Search all thy books and thou shalt find therein
That honour is more hard to hold than win.

Ask Julius Caesar if this tale be true,
The man who conquered all the world so wide,
Whose only word commanded all the crew
Of Roman knights at many a time and tide,
Whose pomp was thought so great it could not glide –
At last with bodkins dubbed and doused to death,
And all his glory banished with his breath.

George Gascoigne (1525–77)

Extract B

Not About Heroes, by Stephen MacDonald is about the friendship between Wilfred Owen and Siegfried Sassoon, and their meeting at Craiglockhart hospital. In this extract from the play, Owen has left the hospital and returned to the front, where he was to die.

[*SOUND: the continuous rumbling of war noises. Owen moves to the dug-out position; stands there.*]

SASSOON 'He stood alone in some queer sunless place
Where Armageddon ends. Perhaps he longed
For days he might have lived, but his young face
Gazed forth untroubled . . .'

OWEN I feel confident because I know I came out to help: directly, by leading them as well as an officer can; indirectly, by watching their sufferings so that I may plead for them as well as I can. I have done the first . . .

[*Owen sits on the floor. Sassoon starts to take the blanket from his knees.
SOUND: noises fade down, under the speech.*]

SASSOON [*folding the blanket*] The news from the Front was changing. We began to advance. The German troops had been told that this battle would decide the outcome of the war. They lost it – and with it, their faith in ultimate victory. At the end of September we began the Great Attack, and we passed the Hindenburg Line.

[*SOUND: an explosion – thunder, or a bomb, or gun. War noises continue.*]

OWEN Very dear Siegfried. I have been in action some days. Our experiences passed the limits of abhorrence: I lost all my earthly faculties and fought like an angel. You'll guess what happened when I say that I am now commanding the Company – and in the line I had a seraphic boy-lance-corporal as my sergeant-major.

I have mentioned my excellent batman, Jones. In the first wave of the attack he was shot in the head and thrown on top of me. He lay there, dead, his blood soaking my shoulder for half an hour. It's still there, crimson, on my tunic.

[*SOUND: fades down as SASSOON speaks.*]

SASSOON

'I saw his round mouth's crimson deepen as it fell,
Like a Sun, in his last deep hour;
Watched the magnificent recession of farewell,
Clouding, half gleam, half glower,
And a last splendour burn the heavens of his cheek,
And in his eyes
The cold stars lighting, very old and bleak,
In different skies.'

[*SOUND: an explosion. Noises continue.*]

OWEN

I can't say I suffered anything – having let my brain grow dull. My nerves, then, are in perfect order. My senses are charred. I shall feel again as soon as I dare, but now I must not. I don't take the cigarette out of my mouth when I write 'Deceased' across their letters . . .

Siegfried, I don't know what you'll think, but I've been recommended for the M.C. – and I've recommended every single N.C.O. who was with me. I'm glad of it – for the confidence it will give me at home.

[*SOUND: an explosion. Noises continue. While Sassoon reads the official citation, Owen pins on the medal ribbon.*]

SASSOON

'For conspicuous gallantry and devotion to duty in the attack on the Fonsomme Line on 1st/2nd October 1918. On the Company Commander becoming a casualty, he assumed command and showed fine leadership and resisted a heavy counter-attack. He personally manipulated a captured enemy Machine Gun in an isolated position and inflicted considerable losses on the enemy. Throughout he behaved most gallantly.'

Extract C

Goodbye To All That is the autobiography of Robert Graves, in which he writes about his experiences as a young officer in the First World War.

We had spent the day after the attack carrying the dead down for burial and cleaning the trench up as best we could. That night the Middlesex held the line, while the Royal Welch carried all the unbroken gas-cylinders along to a position on the left flank of the brigade, where they were to be used on the following night, September 27th. This was worse than carrying the dead; the cylinders were cast-iron, heavy and hateful. The men cursed and sulked. Only the officers knew of the proposed attack; the men must not be told until just beforehand. I felt like screaming. Rain was still pouring down, harder than ever. We knew definitely, this time, that ours would be only a diversion to help troops on our right make the real attack.

The scheme was the same as before: at 4 p.m. gas would be discharged for forty minutes, and after a quarter of an hour's bombardment we should attack. I broke the news to the men about three o'clock. They took it well. The relations of officers and men, and of senior and junior officers, had been very different in the excitement of battle. There had been no insubordination, but a greater freedom of speech, as though we were all drunk together. I found myself calling the adjutant 'Charley' on one occasion; he appeared not to mind in the least. For the next ten days my relations with my men were like those I had in the Welsh Regiment; later, discipline reasserted itself, and it was only occasionally that I found them intimate.

At 4 p.m. then, the gas went off again with a strong wind; the gas-men had brought enough spanners this time. The Germans stayed absolutely silent. Flares went up from the reserve lines, and it looked as though all the men in the front trench were dead. The brigadier decided not to take too much for granted; after the bombardment he sent out a Cameronian officer and twenty-five men as a feeling-patrol. The patrol reached the German wire; there came a burst of machine-gun and rifle fire, and only two wounded men regained the trench.

We waited on the fire-step from four to nine o'clock, with fixed bayonets, for the order to go over. My mind was a blank, except for the recurrence of *S'nice S'mince S'pie, S'nice S'mince S'pie . . . I don't like ham, lamb or jam, and I don't like roley-poley . . .*

The men laughed at my singing. The acting C.S.M. said: 'It's murder, sir.'

'Of course it's murder, you bloody fool,' I agreed. 'But there's nothing else for it, is there?' It was still raining. *But when I sees a s'nice s'mince s'pie, I asks for a helping twice . . .*

At nine o'clock brigade called off the attack; we were told to hold ourselves in readiness to go over at dawn.

No order came at dawn, and no more attacks were promised us after this. From the morning of September 24th to the night of October 3rd, I had in all eight hours of sleep. I kept myself awake and alive by drinking about a bottle of whisky a day. I had never drunk it before, and have seldom drunk it since; it certainly helped me then. We had no blankets, greatcoats, or waterproof sheets, nor any time or material to build new shelters. The rain poured down. Every night we went out to fetch in the dead of the other battalions. The Germans continued indulgent and we had few casualties. After the first day or two the corpses swelled and stank. I vomited more than once while superintending the carrying. Those we could not get in from the German wire continued to swell until the wall of the stomach collapsed, either naturally or when punctured by a bullet; a disgusting smell would float across. The colour of the dead faces changed from white to yellow-grey, to red, to purple, to green, to black, to slimy.

On the morning of the 27th a cry arose from No Man's Land. A wounded soldier of the Middlesex had recovered consciousness after two days. He lay close to the German wire. Our men heard it and looked at each other. We had a tender-hearted lance-corporal named Baxter. He was the man to boil up a special dixie for the sentries of his section when they came off duty. As soon as he heard the wounded Middlesex man, he ran along the trench calling for a volunteer to help fetch him in. Of course, no one would go; it was death to put one's head over the parapet. When he came running to ask me I excused myself as being the only officer in the company. I would come out with him at dusk, I said – not now. So he went alone. He jumped quickly over the parapet, then strolled across No Man's Land, waving a handkerchief; the Germans fired to frighten him, but since he persisted they let him come up close. Baxter continued towards them and, when he got to the Middlesex man, stopped and pointed to show the Germans what he was at. Then he dressed the man's wounds, gave him a drink of rum and some biscuit that he had with him, and promised to be back again at nightfall. He did come back, with a stretcher-party, and the man eventually recovered. I recommended Baxter for the Victoria Cross, being the only officer who had witnessed the action, but the authorities thought it worth no more than a Distinguished Conduct Medal.

The Actor and I had decided to get in touch with the battalion on our right. It was the Tenth Highland Light Infantry. I went down their trench some time in the morning of the 26th and walked nearly a quarter of a mile without seeing a sentry or an officer. There were dead men, sleeping men, wounded men, gassed men, all lying anyhow. The trench had been used as a latrine. Finally I met a Royal Engineer officer who said: 'If the Boche knew what an easy job he had, he'd just walk over and take this trench.'

Extract D

Siegfried Sassoon served as an officer in the First World War. This poem was written in hospital, ten days after he was wounded in action.

THE REAR-GUARD

(HINDENBURG LINE, APRIL 1917)

Groping along the tunnel, step by step,
He winked his prying torch with patching glare
From side to side, and sniffed the unwholesome air.

Tins, boxes, bottles, shapes too vague to know;
A mirror smashed, the mattress from a bed;
And he, exploring fifty feet below
The rosy gloom of battle overhead.

Tripping, he grabbed the wall; saw some one lie
Humped at his feet, half-hidden by a rug,
And stooped to give the sleeper's arm a tug.
'I'm looking for headquarters.' No reply.
'God blast your neck!' (For days he'd had no sleep)
'Get up and guide me through this stinking place.'

Savage, he kicked a soft, unanswering heap,
And flashed his beam across the livid face
Terribly glaring up, whose eyes yet wore
Agony dying hard ten days before;
And fists of fingers clutched a blackening wound.

Alone he staggered on until he found
Dawn's ghost that filtered down a shafted stair
To the dazed, muttering creatures underground
Who hear the boom of shells in muffled sound.
At last, with sweat of horror in his hair,
He climbed through darkness to the twilight air,
Unloading hell behind him step by step.

22 April 1917

Answer **all** questions.

1a Basing your answer on Extract A and *either* **Extract B** or **Extract C**, write a comparison of the ways the writers present glory and heroism in war.

How far do you agree with the view that Gascoigne is more interested in 'kings and captains' than the harsh realities of war?

1b By comparing **Extracts B, C and D**, and by referring to your own wider reading, examine how typical in both style and treatment of subject matter these writings are of literature from or about the First World War.

You should consider:

- language, form and structure
- the ways the writers use the genre of their choice to express their thoughts and feelings
- the writers' attitudes to war and the feelings of characters about war
- the influence of the time of composition.

Achieving top marks in the mark schemes

Assessment Objectives 1, 2 and 3 are tested in both **1a** and **1b**. These are the descriptors for achievement in these Assessment Objectives in Band 4, 16–20 marks out of 20:

- analysis of texts in detail
- extended and illuminating comparison
- technically accurate
- telling and accurate use of appropriate critical vocabulary
- sophisticated analysis of ways in which form, structure and language shape meanings.

In addition, **1a** tests AO4. The Band 4 descriptors are:

- cogent, well-structured argument
- mature and confident judgement based on informed consideration of various possibilities.

1b tests AO5ii. The Band 4 descriptors are:

- specific detailed and illuminating connections between texts and context
- understanding of texts in tradition
- analysis of importance of contextual factors in writing.

Glossary

Alchemy chemistry of the Middle Ages in which there was an attempt to change base metals into gold, as in Jonson's *The Alchemist.*

Antithesis a contrast of ideas presented by strongly contrasted words.

Archetype the prototype or original model.

Bathos a movement from the sublime to the ridiculous, as in Byron's *Don Juan.*

Caricature a grotesque presentation of a person or thing which relies on over-exaggeration of one particular trait.

Context in AS literary study this is the fifth Assessment Objective. Contexts are the important facts, events or processes which have helped to shape literary works.

Demotic popular, colloquial or vulgar language.

Denoting a literary text structured upon a series of events.

Diabolical words, thoughts or actions connected in some way to the devil.

Dialect a form of language related to a particular place, class or person which has distinctive forms of speech and expression.

Didactic in literature, that which has the intention to instruct.

Discourses two philosophical poems by Rousseau. The first is entitled 'Discourses sur les Sciences et les Arts', 1750. The second is 'Discourses sur l'origin de l'inequalite', 1755.

Divine right of kings the belief that God, independent of subjects' wills, selected the ruler.

Episodic denoting a literary text structured upon a series of events.

Expiation making amends for something, as Leontes does in Shakespeare's *The Winter's Tale.*

Fall from Paradise mankind's fall from the Garden of Eden when Adam and Eve ate the forbidden fruit.

Generic relating to genre.

Genre specific type or style of literature or art.

Half-rhyme a type of versification when the rhyme is not full, for example, rhyme created by assonance.

Heroic rhyming couplet iambic pentameters rhyming in pairs, originally used by Pope and Dryden, but also by writers such as Chaucer and Keats.

Humours a part of the medieval belief that the body was composed of four main fluids: blood, phlegm, choler and melancholy. The dominant fluid determined a person's temperament, as in Ben Jonson's play, *The Alchemist*.

Incantatory language which sounds as though it is the recitation of a spell or a charm.

Legalism a preference for the law itself rather than the principles of the Bible and Christian virtue, as in Shakespeare's *Measure for Measure*.

Machiavelli Niccolo Machiavelli (1469–1527) was an Italian writer and statesman who advocated the use of ruthless means to secure wealth and retain power. The adjective *Machiavellian* is used to describe a person who practises duplicity and scheming in order to win political power.

Medieval/medievalism in nineteenth-century poetry, the practice of imitating the Middle Ages.

Milieu the particular environment, social, academic, literary, etc., in which a writer lives.

Motif a dominant idea or image which reappears throughout a work, such as the use of floral images in the *Winter's Tale*.

Morality play medieval drama in verse in which abstractions such as Vice and Virtue were presented on stage, for example, *Everyman*.

Mystery play medieval drama in verse in which biblical stories are retold.

Narrative poem a poem in which a story is told.

Natural universe all existing things which relate to nature. This may be a contrast to the divine universe, in which all of creation is related to God.

Orthodox 'correct' or generally accepted opinions, especially related to religion.

Ottava rima an eight-line stanza in iambic pentameter, rhyming ab ab ab cc: such as Byron used in *Don Juan*.

Pantheism a doctrine which holds that God may be perceived in all things, and that all things are divine.

Paradox a self-contradictory statement or series of statements.

Pastoral poems which portray country life.

Penance an act of contrition carried out after committing a sin as Leontes does in Shakespeare's *The Winter's Tale*.

Pentecost another name for Whit Sunday, when the Holy Spirit is said to have come down as flames to give wisdom to the Apostles.

Register a set of words used in specific circumstances or time period.

Reign of Terror the dreadful events in France after the Revolution in 1792 when thousands of innocent people were slaughtered.

Romance a genre of literature in which restrictions are removed from human actions and from situations, often by the use of magic, so that a moral point may be made. This is evident in Shakespeare's play, *A Winter's Tale*.

Satire literary work in which the aim is to amuse, criticise or correct by means of ridicule, for example, Jonson's *The Alchemist*.

Sensual related to the senses or sensations, usually with a sexual connotation rather than spiritual or intellectual.

Sensuous appealing to the senses, not restricted to fleshy or sexual pleasure.

Seven deadly sins in theology, the seven sins for which, if unrepented, mankind will go to Hell. They are: Pride, Covetousness, Lust, Gluttony, Anger, Envy and Sloth.

Slapstick a form of boisterous, rough comedy, as at times in Jonson's *The Alchemist*.

Social hierarchy the different ranks of people within society.

Socialist a person who approves of the state ownership of the means of production and distribution, and financial exchanges of goods and money.

Soliloquise to speak alone or to oneself. Used as a theatrical device in plays for characters to give speeches without the presence of others on the stage.

Spatial used for example to explain how ideas can be developed across an act of a play rather than being developed in a chronological sequence, as in Shakespeare's *The Winter's Tale*.

Specification the syllabus for a subject issued by an examination board.

Stock standard or typical; (often used of a character in a play).

Sublime having a quality of grandeur which inspires awe, as Wordsworth perceives in nature.

Swedenborg Edward Swedenborg was the philosophical writer who influenced Blake with social writings such as *Wisdom of Angels: Concerning Divine Love and Divine Wisdom*, 1789.

Syntax the grammatical arrangement of words in a sentence or in speech.

Tragicomedy a genre of drama which is a blend of tragedy and comedy such as Shakespeare's play *Measure for Measure*.

Vice figure the character(s) representing evil, originally on the medieval stage.

Visionary a person given to seeing visions or holding fanciful theories; things which exist only in the imagination.

Visionary poems poems by William Blake in which he rewrites the Creation of the World. These include: *America: a Prophecy* (1793); *Visions of the Daughters of Albion* (1793); *The Four* Zoas (1797), *Jerusalem* (1804–20); *The Book of Urizen* (1794) and *The Book of Los* (1795).